Patent Law and Women

This book analyses the gendered nature of patent law and the knowledge governance system it supports.

The vast majority of patented inventions are attributed to male inventors. While this has resulted in arguments that there are not enough women working in science, technology, engineering and mathematics, this book maintains that the issue lies with the very nature of patent law and how it governs knowledge. The reason why fewer women patent than men is that patent law and the knowledge governance system it supports are gendered. This book deconstructs patent law to reveal the multiple gendered binaries it embodies, and how these in turn reflect gendered understandings of what constitutes science and an invention, and a scientist and an inventor. Revealing the inherent biases of the patent system, as well as its reliance on an idea of the public domain, the book argues that an egalitarian knowledge governance system must go beyond socialised binaries to better govern knowledge creation, dissemination and maintenance.

This book will appeal to scholars and policymakers in the field of patent law, as well as those in law and other disciplines with interests in law, gender and technology.

Jessica C. Lai is Associate Professor of Commercial Law, Victoria University of Wellington, New Zealand.

Patent Law and Women

Tackling Gender Bias in Knowledge Governance

Jessica C. Lai

Routledge
Taylor & Francis Group
LONDON AND NEW YORK

First published 2022
by Routledge
2 Park Square, Milton Park, Abingdon, Oxon OX14 4RN

and by Routledge
605 Third Avenue, New York, NY 10158

Routledge is an imprint of the Taylor & Francis Group, an informa business

British Library Cataloguing-in-Publication Data
A catalogue record for this book is available from the British Library

Library of Congress Cataloging-in-Publication Data
A catalog record has been requested for this book

ISBN: 978-0-367-65227-2 (hbk)
ISBN: 978-1-032-07957-8 (pbk)
ISBN: 978-1-003-12850-2 (ebk)

DOI: 10.4324/9781003128502

Typeset in Bembo
by Taylor & Francis Books

Contents

Illustrations

Figures

Tables

Acknowledgements

This is for my parents, Siau Ngui Tham, who later became Jane Yen Yu Lai when she moved her life from Indonesia to New Zealand and married my father, Peter James Lai, born Sheu Len Lai. Both of my parents sacrificed a lot for their children, including their names, thinking (correctly, studies show) they needed to do this to flourish. It was always clear that they wanted me to "succeed" (read: earn well) and be happy (read: marry a nice Chinese man and have children). Their ideals of success and happiness conform to the gender normative role of a "good Chinese daughter". They never quite knew what to do with their questioning, boundary-pushing, lesbian daughter, who chose to become an academic rather than a "real lawyer". But they always saw the importance of their daughters being well-educated and their love was unwavering. Moreover, they gave up parts of their identities so that I could live mine with impunity. I am forever indebted to them for this.

I would also like to acknowledge all the women who have supported and mentored me throughout my life. I have always wondered at my incredible luck in this respect. I would not be where I am today if Susy Frankel had not made me fall in love with the intricacies of patent law and encouraged me to join the world of academia, if Susan Corbett had not supported my move back to New Zealand and entry into my first academic role, and if Lisa Marriott were not a steady champion in my corner.

Of no less importance, I am extremely grateful for the emotional and intellectual sustenance that I get from Dorothea Endres, who continuously challenges me to think about things in different ways, and my sister, Michelle Lai, who is my constant reality check. Both of these women love me for who I am – they are my constants – and that is the greatest gift.

Finally, there have been incredible men in my life, who have never thought that I should be a certain way because of my sex or the colour of my skin. Thomas Borrmann and Michael Richardson supervised my Master's in Chemistry and – as Thomas has since told me – they realised early on that the best thing they could do was to not get in my way. We remain good friends and I delight in having them in my life. Christoph Graber and Vaios Karavas were my doctoral and postdoctoral supervisors. They patiently seeded my interest in legal sociology and legal philosophy – a seed that is now bearing fruit.

Introduction

> Asking the woman question reveals the ways in which political choice and institutional arrangement contribute to women's subordination. … The woman question reveals how the position of women reflects the organization of society rather than the inherent characteristics of women … In exposing the hidden effects of laws that do not explicitly discriminate on the basis of sex, the woman question helps to demonstrate how social structures embody norms that implicitly render women different and thereby subordinate.[1]

This book asks the "woman" question with respect to patent law. Patents are a type of intellectual property that protect "technical" inventions with up to 20 years of exclusive rights. The 20 years of exclusivity are theorised to incentivise inventive activity. Being property, patent owners ("patentees") use their patents to structure transactions, such as technology transfer or licensing agreements. The patent system, thus, lies at the centre of knowledge governance in the Western (and increasingly global) world,[2] affecting the generation, protection and dissemination of knowledge.[3] The subject matter of patents is seemingly objective and without gender. Yet, empirical studies show that patenting rates differ vastly between the sexes. Patenting is gendered. This book examines why this is the case and how we might create a more egalitarian knowledge governance system.

The bulk of existing literature on patents and gender is not legal, but looks at the socio-cultural and institutional reasons why women do not or cannot seek patents. Much of this reflects the "women in science, technology, engineering

1 Katharine T Bartlett, "Feminist Legal Methods" (1990) 103 *Harvard Law Review* 829, 843.

2 All Member States of the World Trade Organization must protect technological inventions with patents for twenty years. See WTO, Agreement on Trade-Related Aspects of Intellectual Property Rights, Marrakesh Agreement Establishing the World Trade Organization, Annex 1C, 1869 UNTS 299; 33 ILM 1197 (adopted on 15 April 1994, entered into force 1 January 1995), Art. 27.

3 See Peter Drahos, *The Global Governance of Knowledge: Patent Offices and their Clients* (Cambridge University Press, 2010), who details this knowledge governance system and examines its private capture.

DOI: 10.4324/9781003128502-1

and mathematics (STEM)" rhetoric, relating to the fact that more males do the kinds of inventing that are protected by patents.[4] This literature focuses on why there are not more women in STEM, with the primary goal of ameliorating the dearth of females in many STEM fields. This literature addresses the high attrition rates of women from STEM, which increase between secondary, tertiary and postgraduate education, and between junior and senior roles.[5] Yet, the average inventors of patented inventions are typically mid-career.[6] Some of this literature explains these attrition rates by stating that females do not have the same brains and/or interests as males due to "nature". However, the more nuanced commentators note that "nurture" affects interests and life "choices".

The focus on women in STEM is a red herring. It is akin to earlier beliefs that more women in the work force would lead to emancipation. However, this focus fails to account for the fact that women and men have different experiences in the work force, including in STEM fields. Invention and innovation take place in gendered environments, wherein there are multiple institutional, structural and organisational biases against women. For example, women are disproportionately burdened with administrative tasks and "soft" jobs,[7] there are few female mentors available[8] and, of course, women's careers

4 Erin Leahey and Amelia Blume, "Elucidating the Process: Why Women Patent Less than Men" in Albert N Link (ed.), *Gender and Entrepreneurial Activity* (Edward Elgar, 2017) 159; Sharmishta Barwa and Shirin M Rai, "Knowledge and/as Power: A Feminist Critique of Trade Related Intellectual Property Rights" (2003) 7(1) *Gender, Technology and Development* 91; Shlomit Yanisky-Ravid, "Eligible Patent Matter – Gender Analysis of Patent Law: International and Comparative Perspectives" (2011) 19(3) *American University Journal of Gender, Social Policy & the Law* 851.

5 E.g. Helen Shen, "Mind the Gender Gap" (2013) 495 *Nature* 22, 22; Rachael D Robnett, "Gender Bias in STEM Fields: Variation in Prevalence and Links to STEM Self-Concept" (2016) 40(1) *Psychology of Women Quarterly* 65; Marc J Lerchenmueller and Olav Sorenson, "The Gender Gap in Early Career Transitions in the Life Sciences" (2018) 47 *Research Policy* 1007.

6 Paola Giuri et al., "Inventors and Invention Processes in Europe: Results from the PatVal-EU Survey" (2007) 36 *Research Policy* 1107, 1111–12.

7 Leahey and Blume (n 4) 155; Waverly L Ding, Fiona Murray and Toby E Stuart, "Gender Differences in Patenting in the Academic Life Sciences" (2006) 313 *Science* 665, at 666–7; and Sue V Rosser, "The Gender Gap in Patenting: Is Technology Transfer a Feminist Issue?" (2009) 21(2) *National Women's Studies Association Journal* 65, 77.

8 Naomi C Chesler and Mark A Chesler, "Gender-Informed Mentoring Strategies for Women Engineering Scholars: On Establishing a Caring Community" (2002) *Journal of Engineering Education* 49, 50–1. See also Kris de Welde and Sandra L Laursen, "The Glass Obstacle Course: Informal and Formal Barriers for Women PhD Students in STEM Fields" (2011) 3(3) *International J. of Gender, Science and Technology* 571, 583–5.

are taxed because of their biological role as child bearer and socially assigned role of caretaker,[9] which subsidises men's careers.[10]

Moreover, patent law itself is gendered.[11] While feminist scholars have critically analysed many areas of the law, patent law remains at the fringes. This is unlike copyright, patent law's running partner, which has attracted significantly more critical attention.[12] This divergence between the two fields of intellectual property likely lies in the fact that copyright law is seemingly more directly connected to culture, as it is about the artistic or the aesthetic. Inherently subjective, it is obvious subject matter for critical analysis through the social sciences. In contrast, patents are understood as dealing with the technical sciences. That which is technical is perceived as being objective and non-cultural, and thus not innately open to deconstruction. However, rather than being objective, patent law reflects dominant cultural norms, embodying multiple socially constructed binaries,[13] such as

9 Kjersten Bunker Whittington, "Mothers of Invention? Gender, Motherhood, and New Dimensions of Productivity in the Science Profession" (2011) 38(3) *Work and Organisations* 417, 442, who shows that, in academia, mothers patent less than women without children and men in general. In contrast, there is a fatherhood premium in both industry and academia. The author hypothesises that academic mothers are affected more than mothers in industry are because (whilst viewed positively) patenting is still considered optional in academia, whereas it is part of commercial life in industry (at 447–8).

10 Heidi I Hartmann, "The Unhappy Marriage of Marxism and Feminism" (1979) 3 (2) *Capital and Class* 1, 14–22.

11 See e.g. Dan L Burk, "Feminism and Dualism in Intellectual Property" (2007) 15(2) *American University Journal of Gender, Social Policy & the Law* 195; Dan L Burk, "Do Patents Have Gender?" (2011) 19 *American University Journal of Gender, Social Policy & the Law* 881; Yanisky-Ravid (n 4).

12 See e.g. Dan L Burk, "Copyright and Feminism in Digital Media" (2006) 14(3) *American University Journal of Gender, Social Policy & the Law* 519; Carys J Craig, Joseph F Turcotte and Rosemary J Coombe, "What is Feminist About Open Access?: A Relational Approach to Copyright in the Academy" (2011) 1(1) *Feminists@law* 1; Carys J Craig, "Reconstructing the Author-Self: Some Feminist Lessons for Copyright Law" (2007) 15(2) *American University Journal of Gender, Social Policy & the Law* 207; Carys J Craig, "Feminist Aesthetics and Copyright Law: Genius, Value, and Gendered Visions of the Creative Self" (2014) 10(1) *Osgoode Legal Studies Research Paper* No. 42; Anne Bartow, "Fair Use and the Fairer Sex: Gender, Feminism, and Copyright Law" (2006) 14(3) *American University Journal of Gender, Social Policy & the Law* 551; B Courtney Doagoo, "Feminist Anthropology and Copyright: Gauging the Application and Limitations of Oppositions Models" in B Courtney Doagoo et al. (eds), *Intellectual Property for the 21st Century: Interdisciplinary Approaches* (Publisher Irwin Law, 2014); Anthea Kraut, *Choreographing Copyright: Race, Gender, and Intellectual Property Rights in American Dance* (Oxford University Press, 2016); Kevin J Greene, "Intellectual Property at the Intersection of Race and Gender: Lady Sings the Blues" (2008) *American University Journal of Gender, Social Policy & the Law* 165; Rebecca Tushnet, "Symposium: My Fair Ladies: Sex, Gender, and Fair Use in Copyright" (2007) 15(2) *American University Journal of Gender, Social Policy & the Law* 273.

13 For a summary of social construction, see Wolfgang Detel, "Social Constructivism" in James D Wright (ed.), *International Encyclopedia of the Social & Behavioral Sciences* (2nd edn, Elsevier, 2015, vol. 22) 228.

"made" (patentable) or "natural" (not patentable). Furthermore, there are numerous stakeholders with converging/conflicting interests, including inventors, contributors, users, competitors, the state and the public at large. One should also not forget that patents are textual documents.[14] Thus, patent law theorists should be contemplating the same issue as those in all other areas of law – "how to challeng[e] and undermin[e] dominant legal conventions and [develop] alternative conventions which take better account of women's experiences and needs".[15]

The dearth of critical analysis of patent law vis-à-vis "the woman question" has led Dan Burk to note that this essentially places the discourse at the beginning of the second wave of feminism.[16] In terms of the black letter law, males and females have the same rights vis-à-vis patents. That is, they have technical equality. This was achieved through the first wave of feminism, which resulted in females being able to own property and, thus, own patents. Furthermore, technological inventions are seemingly genderless and free from gender relations, which adds to the veneer of equality. The discourse around "women in STEM" is a shift towards trying to get equal participation in the knowledge economy. This is second wave feminism.

What is only burgeoning is the recognition that mere neutrality and numbers do not equate to equality and equity.[17] Instead, we need to recognise the way that patent law and the knowledge governance system it creates are gendered and biased against women, because of the constructed roles cast upon women. As discussed in this book, patent law has been developed around Western-masculine-centric modes of invention and innovation,[18] holding these out as standards of "invention" and "innovation". Another way to view this is that men do the kinds of inventing that are protected by patents, because patents protect traditionally masculine kinds of inventing. Patent law protects the interests of its creators, leaving the knowledge of the disempowered (women and non-Western

14 On the performative nature of patents, see Dan L Burk, "Patent Performativity" (2021) 26 *Journal of Technology Law and Policy*.

15 Bartlett (n 1) 831.

16 Burk, "Patent Performativity" (n 14).

17 In contexts other than patent law, see e.g. Abigail C Saguy, Juliet A Williams and Mallory Rees, "Reassessing Gender Neutrality" (2020) 54(1) *Law and Society Review* 7.

18 The term "Western" is used cautiously, keeping in mind its origin in centring perspective, and the homogenising effect it has through creating a binary of Western and non-Western. See e.g. Chandra Talpade Mohanty, "Under Western Eyes: Feminist Scholarship and Colonial Discourses" (1988) 30 *Feminist Review* 61; and Chandra Talpade Mohanty, "'Under Western Eyes' Revisited: Feminist Solidarity through Anticapitalist Struggles" (2002) 28(2) *Signs: Journal of Women in Culture and Society* 499.

Regarding the patent law race and gender dynamic, see Laura A Foster, "Patents, Biopolitics, and Feminisms: Locating Patent Law Struggles over Breast Cancer Genes and the Hoodia Plant" (2012) 19 *International Journal of Cultural Property* 371; Laura A Foster, "Situating Feminism, Patent Law, and the Public Domain" (2011) 20 *Columbia Journal of Gender & Law* 262; and Terra L Gearhart-Serna, "Women's Work, Women's Knowing: Intellectual Property and the Recognition of Women's Traditional Knowledge" (2010) 21(2) *Yale Journal of Law and Feminism* 372.

peoples)[19] free to be taken, filtered through the masculine and patented. This reproduces the socialised devaluing of feminine modes and fields of invention, and of female inventors.

Thus, the issue of not enough "women in STEM" is an aesthetic, superficial problem. The deeper questions are: why do women need to be in STEM to patent? And how do we create a less gendered knowledge governance for a less gendered society?

It is important at this point to explain the terminology used in this book. The terms "sex" and "gender" are commonly used interchangeably. However, they are not considered synonymous within the social sciences.[20] The exact definitions of sex and gender, and the relationship between sex, gender and the body, are highly contested. Generally, "sex" refers to biological sex (male or female), though this is of course complex and non-binary.[21] "Gender" refers to one's social identity (man or woman). Rather than being essential (or dictated by sex), the way that one "does" or "performs" one's gender, through behaviour and actions, is learnt.[22] Masculine or feminine behaviours and actions are those that a given society or culture has coded as being performed by men or women, respectively.[23] According to Candace West and Don Zimmerman, one's gender is "an ongoing situated process, a 'doing' rather than a 'being'".[24] One is not a gender. One does gender. The behaviour and actions are performative, as through their doing is gender performed. Gender is constructed by the doing.[25]

The construction of gender is self-perpetuating through its prescriptive nature – it dictates how one should behave. That is, males and females are expected to play out their gendered roles as men and women, reflecting masculinity and femininity, as defined by a given socio-cultural, historical and political context. Using the imagery

19 "Indigenous" is a contested term. It is used here, for want of a better word, to generally refer to peoples who were colonised by a Western power and who are politically, socially and culturally marginalised.

20 E.g. Gayle Rubin, "The Traffic in Women: Notes on the 'Political Economy' of Sex" in Rayna Reiter (ed.) *Toward an Anthropology of Women* (Monthly Review Press, 1975) 165, where sex is determined by biological raw material and gender is "a set of arrangements by which this 'is shaped by human, social intervention'". Gender is the "socially imposed division of the sexes" (at 179) and women are oppressed *as women* and "by having to *be* women" (at 204).

21 See e.g. Claire Ainsworth, "Sex Redefined" (2015) 518 *Nature* 288.

22 Simone de Beauvoir, *The Second Sex* (Howard M Parshley trans., Vintage, 1974); Candace West and Don H Zimmerman, "Doing Gender" (1987) 1(2) *Gender & Society* 125; Judith Butler, "Performative Acts and Gender Constitution: An Essay in Phenomenology and Feminist Theory" (1988) 40(4) *Theatre Journal* 519.

23 See Butler, "Performative Acts and Gender Constitution" (n 22).

24 Candace West and Don H Zimmerman, "Accounting for Doing Gender" (2009) 23(1) *Gender & Society* 112, 114.

25 The extent to which gender is socially constructed is contentious. That is, the exact relationship between sex and gender is highly debated. Some theorists argue that sex itself is socially constructed. Others argue that sex (that is, biology) must dictate some parts of gender. On the various theories of social constructivism, see Detel (n 13).

of theatre, Judith Butler noted that the stage has been set for social actors and the audience punishes and marginalises deviation from the script.[26] Thus, while sex might not dictate behaviour, social, cultural and political context defines the behaviours one observes, imitates, repeats and inhabits. Failure to conform to gendered expectations comes with negative repercussions – "what is called gender identity is a performative accomplishment compelled by social sanction and taboo".[27] For example, women who display masculine traits might be considered social deviants. Similarly, men viewed as effeminate might be deemed "not real men".

While gender is socially constructed, it has the appearance of essentiality. This is because "[g]ender activities emerge from and bolster claims to membership in a sex category".[28] West and Zimmerman stated:

> But doing gender also renders the social arrangements based on sex category accountable as normal and natural, that is, legitimate ways of organizing social life. Differences between women and men that are created by this process can then be portrayed as fundamental and enduring dispositions. In this light, the institutional arrangements of a society can be seen as responsible to the differences – the social order being merely an accommodation to the natural order. Thus if, in doing gender, men are also doing dominance and women are doing difference … The resultant social order, which supposedly reflects "natural differences," is a powerful reinforce and legitimator of hierarchical arrangements.[29]

They continued:

> The sex category/gender relationship links the institutional and interactional levels, a coupling that legitimates social arrangements based on sex category and reproduces their asymmetry in face-to-face interaction. Doing gender furnishes the interactional scaffolding of social structure, along with a built-in mechanism of social control. In appreciating the institutional forces that maintain distinctions between women and men, we must not lose sight of the interactional validation of those distinctions that confers upon them their sense of "naturalness" and "rightness."[30]

Or, in Butler's words:

> Because there is neither an "essence" that gender expresses or externalizes nor an objective ideal to which gender aspires; because gender is not a fact,

26 Butler, "Performative Acts and Gender Constitution" (n 22) 526–7.
27 See ibid., 520.
28 West and Zimmerman, "Doing Gender" (n 22) 127. See also Pierre Bourdieu, "Structuralism and Theory of Sociological Knowledge" (1968) 35(4) *Social Research* 681, 689.
29 West and Zimmerman, "Doing Gender" (n 22), 146.
30 Ibid., 147.

> the various acts of gender creates the idea of gender, and without those acts, there would be no gender at all. Gender is, thus, a construction that regularly conceals its genesis. The tacit collective agreement to perform, produce, and sustain discrete and polar genders as cultural fictions is obscured by the credibility of its own production. The authors of gender become entranced by their own fictions whereby the construction compels one's belief in its necessity and naturalness. The historical possibilities materialized through various corporeal styles are nothing other than those punitively regulated cultural fictions that are alternately embodied and disguised under duress.[31]

This means, for example, that most males identify as men and attempt to behave masculine in line with societal expectations, though this need not be the case. A female can identify as a man and behave masculine or identify as a woman and behave masculine. Or, more pertinent for our purposes, men and women typically create masculine and feminine knowledge, respectively, because of their gender-normative roles. Knowledge is not inherently gendered and females can create masculine knowledge through masculine ways of knowing. However, deviation from expected behaviour could be met with punishment and/or marginalisation.

The recognition that knowledge is not inherently gendered is important as the point of this book is not to argue that the law should protect "feminine knowledge". Such an argument would require defining "feminine knowledge" and in doing so underscore the dichotomisation between the masculine and the feminine.[32] Instead, this book highlights that multiple gendered binaries are entrenched in patent law and the knowledge governance system it creates, to give value to the masculine over the feminine. Thus, gender relations can mirror power relations.[33] Yet, binaries like masculine and feminine are socially constructed, and their dichotomisation constrain males as well as females. Thus, rather than protecting "feminine knowledge" and reinforcing the binary, we need to recognise that the law embodies socially constructed gender differences, to the detriment of the lived experiences of women, before trying to undermine the dichotomy and develop law and a knowledge governance system that is less-gendered and egalitarian.[34]

31 Butler, "Performative Acts and Gender Constitution" (n 22) 522.

32 Kathy Bowrey and Jane Anderson have made similar arguments with respect to Indigenous and non-Indigenous, and "traditional knowledge" and intellectual property; Kathy Bowrey and Jane Anderson, "The Politics of Global Information Sharing: Whose Cultural Agendas are Being Advanced?" (2009) 18(4) *Social & Legal Studies* 479, 4901.

33 RW Connell, *Gender & Power* (Allen & Unwin, 1987) 107–11.

34 On how equality does not require sameness, see Joan W Scott, "Deconstructing Equality-versus-Difference: Or, the Uses of Poststructuralist Theory for Feminism" (1988) 14(1) *Feminist Studies* 33. A contingent of the feminist movement aims to create a "genderless (though not sexless) society, in which one's sexual anatomy is irrelevant to who one is, what one does, and with whom one makes love"; Rubin (n 20) 204.

In this vein, sex and gender should not be viewed dichotomously as embodiments of nature and nurture. To a certain extent, gender is culture transcribed on the body.[35] That is, social, cultural and historical locations affect gender which affects the body. In Anne Fausto-Sterling's words, "the body's matter responds to experiential input" and "[a]cquiring gender is … nothing if not a scripted cultural task that starts before birth and continues throughout the lifecycle".[36] At the same time, though gender is socially constructed, it is affected by sex. To illustrate, if most males exhibit a certain trait and this becomes socialised as connected to power, it is coded masculine. Physical strength or aggression are examples.[37] As a further illustration, that it is only females who are biologically capable of bearing children and then breastfeeding them contributes to the social construction of women as caring and nurturing, which are coded as feminine attributes. But there are of course some females who are stronger than some males, and some males who are more caring and nurturing than some females.

Gender is relational in the sense that it is constituted by and through interrelated and interdependent parts, to create "man" and "woman". One's gender is then constituted dependent on one's location on a web of social relations. As a result, women are often defined relative to men as "other" – they form a dialectic pair.[38] Because gender is social and relational, it is neither static nor indelible. Gender is continually reconstructed. In the words of David Harvey:

> The making-of-the-body is biological, social, political, all of those things, and therefore we can't say that we're simply talking about the social construction of the body in terms of the sort of clothes people wear or something like that. We have to be talking also about the biological making of the body and see the body as an evolutionary project which is unfinished and ongoing; biological processes are transformative, and we are also engaged in transformative activities.[39]

35 Anne Fausto-Sterling, "Against Dichotomy" (2017) 1(1) *Evolutionary Studies in Imaginative Culture* 63.

36 Ibid., 65.

37 There is a correlation between testosterone and aggression. See e.g. Aitken Harris, "Review and Methodological Considerations in Research on Testosterone and Aggression" (1999) 4(3) *Aggression and Violent Behavior* 273; Estrella R Montoya et al., "Testosterone, Cortisol, and Serotonin as Key Regulators of Social Aggression: A Review and Theoretical Perspective" (2011) 36 *Motivation and Emotion* 65; Christoph Eisenegger, Johannes Haushofer and Ernst Fehr, "The Role of Testosterone in Social Interaction" (2011) 15(6) *Trends in Cognitive Sciences* 263; Francis T McAndrew, "The Interacting Roles of Testosterone and Challenges to Status in Human Male Aggression" (2009) 14(5) *Aggression and Violent Behavior* 330; and John Archer, "Testosterone and Human Aggression: An Evaluation of the Challenge Hypothesis" (2006) 30(3) *Neuroscience & Biobehavioral Reviews* 319.

38 Jane Flax, "Postmodernism and Gender Relations in Feminist Theory" (1987) 12(4) *Signs: Journal of Women in Culture and Society* 621, 628–9.

39 David Harvey, "Nature, Politics, and Possibilities: A Debate and Discussion with David Harvey and Donna Haraway" (1995) 13 *Environmental and Planning D: Society and Space* 507, 516.

However, its appearance as essential makes change difficult. Jane Flax noted:

> We live in a world in which gender is a constituting social relation and in which gender is also a relation of domination. Therefore, both men's and women's understanding of anatomy, biology, embodiedness, sexuality, and reproduction is partially rooted in, reflects, and must justify (or challenge) preexisting gender relations. In turn, the existence of gender relations helps us to order and understand the facts of human existence. In other words, gender can become a metaphor for biology just as biology can become a metaphor for gender.[40]

Nevertheless, being situated, dependent on many social variables,[41] what is masculine or feminine within a given social group can change. This depends on the social and political power attributed to particular fields, activities and related behaviours. This is true of people and also of technology, which embodies and affects gender relations.[42] Thus, heteronormative roles are mutable, females can and do invent in masculine ways and fields, and male work can be feminised and vice versa. The recognition that gender constructions are not essential and can be changed is important, as it highlights that knowledge governance need not (and, indeed, should not) be gendered.

In this book, the terms woman and women are not used to maintain gender differences and resultant stigmatisation, marginalisation or oppression, but are employed as an analytical category to explain the varying experiences of females and males.[43] The lived experiences of females and males differ. This is true across many (if not all) social contexts. Ignoring this fact does not make it go away. Social relations that define a society are in large part determined by gender relations, which are dictated by the binaries of male and female, and man and woman. Those binaries, together with other sub-categories of social relations, such as class, race/ethnicity and age, impact an individual's experience, expression of identity and the distribution of power.

At the same time, it is important to acknowledge that "women" are not unified in their experiences.[44] Gender is but one characteristic that defines the

40 Flax (n 38) 637.

41 See e.g. Kalissa Alexeyeff and Niko Besnier, "Gender on the Edge. Identities, Politics, Transformations" in Kalissa Alexeyeff and Niko Besnier (eds), *Gender on the Edge: Transgender, Gay, and Other Pacific Islanders* (University of Hawai'i Press, 2014) 1, on gender in the Pacific.

42 Judy Wajcman, "Feminist Theories of Technology" (2010) 34 *Cambridge Journal of Economics* 143, 150–1.

43 This is similarly the case with the usage of the terms "Indigenous" and "Western" – these terms are not used to reify the dichotomy between the two, but as descriptors necessary to identify the empirical differences between Indigenous people and those with a Eurocentric background.

44 E.g. Bartlett (n 1) 834–5 stated "Assuming a unified concept of 'woman' also adopts a view of the subject that has been rendered highly problematic. Poststructural feminists have claimed that woman has no core identity by rather comprises multiple, overlapping social structures and discourses. Using woman as a category of

human experience, together with sexuality, race, able-bodiedness and class, amongst others. These situate a woman's lived experience in a web of social relations and the intersectional, even specifically individual, experience of any person might differ significantly. This makes these characteristics, not just social relations, but discursive power relations.[45]

This book is primarily about the Western female experience – though this is, of course, also not coherent. There are, thus, generalisations made. It is worth noting that a large majority of the literature on the gendered nature of patent law written in the English language originates from the United States. Broadening the scope to literature on women in STEM, one finds work from the United Kingdom and Western Europe.

The statistical patenting gap between males and females, a global phenomenon, reflects a difference based on sex. However, the reasons why the gap developed and persists are attributable to gender. That is, they pertain to socialised constructions of the scientist and the inventor, science and the inventive process, the patentable invention, and the entrepreneur, all of which are coded masculine.[46] Furthermore, patenting is gendered because of gender-normative roles, biases and power dynamics.[47] These are examined in this book. Though this book takes a generic Western perspective (so far as this exists), much of the commentary on power and privilege are likely more broadly generalisable.

Like all law, patent law both allocates and directs the flow of power and wealth. This is particularly true in the knowledge economy, in which patent law plays a pivotal role in the regulation of who owns some of its most valuable assets. The heavily gendered patenting statistics highlight that patent law allocates this power and wealth predominantly to males. At the same time, the gendered nature of patentability directs society towards masculine technologies. This has the effect of valorising it to the detriment of the feminine. Because of socialisation, this largely impacts females negatively – their ability to patent and commercialise inventions – and perpetuates the social construction of inventors and entrepreneurs as male.

There is, thus, unequal participation in the knowledge economy. Yet, those in power do not like to loosen their grip on it. Men and masculine entities that are patent rich and control the knowledge economy will not allow for change

analysis implies a rejection of these claims, for it suggest that members of the category share a set of common, essential, ahistorical characteristics that constitute a coherent identity". See also Flax (n 38) 642.

45 Judith Butler, *Bodies That Matter: On the Discursive Limits of "Sex"* (Routledge, 2011)

46 See e.g. Burk, "Feminism and Dualism in Intellectual Property" (n 11); Burk, "Do Patents Have Gender?" (n 11); Rosser (n 7); Kara W Swanson, "Getting a Grip on the Corset: Gender, Sexuality, and Patent Law" (2011) 23(1) *Yale Journal of Law and Feminism* 57.

47 See n 4 and 7–6; and Jessica C Lai, "Patents and Gender: A Contextual Analysis" (2020) 10(3) *Queen Mary Journal of Intellectual Property* 283.

that would shift the power dynamic. But this is a question of justice.[48] The marginalisation of women in and by the law is ubiquitous.[49] It needs to be rooted out from a system that purports to be objective, and that can determine the "haves" from the "have nots" and who defines what the future looks like, in the knowledge-driven digital age.

While this book is chiefly about the gendered nature of patent law, it draws from analogies with Indigenous peoples' concerns around the protection of their knowledge.[50] This is not to say that women and Indigenous peoples, or even that Western women and Indigenous women, share the same concerns, interests and goals. They do not.[51] No two social groups (arguably even no two women) have the same historical, social, cultural and political context. Furthermore, the development and theorisation of patent law is distinctively Western.[52] Nevertheless, the analogies serve to illustrate the power dynamics at play behind patent law's constructs, which reflect hierarchies of power and privilege. Furthermore, the literature on Indigenous peoples and the colonisation of their knowledge and knowledge systems is more developed than that on patents and gender. Finally, to a certain extent, Indigenous knowledge has been constructed and categorised as feminine in order to deny its patentability.

Looking at Indigenous peoples' experiences with patent law also serves to underscore the fact that patent law has been constructed to reflect hegemonic power. It allows us to look beyond patent law in trying to frame a regulatory system that promotes the egalitarian production and promotion of knowledge.

When we step away from the comforts of the familiar Western knowledge governance system, patent law, the question becomes what kind of invention and innovation a society wishes to incentivise and commercialise, valorise and foster, and how to best do so. The difficulty is answering such a question in an unbiased manner. After all, invention is not neutral but social, as it is determined by societal need, culture, history and technological inertia. The challenge is to frame a knowledge governance system that factors in that knowledge creation and development are contingent, and simultaneously ensures an egalitarian ecosystem that does not predominantly protect the interests of those in power.

This needs to be a system that allows for the multiplicity of ways in which invention and innovation can and do occur, which in turn will require that we

48 Anne Pollack and Banu Subramaniam "Resisting Power, Retooling Justice: Promises of Feminist Postcolonial Technosciences" (2016) 41(6) *Science, Technology, & Human Values* 951.

49 See e.g. Catharine A MacKinnon, "Feminism, Marxism, Method, and the State: Toward Feminist Jurisprudence" (1983) 8(4) *Signs* 635.

50 On the analogous nature of how science treats race and gender, see Nancy Leys Stepan, "Race and Gender: The Role of Analogy in Science" (1986) 77 *ISIS* 261.

51 See e.g. Sandra Harding, "Postcolonial and Feminist Philosophies of Science and Technology: Convergence and Dissonances" (2009) 12(4) *Postcolonial Studies* 401; and Arun Agrawal, "Dismantling the Divide between Indigenous and Scientific Knowledge" (1995) 26 *Development and Change* 413, 421.

52 See e.g. Jessica C Lai, "The Changing Function of Patents: A Reversion to Privileges?" (2017) 37(4) *Legal Studies* 807.

recognise that individuals, groups and communities can behave beyond socially constructed dichotomies. We need to develop such a system to ensure that everyone can participate equally in the knowledge economy and, moreover, have an equal say in what that knowledge economy looks like and whom it benefits.

Moreover, having diverse ways of knowing, knowledges and viewpoints is advantageous for invention and innovation. As noted by Sandra Harding:

> how we live together both enables and limits what we can know, and vice versa. Thus when new kinds of persons "step on the stage of history" to rearticulate how they see themselves and the world, new kinds of sciences, philosophies of science, and epistemologies are both generated and also relied on by their listeners. Of course this insight about the relation between what we do and what we can know is not far from an important conventional feature of scientific method: how one interacts with the world around us both enables and limits what one can know about it.[53]

Mono-cultural, mono-gendered knowledge can only ever be narrow and poor:

> Since societies and their sciences co-constitute each other, it should not come as a surprise to discover that the gender relations of the societies sponsoring and conducting scientific and technological research in colonial and imperial contexts would shape the nature of the knowledge such inquiries produced. The absence of women in these kinds of directorial positions affected the selection of scientific problems, hypotheses to be tested, what constituted relevant data to be collected, how it was collected and interpreted, the dissemination and consequences of the results of research, and who was credited with the scientific and technological work.[54]

Therefore, developing a knowledge governance system that embraces multiplicity is not just egalitarian, it makes sense in terms of creating novel, broad and rich knowledge. The "women in STEM" dialogue is a distraction from this – it perpetuates the idea that masculine modes and fields of industry are of greatest value, forcing women to operate within binary cultures that marginalise and oppress them. It does nothing to change existing modalities to maximise innovative potential. Nor does it do anything to break down the dichotomy between the masculine and the feminine.

Chapter 1 of this book examines gendered patenting. That is, the empirical data around how patenting rates differ for males and females, based on jurisdiction, industry and other variables. Chapter 2 follows with an analysis of the

53 Harding (n 51) 403. See also Evelyn Fox Keller, "Feminism and Science" in Evelyn Fox Keller and Helen E Longino, *Feminism and Science* (Oxford University Press, 1996) 28.

54 Harding (n 51) 408.

gendered binaries embodied within patent law, in particular what is patentable. The gendered nature of patent law results in male-dominated STEM being fields that produce patentable inventions. This, in turn, means that women must be in STEM if they wish to partake in the knowledge economy. Yet, the contexts within which invention and innovation take place are heavily gendered and biased against women. This is addressed in Chapter 3, which highlights how the entire system created around patents sets up women to fail. This has many negative consequences for women's financial position, reputation as inventors, and what knowledge is commercialised and perpetuated, which is examined in Chapter 4. The knowledge system created by patent law is by no means otherwise flawless. Chapter 5 discusses the multitude of ways in which patent law reproduces binaries and hegemonic power, and does not reflect how invention and innovation actually take place. Chapter 6 examines different ontological and epistemological theories around knowledge with the aim of better understanding "knowledge" existentially and empirically. Chapter 7 looks at how we might develop an egalitarian knowledge governance system that reflects how creativity occurs in practice. It does so by asking what the legal system can learn from feminist theory and ontology/epistemology.

Ultimately, this book is about the power relations that undergird the patent system and how the predominant knowledge governance system reflects the hegemony of white, middle-class males. Perhaps in creating an egalitarian knowledge governance system, freer of constructed gendered binaries as to what is deemed an invention and who is deemed an inventor, we might contribute to chipping down the masculine/feminine dichotomy.

1 Gendered patenting

Intellectual property regulates certain intangible "things". While trade mark law protects registered marks used in trade, copyright law and patent law are more geared toward protecting the creative. The distinction between the subject matter of copyright and patents is by no means hard and fast, and (as discussed in Chapter 7) it is a constructed difference. Generally (or legally speaking), copyright protects the artistic and aesthetic, such as artwork, literature and musical works. In contrast, patents protect industrial and technical inventions, such as machines and pharmaceuticals. If granted, a patent owner (or patentee) has up to 20 years of exclusive rights.

Women can apply for and be granted patents. There is nothing in the law that is apparently unequal. Furthermore, because patents are granted for industrial and technical inventions, they are outwardly objective in appearance. Yet, multiple data sets from around the world show that patents are predominantly attributed to male inventors. Patenting is gendered. Chapters 2 and 3 examine why it is that patenting is gendered. This chapter outlines the nature of the patent gender gap.

1 General statistics

Every jurisdiction has slightly different rules for what is patentable. International law and globalisation of trade have resulted in a certain degree of harmonisation. However, the differences in patentability across jurisdictions mean that data from different countries are not directly comparable. However, the gender patenting gap exists around the world.[1]

As illustrated in Table 1.1, the gender patenting gap is exhibited in patent applications made through the international filing system. This is via the World Intellectual Property Organization (WIPO) Patent Cooperation Treaty (PCT).[2] This does not offer international patents. Patents are territorial (that is,

1 Gema Lax Martine, Julio Raffo and Kaori Saito, "Identifying the Gender of PCT Inventors" (November 2016) *Economic Research Working Paper* No. 33, WIPO Economics and Statistics Series, 11.

2 Through the Patent Cooperation Treaty. See Lax Martine, Raffo and Saito (n 1) 8. See also UKIPO, "Gender Profiles in Worldwide Patenting: An Analysis of Female Inventorship" (September 2019), 8–12; and Rainer Frietsch et al., "Gender-Specific Patterns in Patenting and Publishing" (2009) 38 *Research Policy* 590.

DOI: 10.4324/9781003128502-2

jurisdictionally bound). However, applicants in PCT contracting states can file "PCT applications" through their local patent office. These are passed on to WIPO, which then has an administrative role in distributing these to selected foreign patent offices. In 2015, 71 per cent of PCT filings named only male inventors, and males constituted 85 per cent of inventors.[3]

Similar statistics can be seen in applications made to the European Patent Office (EPO).[4] The EPO grants a bundle of national patents, based on the European Patent Convention. A national patent granted through the EPO can be ruled invalid by the national courts. From 2001–2003, only 8 per cent of inventors on EPO applications were female.

Unsurprisingly, similar statistics exist at the national level. To illustrate, of patents granted by the United States Patent and Trademark Office (USPTO) in 2019, only 12.8 per cent of inventors were female and 78.1 per cent of the patents named only male inventors.[5] Similarly, in the United Kingdom, 69 per cent of applications in 2015 named only male inventors and only 11 per cent of

Table 1.1 Comparison of inventors

	% female inventors of total inventors	*% applications/ patents with only male inventors*	*% applications/ patents with only female inventors*
United Kingdom (UK), 2017, applications.[6]	11	69	4.9
United States (US), 2019, granted patents.[7]	12.8	78.1	4 (2016 data)[8]

3 Lax Martine, Raffo and Saito (n 1) 8.
4 Fulvio Naldi et al., "Scientific and Technological Performance by Gender" in Henk F Moed et al. (eds), *Handbook of Quantitative Science and Technology Research* (Springer, 2005) 299; Paola Giuri et al., "Inventors and Invention Processes in Europe: Results from the PatVal-EU Survey" (2007) 36 *Research Policy* 1107, 1111; European Studies on Gender Aspects of Inventions, "Statistical Survey and Analysis of Gender Impact on Inventions" (2009) EUR 036671; Kordula Kugele, "Analysis of Women's Participation in High-Technology Patenting" in Pooran Wynarczyk and Susan Marlow (eds), *Innovating Women: Contributions to Technological Advancement* (Emerald Group Publishing, 2010) 123, 134–5.
5 USPTO, "Progress and Potential: 2020 Update on U.S. Women Inventor-Patentees" (2020) Office of the Chief Economist, *IP Data Highlights* No. 4, 3 (hereinafter USPTO 2020 Update); Cassidy R Sugimoto et al., "The Academic Advantage: Gender Disparities in Patenting" (2015) 10(5) *PLoS ONE* e0128000, 5; and Waverly L Ding, Fiona Murray and Toby E Stuart "Gender Differences in Patenting in the Academic Life Sciences" (2006) 313 *Science* 665; Jessica Milli et al., "Equity in Innovation: Women Inventors and Patents" (2016) *Institute for Women's Policy Research.*
6 UKIPO (n 2) 13.
7 USPTO 2020 Update (n 5) 3.
8 USPTO, 'Progress and Potential: A Profile of Women Inventors on US Patents' (2019) Office of the Chief Economist, *IP Data Highlights* No. 2 (hereinafter USPTO 2019).

	% female inventors of total inventors	*% applications/patents with only male inventors*	*% applications/patents with only female inventors*
Australia, 2016, applications.[9]	Not available	74	5
European Patent Office (EPO), 2001–2003, applications.[10]	8	Not available	Not available
WIPO Patent Cooperation Treaty (PCT), 2015, applications.[11]	15	71	4.3

inventors were female. Finally, in Australia, 74 per cent of patent applications from 2016 had no female inventors. The national-level statistics presented here are from Western, English-speaking countries. This is due to the perspective of this book. However, it is worth noting that the statistics are similar around the world, as exhibited by the international filing data and the national breakdowns one finds in that data.

If a patent application or grant names a female inventor, this is typically among a group of male inventors.[12] That is, only a small percentage of patented inventions have solely female inventors (whether as individuals or in teams).[13] This is also shown in Table 1.1. Of WIPO PCT applications in 2015, only 4.3 per cent of applications were attributed to female-only inventors. In the UK, this statistic was 4.9 per cent in 2017.

Females also tend to patent in larger teams than males.[14] This potentially indicates that females are more likely to work in teams and/or tend to only patent when males are involved. Furthermore, if a patent names a female inventor, that female is seldom listed as the first inventor.[15] As discussed further in Chapter 3, patenting in larger teams and not as first inventors negatively affects the reputational gains that females might get from patenting. The more inventors there are,

9 IP Australia, 'Australia is Closing the Gender Gap on Female Inventors' (8 March 2018) <https://www.ipaustralia.gov.au/about-us/news-and-community/news/australia-closing-gender-gap-female-inventors>.

10 European Studies on Gender Aspects of Inventions (n 4).

11 Lax Martine, Raffo and Saito (n 1) 8.

12 Ibid.; UKIPO (n 2) 13–4; Naldi et al. (n 4) 299–314; Yu Meng and Phillip Shapira, "Women and Patenting in Nanotechnology: Scale Scope and Equity" in Susan E Cozens and Jameson M Wetmore (eds), *Nanotechnology and the Challenges of Equity: Equality and Development* (Springer, 2011) 23, 33; and European Studies on Gender Aspects of Inventions (n 4).

13 Lax Martine, Raffo and Saito (n 1) 13–14; Naldi et al. (n 4) 307; Meng and Shapira (n 12) 34; and G Steven McMillan, "Gender Differences in Patenting Activity: An Examination of the US Biotechnology Industry" (2009) 80(3) *Scientometrics* 683, 686.

14 UKIPO (n 2) 13; and USPTO 2019 (n 8) 11–12.

15 Catherine Ashcraft and Tony Breitzman, "Who Invents IT? Women's Participation in Information Technology Patenting" (2012) National Center for Women & Information Technology, at 9.

the less reputational gain additional inventors get. The first inventor tends to become associated with the invention and all other inventors are cast into the oblivion of "et al".

2 Field of technology

The exact gender patenting gap differs country to country.[16] One would presume that this reflects how socially progressive a country is. For example, that a country that scores high generally on gender equality should have a smaller gender patenting gap. However, this is not the case. Instead, jurisdictional disparities in the gender patenting gap are largely due to: (1) differences in employment in a given science, technology, engineering and mathematics (STEM) field; and (2) the strength of particular industries within a jurisdiction.

The gender patenting gap is not as stark in fields that have more female representation. That is, there are more females in certain STEM fields and, thus, more patents naming female inventors from those fields. The fields with more gender parity in patenting are chemistry, pharmaceutical or biotechnology, as well as health-related disciplines.[17] Jurisdictions strong in these fields will have relatively smaller gender patenting gaps. For example, 2015 PCT filings show that 57.6 of biotechnology patent applications named a female inventor.[18] Applications in pharmaceuticals, organic fine chemistry and food chemistry were similarly high.[19] As a further illustration, in the period 2007–2019, women made up 11 per cent of inventors of USTPO-granted patents.[20] This percentage was higher for patents relating to healthcare products and pharmaceuticals but was markedly lower for electrical and mechanical engineering technologies.[21]

This leads to the flipside of the coin, which is that the gender gap in patenting is larger in fields with low female participation, such as computer and engineering fields, transport and machine construction.[22] Furthermore, the gap is more apparent in industries that are notoriously hostile environments for females, such

16 Lax Martine, Raffo and Saito (n 1) 9.
17 Ibid., 11–14; UKIPO (n 2) 18–22; and Annette I Kahler "Examining Exclusion in Woman-Inventor Patenting: A Comparison of Educational Trends and Patent Data in the Era of Computer Engineer Barbie" (2011) 19(3) *American University Journal of Gender, Social Policy & the Law* 773; Ulrike Busolt, Kordula Kugele and Iris Tinsel, "European Studies on Gender Aspects of Inventions – Statistical Survey and Analysis of Gender Impact on Inventions (ESGI)" (2008), 3; and Naldi et al. (n 4) 309–11. See also Susan C Eaton, "Surprising Opportunities: Gender and the Structure of Work in Biotechnology Firms" (1999) 869 *Annals New York Academy of Sciences* 175; Kjersten Bunker Whittington and Laurel Smith-Doerr, "Women Inventors in Context: Disparities in Patenting Across Academia and Industry" (2008) 22(2) *Gender & Society* 194.
18 Lax Martine, Raffo and Saito (n 1) 11
19 See also UKIPO (n 2) 18–9.
20 USPTO 2020 Update (n 5) 6
21 USPTO 2020 Update (n 5) 7.
22 Busolt, Kugele and Tinsel (n 17) 3. See also UKIPO (n 2) 18–22.

as engineering and the computer sciences, analysed further below. To illustrate, PCT filings from 2015 showed that only 10.9 per cent of patent applications in the field of mechanical elements named a female inventor.[23] Patent applications in the fields of civil engineering, engines, pumps, turbines, machines tools and transport were similarly low. Jurisdictions focused on these disciplines will have relatively larger gender patenting gaps.

This explains why countries known to have relatively better gender equality might nevertheless have large gender patenting gaps.[24] Germany exemplifies this. Germany is known for being relatively socially progressive vis-à-vis gender. Yet only 9.1 per cent of inventors named on 2011–2015 PCT fillings from Germany were female.[25] Part of the reason for this was that Germany has strong transport and mechanical engineering industries. These are male-dominated fields that tend to ostracise women.

The statistics from this section form the basis for the "women in STEM" rhetoric, which argues that the gender patenting gap is attributable to under-representation of women in STEM. As discussed below (and throughout this book), not enough "women in STEM" resulting in fewer female inventors is only a symptom of systemic and social inequity.

3 Institution type

Applications from universities and public institutes are more likely to name a female inventor than applications from industry.[26] This is true across almost all disciplines.[27] PatStat data (collecting data from multiple patent offices, including all the major patent offices) from 1998–2017 showed that around 15 per cent of inventors from universities were female, whereas only around 9 per cent of inventors from industry were female.[28]

Problematically, there are far more patent applications from industry than universities or the public sector,[29] and there are proportionately fewer female researchers in the former than in the latter.[30] That is, industry figures, which are more gendered than university and public-sector figures, dominate overall figures. Exact numbers are also discipline specific. To illustrate, within the life sciences in the US, taking into account the number of researchers, the gender patenting gap is significantly smaller in industry than it is in academia.[31]

23 Lax Martine, Raffo and Saito (n 1) 11.
24 Ibid., 9.
25 Ibid., 10.
26 European Studies on Gender Aspects of Inventions (n 4); and Lax Martine, Raffo and Saito (n 1) 15.
27 Sugimoto et al. (n 5) 5–6.
28 UKIPO (n 2) 24.
29 Lax Martine, Raffo and Saito (n 1) 15.
30 Busolt, Kugele and Tinsel (n 17); USPTO 2019 (n 8) 9.
31 Kjersten Bunker Whittington and Laurel Smith-Doerr, "Gender and Commercial Science: Women's Patenting in the Life Sciences" (2005) 30 *Journal of Technology*

4 Relative to other numbers

International and national data shows that the gender patenting gap has decreased over time.[32] However, as outlined in the foregoing, it remains clearly apparent. Indeed, the increase in female patenting rates does not match the growth of females attending university and achieving postgraduate education.[33] As indicated in the foregoing, the patenting gap exists, in part, due to the fact that there are fewer females in the patent-heavy STEM fields. The issue has become less about education levels and more about whether females remain in STEM.[34] The absence of employment equality in these fields naturally means that fewer females patent than males.[35]

Nevertheless, as alluded to above, that there are not enough "women in STEM" is not the core problem. This is exemplified by the fact that, even factoring in that there are fewer females in STEM fields, the number of females patenting in STEM is disproportionately low.[36] This is true even in the STEM fields with more employment parity, such as chemistry and biotechnology.[37]

Transfer 355; and Bunker Whittington and Smith-Doerr, "Women Inventors in Context" (n 17).

32 E.g. Milli et al. (n 5) 4 and 7; Jennifer Hunt et al., "Why Don't Women Patent?" (2012) *NBER Working Paper* No. 17888, www.nber.org/papers/w17888.

33 Yun Ling Li and Anthony A Peguero, "Professional Women's Dilemma Between Work and Family: An Examination of the Advance Program" (2015) 19(2) *Gender, Technology and Development* 119, 123; Taehyun Jung and Olof Ejermo, "Demographic Patterns and Trends in Patenting: Gender, Age, and Education of Inventors" (2014) 86 *Technological Forecasting Social Change* 110, 117; and Kahler (n 17) 784–90.

34 Jennifer Hunt et al., "Why Are Women Underrepresented Amongst Patentees?" (2013) 42 *Research Policy* 831, looked at patenting and commercialisation rates against education in science and engineering. They found that women with a degree in these fields patent little more than women without such a degree. Furthermore, the underrepresentation of women in science and technology only contributes 7 per cent of the lower rates of female patent commercialisation. They conclude that the issue is not that women are not educated in these fields, but that they do not stay in the field, especially in electrical and mechanical engineering (high patenting fields, even within STEM). Furthermore, women do not have development and design positions. See also Lisa D Cook and Chaleampong Kongcharoen, "The Idea Gap in Pink and Black" (September 2010) *NBER Working Paper* No. 16331, 14–17, www.nber.org/papers/w16331.

35 Erin Leahey and Amelia Blume "Elucidating the Process: Why Women Patent Less than Men" in Albert N Link (ed), *Gender and Entrepreneurial Activity* (Edward Elgar, 2017) 151, 159; Giuri et al. (n 4) 1111; and Ann Bartow, "Patent Law, Copyright Law, and the Girl Germs Effect" (2016) 90 *St John's Law Review* 578, 583–8.

36 Giuri et al. (n 4) 1111; Kugele (n 4) 135; and Sue V Rosser, "The Gender Gap in Patenting: Is Technology Transfer a Feminist Issue?" (2009) 21(2) *National Women's Studies Association Journal* 65, 67.

37 Ding, Murray and Stuart (n 5); European Studies on Gender Aspects of Inventions (n 4); Meng and Shapira (n 12) 22–7; and Kara W. Swanson, "Intellectual Property and Gender: Reflections on Accomplishments and Methodology" (2015) 24(1) *American University Journal of Gender, Social Policy & the Law* 175, 183.

Table 1.2 Kugele's comparison of female researchers and female inventors in Europe

	Female researchers	*Female inventors*
pharmaceuticals, medicinal chemicals and botanical products	44%	18%
chemicals and chemical products	35%	15%
electrical and optical equipment	10%	5%

That is to say, the percentage of females listed as inventors on patents is lower than the percentage of females working in STEM, regardless of the exact field.

By way of illustration, Kordula Kugele examined the number of researchers compared to the number of inventors in three European contexts in 2003: pharmaceuticals, medicinal chemicals and botanical products; chemicals and chemical products; and electrical and optical equipment.[38] In all three groups of technology fields, there were statistically at least twice as many female researchers than there were inventors. Her results are summarised in Table 1.2.

Analogously, looking at patents granted in the US in 2019, the USPTO noted that female inventor rate of 12.8 per cent was:

> substantially lower benchmarks of women's education and employment as scientists and engineers. In 2017, women held about 2 million science and engineering jobs, but only 27,000 women were inventor-patentees in that year. The share of male science and engineering job holders who are inventor-patentees was three times higher.[39]

If the issue were merely that women are underrepresented in STEM, we would not expect to see these disparities between the proportion of researchers and the proportion of inventors. The issue goes beyond there not being enough women in STEM. Thus, regarding the 2019 data, the USPTO continued that "[t]hese data suggest that expanding the pipeline through education and science and engineering jobs, while necessary, is not sufficient to increase the participation of women as inventor-patentees".[40]

More still, the fact that females in STEM tend to be in medicine, pharmaceuticals, chemistry and the life sciences also impacts their ability to own patents.[41] This is because these are fields that have lower application acceptance rates. In contrast, fields like mechanics, engineering and electronics, which are male dominated, have higher application acceptance rates.[42] There is empirical

38 Kugele (n 4) 134–5.
39 USPTO 2020 Update (n 5) 3.
40 USPTO 2020 Update (n 5) 3.
41 Milli et al. (n 5) 11–12.
42 Michael Carley, Deepak Hedge and Alan Marco. "What Is the Probability of Receiving a US Patent? USPTO Economic Working Paper" (2014) Office of Chief Economist, USPTO, Working Paper No. 2013–2, 8, https://papers.ssrn.com/sol3/papers.cfm?abstract_id=2849631.

evidence to support that biases within patent offices result in male-dominated fields having higher success rates than female-dominated fields (discussed in Chapter 3). This implies that having "women in STEM" is not sufficient. The systemic gendered nature of knowledge governance (as centred on patents) and the power dynamics involved in gender relations means that the system will not treat women as it treats men (see Chapters 2 and 3). Thus, even as women move into STEM, the system finds ways to deny them patents and thereby wealth and power (see Chapters 3 and 4).

5 Conclusion

Patenting is gendered. The data is very clear. The exact numbers depend on the country, field and institution type. There tends to be more gender equity in patenting in the "soft" sciences, such as chemistry and biology. The gender patenting gap is larger in the "hard" sciences, such as engineering. This has been attributed to the fact that there are more women in the former and fewer in the latter. That is, the more women in a field, the more female inventors there are in that field, and vice versa. This contributes towards the rhetoric that we need more "women in STEM" and that this will remove the gendered patenting gap. However, the relationship between representation in a field and patent inventorship in that field is a correlation. The relationship is not proportionate. It is not one of simple causation.

Therefore, increasing the number of females in currently patent-heavy fields is unlikely to ever proportionately increase the number of female inventors named on patents.[43] While part of the gender patenting gap can be attributable to the number of women in STEM (because quite obviously if women are not in STEM they cannot get patents in STEM), patent law is not a neutral bystander. What is patentable and the construction of "science" and "technology" are gendered to be biased against women. Thus, there is a deeper inquiry at issue: why do females need to be in STEM to patent? The gendered nature of patent law is discussed in the following chapter. Chapter 3 then examines the social, cultural and institutional context within which invention and innovation take place, showing how they reinforce the masculine construction of "science" and "technology".

43 Cf. n 34.

2 The organising force of gender

> … ideologies of gender play (and have played) [a role] in the abstract schema underlying our modes of organization. … [One should try to understand] the genesis of the sexual and emotional division of labour, so conspicuously prevalent … that labelled mind, reason, and objectivity as "male", and heart (and body), feeling, and subjectivity as "female", and hence, that underlay the historic exclusion of women from the scientific endeavour.[1]

> … those with power pretend that their interest are natural, objective and inevitable, they supress and ignore other diverse perspectives.[2]

1 Introduction

Chapter 1 reviewed statistics around patenting relative to sex. It showed that around the world the vast majority of inventors named on patent applications are male. This chapter and the following chapter elucidate why there is a gender patenting gap.

The gender patenting gap is larger in fields that are stereotypically few in, and hostile towards, women, such as engineering. The natural corollary to these kinds of statistics is a discussion around there being not enough "women in science, technology, engineering and mathematics (STEM)". The discourse is narrowly focused on how to get more women in STEM.[3] However, even in industries and countries with more employment parity, such as biotechnology and chemistry, females patent disproportionately less than males. These are important statistics as they evidence that the issue goes beyond there not being enough women in STEM. The deeper problems are, firstly, that patent law protects the masculine rather than the feminine, which means that creations from masculine production embodied in STEM constitute patentable inventions, but not feminine inventions.

1 Evelyn Fox Keller, "What Impact, if Any, Has Feminism Had on Science?" (2004) 29(1) *Journal of Biosciences* 7.
2 Katharine T Bartlett, "Feminist Legal Methods" (1990) 103 *Harvard Law Review* 829, 885–6.
3 See e.g. Vikki Hazelwood et al., "What Might We Do to Encourage More Women to Write Patents?" (2019) 32 *Technology and Innovation* 43.

DOI: 10.4324/9781003128502-3

This is discussed in this chapter. The consequence of gendered patentability is that females must be in STEM to patent. However, the second problem is that women face numerous biases when they operate in STEM. Chapter 3 discusses the social, institutional, structural and organisational biases against women scientists in inventing, patenting and commercialising.

This chapter addresses how patent law itself is gendered to the advantage of the masculine and disadvantage of the feminine.[4] It underscores how patent law has been crafted and interpreted to protect and enhance the power that created it. As indicated by the quotes at the beginning of the chapter, part of the gender patenting gap is attributable to binaries embedded in patent law that are detrimental to women, yet have the appearance of being essential. Furthermore, as property, patent rights are (in part) justified through natural rights theory.[5] This gives patents an air of neutrality.[6] However, no law is neutral.[7] Law is a reflection of its author, and the cultural, social, political and philosophical context in which it is created. Regarding gender, Catharine MacKinnon stated:

> I propose that the state is male in the feminist sense. The law sees and treats women the way men see and treat women. The liberal state coercively and authoritatively constitutes the social order in the interest of men as a gender, through its legitimizing norms, relation to society, and substantive policies. … Substantively, the way the male point of view frames an experience is the way it is framed by state policy. … Gender, elaborated and sustained by behavioral patterns of application and administration, is maintained as a division of power.[8]

4 A simplified and shorter version of this chapter was published in Jessica C Lai, "Gendered 'Objective' Patent Law: Of Binaries and a Singularity" (2020) 47(3) *Journal of Law and Society* 441.

5 In the English-speaking world, this is typically through applying Lockean labour theory; John Locke, *Two Treatises of Government* (Peter Laslett ed., 2nd edn, Cambridge University Press, 1960) sect. 27; and Adam Mossoff, "Rethinking the Development of Patents: An Intellectual History, 1550–1800" (2001) 52 *Hastings Law Journal* 1255, 1288–315. In Continental Europe, a natural rights basis for intellectual property is largely attributable Kantian and Hegelian natural rights theories related to personality and individuality; Immanuel Kant, "On the Injustice of Counterfeiting Books" (1785), reprinted in JAL Sterling, *World Copyright Law* (2nd edn, Sweet & Maxwell, 2003); Georg Wilhelm Friedrich Hegel, *Philosophy of Right* (Thomas M Knox trans., Oxford University Press, 1967).

6 Laura A Foster, "Decolonizing Patent Law: Postcolonial Technoscience and Indigenous Knowledge in South Africa" (2017) 28(3) *Feminist Formations* 148, 151.

7 Kara W Swanson, "Intellectual Property and Gender: Reflections on Accomplishments and Methodology" (2015) 24(1) *American University Journal of Gender, Social Policy & the Law* 175, 182.

8 Catharine A MacKinnon, "Feminism, Marxism, Method, and the State: Towards Feminist Jurisprudence" (1983) 8(3) *Journal of Women in Culture and Society* 635, 644.

More specific to our purposes, "patents (and science) are not objective, natural rights but historical and contingent processes open to change".[9] In the words of Dan Burk, patent law "is infected with a prevailing set of attitudes about the social role of women".[10] This is reflected in what is deemed to be patentable. It is important to critically analyse this, as failure to do so allows false neutral notions of science (discussed in Chapter 3) to be bolstered by *prima facie* neutral law – "The formal norm of legal neutrality conceals the way in which legal rules participate in the construction of [gendered] meanings".[11] The law has a naturalising effect.

This chapter analyses patentability through a gender frame, addressing the four core requirements for patentability and how they embody multiple constructed and gendered binaries.[12] Patents are granted for "inventions" of the "technical arts", rather than the "aesthetic arts". Copyright law protects the latter, such as books, poetry, paintings, sculptures, dance choreography and

9 Foster, "Decolonizing Patent Law" (n 6) 153–4.

10 Dan L Burk, "Do Patents Have Gender?" (2011) 19 *American University Journal of Gender, Social Policy & the Law* 881, 888. See also Laura A Foster, "The Making and Unmaking of Patent Ownership: Technicalities, Materialities, and Subjectivities" (2016) *PoLAR* 127.

11 Mary Joe Frug, *Postmodern Legal Feminism* (Routledge, 1992) 129.

12 There is very little written on patentability and gender. See, however, Dan L Burk, "Feminism and Dualism in Intellectual Property" (2007) 15(2) *American University Journal of Gender, Social Policy & the Law* 195; Burk, "Do Patents Have Gender?" (n 10); Shlomit Yanisky-Ravid, "Eligible Patent Matter – Gender Analysis of Patent Law: International and Comparative Perspectives" (2011) 19(3) *American University Journal of Gender, Social Policy & the Law* 851; and Annette I Kahler, "Examining Exclusion in Woman-Inventor Patenting: A Comparison of Educational Trends and Patent Data in the Era of Computer Engineer Barbie" (2011) 19(3) *American University Journal of Gender, Social Policy & the Law* 773.

There is considerably more literature on copyright law and gender. See e.g. Dan L Burk, "Copyright and Feminism in Digital Media" (2006) 14(3) *American University Journal of Gender, Social Policy & the Law* 519; Carys J Craig; Joseph F Turcotte and Rosemary J Coombe, "What is Feminist About Open Access?: A Relational Approach to Copyright in the Academy" (2011) 1(1) *Feminists@law* 1; Carys J Craig, "Reconstructing the Author-Self: Some Feminist Lessons for Copyright Law" (2007) 15(2) *American University Journal of Gender, Social Policy & the Law* 207; Carys J Craig, "Feminist Aesthetics and Copyright Law: Genius, Value, and Gendered Visions of the Creative Self" (2014) 10(1) *Osgoode Legal Studies Research Paper* No. 42; Ann Bartow, "Fair Use and the Fairer Sex: Gender, Feminism, and Copyright Law" (2006) 14(3) *American University Journal of Gender, Social Policy & the Law* 551; B Courtney Doagoo, "Feminist Anthropology and Copyright: Gauging the Application and Limitations of Oppositions Models" in B Courtney Doagoo et al. (eds), *Intellectual Property for the 21st Century: Interdisciplinary Approaches* (Irwin Law, 2014) 163; Anthea Kraut, *Choreographing Copyright: Race, Gender, and Intellectual Property Rights in American Dance* (Oxford University Press, 2016); Kevin J Greene, "Intellectual Property at the Intersection of Race and Gender: Lady Sings the Blues" (2008) 16(3) *American University Journal of Gender, Social Policy & the Law* 165.

musical works.[13] To be patentable, the invention must be: (1) novel; (2) non-obvious (or embody an inventive step); (3) have utility or use (or industrial application); and (4) constitute patent-eligible subject matter. The first two of these judge the claimed invention relative to certain reference points – the "prior art" and the "common general knowledge". The latter two involve an assessment of the invention itself and whether it embodies the "right kind" of subject matter and related use.

One has to apply to a patent office for a patent. The patent application includes an explanation of the field, a description of the invention and "claims". If granted, the scope of the patentee's property is embodied in the claims. The claims are separate but related inventions. For example, Claim 1 of an application might be for a chemical compound, Claim 2 could be a specific formulation of the compound, and Claim 3 might pertain to a specific method of using that compound. Patent examiners examine the application and each claim individually for the four requirements listed in the foregoing. All four of these requirements must be met. For example, one might create something new that is very inventive and useful, but it will not be patentable if it does not qualify as patent-eligible subject matter. Patents are territorial, meaning that having a patent from one country only has effect in that country.[14]

This chapter offers a primer on the core binaries embodied in patent law. These are namely: public/private, mind/body and culture/nature. The chapter then demonstrates that the novelty standard reflects the private/public dichotomy, where women operate in the private sphere and only men may move between the two spheres. Relegated to the private sphere, the patent system ignores feminine modes of invention. It is masculine knowledge in the public sphere that is perceived as new. However, while women's knowledge is given, it does not form part of the common general knowledge, which is constructed masculine. The common general knowledge is the knowledge base used to assess whether an invention is non-obvious. If feminine knowledge is not part of the common general knowledge, it is open to be taken, transformed through the masculine and patented. The derived invention is non-obvious because the feminine knowledge was not common general knowledge.

13 The distinction between the "technical arts" and the "aesthetic arts" is a human construct. Indeed, it is a Western construct and many peoples, such as Indigenous peoples, do not draw such a distinction. Instead, Indigenous peoples tend to view everything more holistically and their knowledge systems tend not to distinguish between different kinds of "intellectual knowledge", or between the tangible, intangible and spiritual. See e.g. Michael Blakeney, "The Negotiations in WIPO for International Conventions on Traditional Knowledge and Traditional Cultural Expressions" in Jessica C Lai and Antoinette Maget Dominicé (eds), *Intellectual Property and Access to Im/material Goods* (Edward Elgar, 2016) 227, 247–54.

14 There is no such thing as an "international patent", though the Patent Cooperation Treaty (1160 UNTS 231; 9 ILM 978 (1970)) means that there is cooperation between the different patent offices, and there are some regional patent offices, such as the European Patent Office (EPO, which has the ability to grant national patents for that region).

The requirements that an invention must have utility and must be a certain kind of subject matter also reflect the private/public binary. The law deems the industrial to be useful and patent-eligible. The industrial is the masculine, which has been made in the public sphere. Moreover, patent-eligible subject matter reflects the cultural – the "made". Natural products and laws are not patentable, yet women are constructed as being closer to nature.

It is worth reiterating that gender (man or woman) and associated behaviour (masculine or feminine) are socially constructed. What is a masculine or feminine way of knowing or kind of knowledge relates to the spheres and roles that society has given men and women. These are not inherent spheres or roles, but the masculine is typically performed by males, and connected to value, power and privilege, while females usually perform feminine, which is attributed less worth, power and advantage.[15] Thus, in the following, when it is concluded that patent law predominantly protects the masculine, this is to say that it predominately grants property over the creations of men and males – creations that they predominantly make because of their gendered roles. The statistics in Chapter 2 confirm that this is the case. But, because gender is a social construct, females can and indeed do perform masculine. However, as discussed in Chapter 3, they are ostracised when they do and "old boys' clubs" and other masculine institutions (including patent offices) ensure that those with power do not have to share their power.

2 A primer on modernity

The Venetian Patent Statute 1474 is typically credited as the first statute in the world relating to patents. The next significant piece of legislation pertaining to patents was the Statute of Monopolies 1623 from the United Kingdom, which was passed to curtail the Crown's ability to grant monopolies. The Statute of Monopolies 1623 included an exception, allowing the Crown to grant patents for inventions that were "manners of new manufacture".[16] This Statute created the foundation for modern patent law across England, England's colonies and the English-speaking world.

Patent law was interpreted and developed significantly by the courts subsequent to the passing of the Statute of Monopolies in 1623. This coincided with the Industrial Revolution, which shaped the modern patent system into what it is today.[17] The Industrial Revolution, in turn, took place within the "modern era" and the socio-political, ontological and epistemological philosophies of this era form the bedrock of modern patent law. Patent law has remained substantively the same since the mid-1800s.[18]

15 This is equally true of "Indigenous knowledge" and "Western science"; see e.g. Arun Agrawal, "Dismantling the Divide between Indigenous and Scientific Knowledge" (1995) 26 *Development and Change* 413.

16 Statute of Monopolies 1623 (UK), s 6.

17 See Christine MacLeod, *Inventing the Industrial Revolution: The English Patent System, 1660–1800* (Cambridge University Press, 1988).

18 Brad Sherman and Lionel Bently, *The Making of Modern Intellectual Property Law: The British Experience, 1760–1911* (Cambridge University Press, 1999).

The "modern era" is considered to include the early modern period from 1500–1800 (encompassing the Age of Enlightenment, the Age of Exploration and the Industrial Revolution), followed by the late modern period (encompassing the Machine Age, Age of Oil, Jet Age, Atomic Age, Digital Revolution, Space Age and Information Age), which continues. It was an Enlightenment era project to find objective truths, which were universal and homogenising. This had the effect of creating "other", or the impure. In Iris Young's words:

> Bringing particular things under a universal essence, for example, depends on determining some attribute of particulars as accidental, lying outside the essence. Any definition or category creates an inside/outside distinction, and the logic of identity seeks to keep those borders firmly drawn. In the history of Western thought the metaphysics of presence has created a vast number of such mutually exclusive oppositions that structure whole philosophies: subject/object, mind/body, culture/nature, male/female.[19]

Thus, modernity is reflected in binary pairs. A pivotal characteristic of "modern" societies is the classification and categorisation of all aspects of the human experience and knowledge architecture, including disciplines of study, creating the mind/body duality.[20] This duality cast the mind (thought and language) as separate from the physical form embodying it. The mind constituted the self, whereas the body was something to be controlled by the mind. The mind/body binary has a sibling in culture/nature, where the mind creates culture, whereas the body is dictated by nature. These dualities in turn birth further binaries, including subject/object and agency/essential. It is the mind that is the subject of observation and that has agency to act upon objects, which are essential and without agency.

Within these binaries, one is only genuine or "pure" in relation to its other.[21] For example, for there to be "culture" and the made, there must be "nature", or for there to be objects of observation, there must be subjects undertaking the observation. Hence, neither part of a binary can stand on its own. They are interdependent.

The social construction of binaries included casting one half of the binaries as masculine (subject, mind, culture) and the other half as feminine (object, body, nature). Binaries were then set up in hierarchies, where the masculine was (and is) favoured ("the pure") over the feminine ("the impure"). As Young stated:

> In the metaphysical tradition the first of these [subject, mind, culture, male] is elevated over the second [object, body, nature, female] because it designates the unified, the self-identical, whereas the second side lies

19 Iris M Young, "The Ideal of Community and the Politics of Difference" (1986) 12 (1) *Social Theory and Practice* 1, 3.

20 René Descartes, "Meditatio Sexta: De rerum materialium existentia, et reali mentis a corpore distinctione" (1641), in John Cottingham (ed. and trans.), *Meditations on the First Philosophy* (Cambridge University Press, 1996) 100.

21 Young (n 19) 3.

> outside the unified, the chaotic, unformed, transforming. Metaphysical thinking makes distinctions and formulates accounts by relying on such oppositions, where one side designates the pure, authentic, good, and the other the impure, inauthentic, bad.[22]

A closely related binary relates to the individual as opposed to the community. Like the binaries discussed thus far, this is also gendered as:

> The culture identifies masculinity with the values associated with individualism – self-sufficiency, competition, separation, the formal equality of rights. The culture identifies femininity, on the other hand, with the values associated with community – affective relations of care, mutual aid, and cooperation.[23]

The individual/community binary creates further dyads:

> The opposition between individualism and community, then, is homologous with and often implies the oppositions masculine/feminine, public/private, calculative/affective, instrumental/aesthetic, which are also present in modern political thinking. This thinking has always valued the first side of these oppositions more highly than the second, and provided them with a dominant institutional expression in the society.[24]

The public/private dichotomy is important for our purposes. As Sandra Harding noted, in the late nineteenth century:

> economic and political activities, located in households and kin relations in premodernity, [were] extracted from households to a "public sphere," leaving the "private sphere" of the household severely politically and economically weakened. [Furthermore], scientific rationality and technological expertise function[ed] as one-way "time machines" that transport[ed] men and all of the institutions of society except the family into the modern, public sphere. Finally, this kind of social transformation [wa]s presented in naturalizing, evolutionary terms; this is how the human species evolve[d] from its childhood in tradition to its maturity in modern civilizations, according to modernization theory.[25]

Modernity leaves behind women. More still, the public/private binary result in women and the feminine being undervalued:

22 Ibid.
23 Ibid., 6.
24 Ibid., 7.
25 Sandra Harding, "Postcolonial and Feminist Philosophies of Science and Technology: Convergence and Dissonances" (2009) 12(4) *Postcolonial Studies* 401, 410.

> The welfare of women and households is abandoned by public institutions as a condition of modernization. Women and households are identified as drags on economic growth and political progress, and as "externals" to economies and their political systems, their welfare undeserving of serious consideration, sometimes deserving gracious handouts, but never positioned as active agents of social progress. Furthermore, male-supremacy and European/white-supremacy are used to metaphorize each other. Women are "outside civilization," non-European men are not really manly. Thus the oppression of each lives on as a natural fact inside representations of the oppression of other.[26]

Thus, modernisation is typically not good for women anywhere or for non-Western men, as they are placed in "the childhood of the species".[27] Indeed, many Indigenous communities do not divide the world in the dualisms identified in the foregoing. They do not, for example, divide culture and nature or mind and body. Instead, Indigenous communities tend to view the world and their place in it more holistically. Being "pre-modern", they are considered "primitive", "other", impure and of less value, and more easily colonised and objectified.[28] In Nancy Hartsock's words:

> Duality, inequality, and domination were established in the name of universality and progress; ironically, power relations were institutionalized in and through a mode of thinking that denied any connections between knowledge and power or between the construction of subjectivity and power. The philosophical and historical creation of devalued Others was the necessary precondition, then, for the creation of the transcendent, rational subject who can persuade himself that he exists outside time and space and power relations. The subject the speaker in Enlightenment philosophy.[29]

Yet, the existence of communities that are "pre-modern" highlights the constructed (rather than essential) nature of binaries. Indeed, Bruno Latour wrote an entire book about how *We Have Never Been Modern*.[30] In this book, Latour argues that we will never understand human beings and their world until we collapse binaries. Modernity sought to purify reality through its binaries, to create universal truths by separating out the other and impure. However, this does not create true knowledge (or reflect practice) and, thus, we have never been modern.

26 Ibid., 410–11.
27 Ibid., 410.
28 Nancy Hartsock, "Rethinking Modernism: Minority vs. Majority Theories" (1987) *Cultural Critique* 187, 191–6.
29 Nancy Harstock, "Postmodern and Political Change: Issues for Feminist Theory" (1989–1990) 14 *Cultural Critique* 15, 18.
30 Bruno Latour, *We Have Never Been Modern* (Catherine Porter trans., Harvard University Press, 1993).

To illustrate, the mind is not separate from the body. Firstly, studies show that the mind does not simply control the body in a purposeful and causal manner – much of the "mind" is unconscious, even in the decision-making process.[31] Secondly, the social location of the bodied subject affects his/her perception of the object.

As to other binaries, culture is not wholly separate from nature and vice versa. In Jane Flax's words:

> What after all, is the "natural" in the context of the human world? … The tendency of Western science is to "disenchant" the natural world. More and more the "natural" ceases to exist as the opposite of "cultural" or social. Nature becomes the object and product of human action; it loses its independent existence.[32]

Flax used the example of vaccinating against diseases to illustrate how humans "disenchant" nature by mixing in culture. Furthermore, setting the individual in opposition to his/her dyadic community does not reflect lived experiences – individuals are not separate from (unaffected by and unaffecting) the communities in which they move. Finally, as analysed in Chapter 5, without the privatised there would be no public domain, and the latter feeds the former – the two are intimately connected.

As discussed further in Chapters 5 and 6, postmodern theorists have deconstructed binaries, showing their social (and semiotic) rather than essential character, and sought to avoid universalities that led to their construction. This necessarily involves understanding that the products of our binaries are equally as socially constructed. This includes the law.

3 Reference points for patentability

3.1 Novelty

The simplest requirement for patentability is that the invention has to be new – it cannot constitute part of the prior art.[33] The prior art is information, knowledge and matter that was publicly available before the date at which the patent applicant or owner asserts priority (usually the application date).

31 E.g. Benjamin Libet, *Mind Time: The Temporal Factor in Consciousness* (Harvard University Press, 2005); and Chun Siong Soon et al., "Unconscious Determinants of Free Decisions in the Human Brain" (2008) 11(5) *Nature Neuroscience* 543. Expectation or anticipation results in "readiness potential" or antecedent brain activity, before any conscious intention is formed.

32 Jane Flax, "Postmodernism and Gender Relations in Feminist Theory" (1987) 12(4) *Signs: Journal of Women in Culture and Society* 621, 634–635.

33 This and the following part update and expand upon content from Jessica C Lai, "Gendered 'Objective' Patent Law: Of Binaries and a Singularity" (2020) 47(3) *Journal of Law and Society* 441.

Generally, the prior art is "universal", meaning that it can come from anywhere, in any form (for example, in any language, written, oral or use-based).[34]

For prior art to destroy the novelty of a claimed invention, it "must contain clear and unmistakeable directions to do what the patentee claims to have invented".[35] In the oft-cited words of Lord Justice Sachs, "A signpost, however clear, upon the road to the patentee's invention will not suffice. The prior inventor must be clearly shown to have planted his flag at the precise destination before the patentee."[36] This is a high standard for a challenger to reach in order to successfully show that an invention is not novel.

Any amount of "newness" vis-à-vis the prior art suffices. Thus, novelty is an ostensibly quantitative standard and is usually easy to overcome. Supposedly quantitative and assessed "universally", the novelty standard appears neutral. However, the conceptualisation of novelty and prior art are value laden.

There is a presumption that the feminine work of women belongs in the public domain. Note that the public domain and prior art are related, but distinct, concepts. Prior art is information or knowledge recognised by the patent system as such. Because it is already known, it is not patentable per se (though it may have been patented in the past). The public domain includes this (so long as it is not covered by a valid patent or other property form), as well as some things that are new but not patentable. This is illustrated with a Venn diagram in Figure 2.1. For example, a valid patent constitutes prior art for the examination of subsequent inventions (the left section of the Venn diagram). Once a patent expires (or fails to be renewed), the information and knowledge it embodies falls into the public domain (the middle section of the Venn diagram).

Feminine knowledge typically falls into the right section of the Venn diagram, as it is something outside of the realm of the propertised, not recognised or protected by any intellectual property. As elaborated upon in the following, the consequence of this is that the patent system often does not deem feminine knowledge to be new. Yet, at the same time, it does not form part of the prior art when assessing the novelty of masculine inventions.

The presumption that feminine knowledge automatically falls into the public domain is consistent with the constructed dichotomy of societal institutions

34 E.g. European Patent Convention on the Grant of European Patents (EPC), 1065 UNTS 199 (adopted 5 October 1973, entered into force 7 October 1977), art. 54; and EPO, Guidelines for Examination in the European Patent Office (November 2019) Part G – Chapter IV; Patents Act 1990 (Cth), sch 1 definition of "prior art base"; and Patents Act 2013 (NZ), s 8.

35 *General Tire & Rubber Co v Firestone Tyre & Rubber Co Ltd* [1972] RPC 457, 486.

36 Ibid. This is the test generally used in England, Australia, New Zealand and Canada; e.g. *Smale v North Sails* [1991] 3 NZLR 19, 39; *ICI Chemicals & Polymers v Lubrizol Corp* (1999) 45 IPR 577, [58]; and *Apotex Inc v Sanofi-Synthelabo Canada Inc* [2008] 3 SCR 265. Showing anticipation through prior art in the United States is also a high standard, requiring that a piece of prior art shows every integer claimed, such that the complete claimed invention is in the piece of prior art; e.g. *Verdegaal Bros v Union Oil Co of California*, 814 F2d 628, 631 (Fed Cir 1987); and *Richardson v Suzuki Motor Co*, 868 F2d 1226 (Fed Cir 1989).

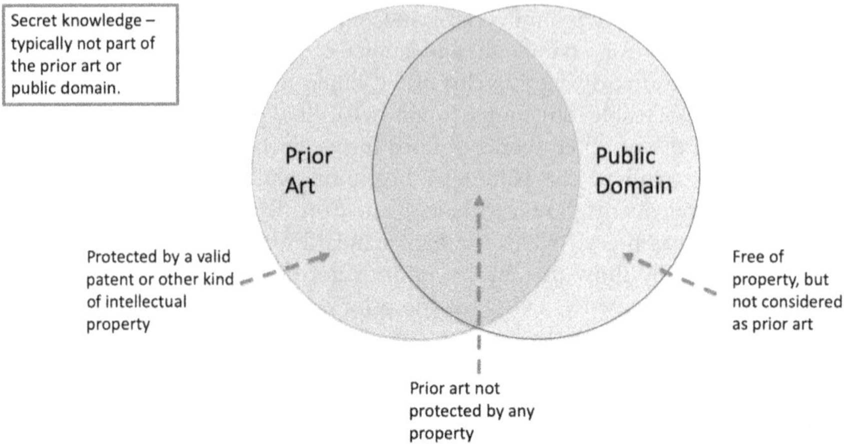

Figure 2.1 Relationship between prior art and the public domain

being either private or public, and that women have traditionally occupied solely the private sphere, whilst men were privy to both the private and the public spheres.[37] The former encompasses the home, while the latter includes the business and commercial world. Within the private sphere, women are expected to perform continual and invisible tasks, such as cleaning and caregiving.[38] Society considers these tasks to be done altruistically as part of the gendered role of the feminine "nurturer", without any commercial goal in mind.[39] Thus, when women invent the feminine (often within the home environment, such as home remedies or cooking methods), the products of their labour are typically not considered capable of propertisation. Such feminine inventions are not perceived as new, but rather better ways to do

37 Jean Bethke Elshtain, *Public Man, Private Woman: Women in Social and Political Thought* (2nd edn, Princeton University Press, 1993); and Michelle Zimbalist Rosaldo, "Woman, Culture, and Society: A Theoretical Overview" in Michelle Zimbalist Rosaldo and Louise Lamphere (eds), *Women, Culture, and Society* (Stanford University Press, 1974) 17–42.

38 There is a strong body of literature on the "free" work that women do, which is necessary for the patriarchal capitalist model to function. See e.g. Penny Griffin, "Feminist Political Economy" in Jill Steans and Daniela Tepe-Belfrage (eds), *Handbook on Gender in World Politics* (Edward Elgar, 2016) 345; Michèle A. Pujol, *Feminism and Anti-feminism in Early Economic Thought* (Vermont, USA: Edward Elgar, 1992); and Libby Assassi, *The Gendering of Global Finance* (Palgrave Macmillan, 2009); Juanita Elias, "Critical Feminist Scholarship in IPE" in Stuart Shields, Ian Bruff and Huw Macartney (eds), *Critical International Political Economy: Dialogue, Debate and Dissensus* (Palgrave Macmillan, 2011) 99.

39 On the relationship between the gendered notion of domesticity and real property, Ellen Gordon-Bouvier "Crossing the Boundaries of the Home: A Chronotopical Analysis of the Legal Status of Women's Domestic Work" (2019) *International Law in Context* 1.

housework, "make-do" or improvisations, or "an extension of the traditional homemaker's role".[40]

Another way to frame the presumption that feminine knowledge is in the public domain stems from the fact that knowledge created in the private sphere is considered to be socially situated. This means that it is dependent on its social location – it is "subjective". The predominant Western view is that socially situated knowledge is not true knowledge, but merely beliefs or opinions – "old wives' tales". "True" (scientific) knowledge must be abstract and "objective" – free from context and values.[41] For example, a method for cooking eggs for a particular period of time would not be patentable, as the exact results differ depending on the exact eggs used. The results are situated and non-universalistic. In contrast, a method of heating two exact amounts of exact chemicals together to make a new chemical would be patentable because this appears objective.[42] The predominant Western perspective, thus, does not view feminine knowledge – created in the private sphere and not stripped of its subjective context – as knowledge.

As a result, science and the patent regime do not recognise such feminine knowledge, relegating it to the public domain, but not designating it as prior art. This leaves feminine knowledge open to be used, filtered through the masculine public sphere where it is turned into "scientific" "inventions",[43] and patented by those formally educated and working in STEM – predominantly males.[44] This is exacerbated by the fact that much feminine knowledge has gone unrecorded, passed on orally.[45] While most jurisdictions technically include the oral as prior art, oral knowledge is notoriously difficult to locate and evidence. Many patent offices have large workloads and/or are under-resourced, resulting in poor patent examination that does not locate oral knowledge.[46] Thus, whilst in the public domain, feminine knowledge often does not constitute prior art when assessing novelty, making it easier to appropriate and patent.

40 Susan A McDaniel, Helene Cummins and Rachelle Sender Beauchamp, "Mothers of Invention? Meshing the Roles of Inventor, Mother, and Worker" (1988) 11(1) *Women's Studies International Forum* 1, 8–9; and Autumn Stanley, "Once and Future Power: Women as Inventors" (1992) 15(2) *Women's Studies International Forum* 193, 197.

41 Sandra Harding, "Rethinking Standpoint Epistemology: What is 'Strong Objectivity?'" (1992) 36(3) *The Centennial Review* 437, 438.

42 Of course, ask any chemist and they will tell you that repeating experiments does not always lead to the same results, from different products to different yields, and this cannot always be explained.

43 The social constructions of the "science" and "invention" are examined in Chapter 3.

44 Laura A Foster, "Situating Feminism, Patent Law, and the Public Domain" (2011) 20 *Colum J Gender & L* 262, 312.

45 See e.g. Vrinda Dalmiya and Linda Alcoff, "Are 'Old Wives' Tales' Justified?" in Linda Alcoff and Elizabeth Potter (eds), *Feminist Epistemologies* (Routledge, 1993) 217.

46 Susy Frankel, *Intellectual Property in New Zealand* (2nd edn, LexisNexis, 2011) 137; and Peter K Yu, "Cultural Relics, Intellectual Property, and Intangible Heritage" (2008) 81 *Temple Law Review* 433, 480.

In fact, in the English-speaking world, married females could not own property (including patents) separately from their husbands until the turn of the twentieth century.[47] Everything women invented was given to the public domain or their husbands. Once females could patent, the idea that they would seek property for their inventions was viewed as being contrary to their private and non-commercial roles. As stated by Autumn Stanley,

> if a man invents a remedy or palliative for some ailment, it will be called a medical invention, and people may expect him to try to patent it or profit from it in some way. However, if a woman invents the same preparation, it will be called a "home remedy" or an "old wives' tale," and people may be surprised or *even disapproving if she tries to patent it rather than passing it on freely to others.*[48]

Women were discouraged from entering the public sphere. Yet, what they invented in the private sphere was generally placed in the public domain. Thus, women could only *give* in the private sphere, and solely men could economically *gain* in the public sphere.[49] Implicit in this, predominantly men benefit from the public domain (discussed further in Chapter 5).[50]

There are analogies between women and Indigenous peoples with respect to novelty and the public domain. The colonisation process often resulted in land being taken from Indigenous people because they did not show the same "bundle of rights" or traits over their land that Western law recognises as constituting "property". In other words, because many Indigenous peoples did not use their land in an exclusive or individual manner, or for cultivation, or did not show continued possession, the colonisers, law and courts perceived that they did not have "property" rights over the land and it was free for the taking.[51] Land was deemed *res nullius*, or more specifically *terra nullius* – the

47 In the UK, this was through the Married Women's Property Act 1882. On the US, see B Zorina Khan, "Married Women's Property Laws and Female Commercial Activity: Evidence from US Patent Records, 1790–1895" (1996) 56 *Journal of Economic History* 356; Deborah Merritt, "Hypatia in the Patent Office: Women Inventors and the Law, 1865–1900" (1991) 35 *American Journal of Legal History* 235, 290, who additionally notes that historically in the United States women could not enter into contracts, so could not licence out their patents (if they could obtain them).

48 Stanley (n 40) 197 (emphasis added).

49 Malla Pollack, "Towards a Feminist Theory of the Public Domain, or Rejecting the Gendered Scope of United States Copyrightable and Patentable Subject Matter" (2006) 12 *William & Mary Journal of Women and the Law* 603, 613 and 615.

50 Anupam Chander and Madhavi Sunder, "The Romance of the Public Domain" (2004) 92 *California Law Review* 1331; and Foster, "Situating Feminism, Patent Law, and the Public Domain" (n 44) 318.

51 See e.g. Carol M Rose, "The Several Futures of Property: Of Cyberspace and Folk Tales, Emission Trades and Ecosystems" (1998) 88 *Minnesota Law Review* 129, 140–141; and Stuart Banner, "Two Properties, One Land: Law and Space in Nineteenth-Century New Zealand" (1999) 24 *Law and Social Inquiry* 807.

people and their use of the land were invisible. In what some have called a second wave of colonisation,[52] there is an automatic presumption that Indigenous peoples' knowledge and works are in the "public domain" (*res nullius*), free for all to use.[53] Furthermore, Indigenous peoples typically have oral traditions. The result is that, even with the best of intentions, Indigenous knowledge is often not located to form part of the prior art base when assessing patentability.

Indigenous peoples and Western women are by no means homogenous in their concerns or desired outcomes. The analogy serves to highlight that patent law is not neutral. It is both gendered and racialised.[54] It protects the creations of its creator – the Western male.

52 Aroha Mead, "Cultural and Intellectual Property Rights of Indigenous Peoples of the Pacific" in Leonie Pihama and Cherryl Waerea-i-te-rangi Smith (eds), *Cultural and Intellectual Property Rights: Economics, Politics & Colonisation* (Auckland, New Zealand: International Research Institute for Māori and Indigenous Education, University of Auckland, 1997, vol. 2) 20, 21; Aroha Mead, "Geneaology, Sacredness, and the Commodities Market" (1996) 20(2) *Cultural Survival: Genes, People and Property*, www.culturalsurvival.org/ourpublications/csq/article/genealogy-sacredness-and-commodities-market; Toni Liddell, "The Travesty of Waitaha: The New Age Piracy of Early Māori History" in Leonie Pihama and Cherryl Waerea-i-te-rangi Smith (eds), *Cultural and Intellectual Property Rights. Economics, Politics & Colonisation* (Auckland, New Zealand: International Research Institute for Māori and Indigenous Education, University of Auckland, 1997, vol. 2) 32, 32 and 42; and Donna Ngaronoa Gardiner, "Hands Off – Our Genes: A Case Study on the Theft of Whakapapa" in Leonie Pihama and Cherryl Waerea-i-te-rangi Smith (eds), *Cultural and Intellectual Property Rights. Economics, Politics & Colonisation* (Auckland, New Zealand: International Research Institute for Māori and Indigenous Education, University of Auckland, 1997, vol. 2) 44, 45–7; and Alejandro Madrazo, "Biocolonialism: TRIPs and the Genetic No Man's Land" (2013) 25 *Geoergetown International Environmental Law Review* 487.

53 Graham Dutfield, "The Public and Private Domains" (2000) 21(3) *Science Communication* 274, 287; Brigitte Vézina, "Are They In or Are They Out? Traditional Cultural Expressions and the Public Domain – Implications for Trade" in Christoph B Graber, Karolina Kuprecht and Jessica C Lai (eds), *International Trade in Indigenous Cultural Heritage: Legal and Policy Issues* (Edward Elgar, 2012) 196, 198–9; WIPO IGC, Secretariat, "Note on the Meanings of the Term 'Public Domain' in the Intellectual Property System with Special Reference to the Protection of Traditional Knowledge and Traditional Cultural Expressions/Expressions of Folklore" (2010) WIPO Doc. WIPO/GRTKF/IC/17/INF/8, [5]; Frankel (n 46) 116; and Mariaan de Beer, "Protecting Echoes of the Past: Intellectual Property and Expressions of Culture" (2006) 12 *Canterbury Law Review* 94, 107.

54 On patents and race, see Keith Aoki, "Distributive Justice and Intellectual Property: Distributive and Syncretic Motives in Intellectual Property Law" (2007) 40 *UC Davis Law Review* 717; Shubha Ghosh, "Globalization, Patents, and Traditional Knowledge" (2004) 17 *Columbia Journal of Asian Law* 73; and Jessica C Lai, *Indigenous Cultural Heritage and Intellectual Property Rights: Learning from the New Zealand Experience* (Springer, 2014) 59–66.

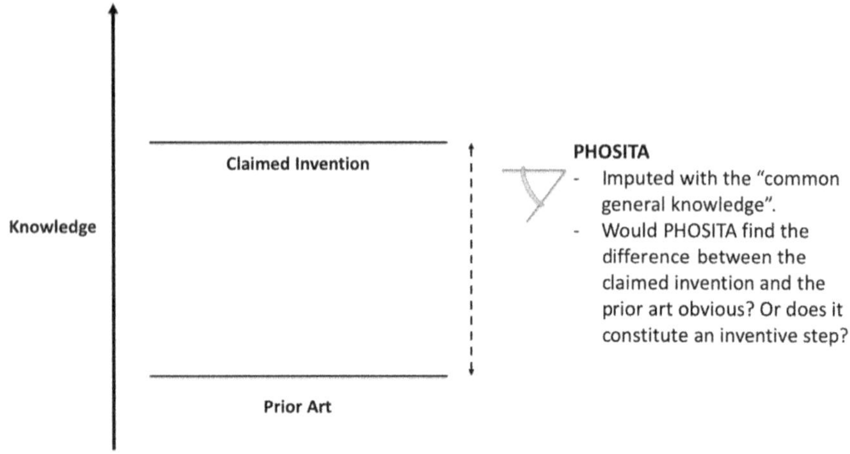

Figure 2.2 Assessment of non-obviousness

3.2 Non-obvious or inventive step

The standard to determine whether an invention is obvious or not differs across jurisdictions. It is a qualitative standard and is considered to be a gatekeeper to patentability. Because of this, the standard is inherently subjective, and law-makers use it to achieve policy objectives, making it easier or harder to get a patent in various fields.[55] Generally, the standard requires that the "person having ordinary skill in the art" (PHOSITA), knowing the common general knowledge, would not find obvious (or would think there is an inventive step in) the difference between the claimed invention and the prior art. This is illustrated in Figure 2.2.

Unlike the prior art used to assess novelty, the common general knowledge is not universal. Instead, it is generally limited to the knowledge that the PHOSITA in the relevant field would know. This allows the standard to be field specific. For example, PHOSITA in "Field A" might know very little, because it is a nascent field. Thus, PHOSITA is more likely to find a claimed invention non-obvious. In contrast, PHOSITA in "Field B", a well-established field, might be expected to know significantly more, perhaps even have knowledge from related fields if PHOSITA in Field B would typically work in an interdisciplinary team.[56]

In light of the gendered development of patent law and its interpretation noted above,[57] and that STEM is predominantly male, it should come as no surprise that courts construct PHOSITA as masculine. Burk has discussed this in depth, including an analysis of the use of gendered conceptualisations and

55 Mark A Lemley and Dan L Burk, "Policy Levers in Patent Law" (2003) 89 *Virginia Law Review* 1575.

56 See e.g. *General Tire & Rubber Co v Firestone Tyre & Rubber Co Ltd* (n 35) 482.

57 Burk, "Do Patents Have Gender?" (n 10) 903–4.

visualisations in case law, particularly in reference to how PHOSITA is conceived.[58]

The result is that an invention must be non-obvious relative to masculine modes of science and invention. In turn, the common general knowledge is also constructed as masculine. In other words, filled with masculine knowledge and ways of knowing. As noted in the discussion on novelty, science and patent law often ignore feminine knowledge. Unseen and unrecorded feminine knowledge and ways of knowing are not part of the common general knowledge. PHOSITA does not have feminine knowledge in mind when comparing the claimed invention to the prior art, which is also blind to the feminine. Feminine knowledge can, thus, be appropriated and propertised through masculine forms of science and invention.[59]

Feminine knowledge is invisible to the patent system. Indigenous peoples and non-Western communities often share this experience. Indigenous and non-Western knowledge is not typically considered "common general knowledge". For example, in the assessment of a patent application for a pharmaceutical chemical, it is unlikely that PHOSITA would be imputed with the knowledge of Indigenous communities. The result is that Indigenous peoples and non-Western communities have often found their knowledge taken, abstracted and patented, without reference to the traditional knowledge or the holders thereof.[60] Only through this abstraction and filtration through the masculine patent system is feminine and Indigenous knowledge considered scientific.

58 See Dan L Burk, "Diversity Levers" (2015) 23(25) *Duke Journal of Gender, Law & Policy* 25, who argues for a separate "women of ordinary skill in the art", as this would take into account the challenges that women face in the inventive process. See also Chris Dent, "The 'Reasonable Man', his Nineteenth-century 'Siblings', and their Legacy" (2017) 44(3) *Journal of Law and Society* 406, 426–7.
See also *Technographic Printed Circuits Ltd v Mills & Rockley (Electronic) Ltd* [1972] RPC 346, 355 Lord Reid and *Windsurfing Int'l Inc v Tabur Marine (GB) Ltd* [1985] 4 RPC 59, 72 – two classic cases with very masculine constructions of PHOSITA.

59 On gender and public use, see Kara W Swanson, "Getting a Grip on the Corset: Gender, Sexuality, and Patent Law" (2011) 23(1) *Yale Journal of Law & Feminism* 57, who analyses the US public use doctrine with respect to *Egbert v Lippmann* (1881) 104 US 333 and patents pertaining to corsets, through a feminist lens.

60 Antony Taubman, "Saving the Village: Conserving Jurisprudential Diversity in the International Protection of Traditional Knowledge" in Keith E Maskus and Jerome H Reichman, *International Public Goods and Transfer of Technology. Under a Globalized Intellectual Property Regime*, eds (2005) 521, 523; Lere Amusan, "Politics of Biopiracy: An Adventure into Hoodia/Xhoba Patenting in Southern Africa" (2017) 14 (1) *African Journal of Traditional, Complementary and Alternative Medicines* 103; and Cormac Sheridan, "EPO Neem Patent Revocation Revives Biopiracy Debate" (2005) 23 *Nature Biotechnology* 511.

4 The invention itself

4.1 Utility or industrial application

To be patentable, an invention must have utility (be useful) or have industrial application. Anglo-American jurisdictions have adopted the term "useful", whereas European states use an "industrial application" standard. The utility and industrial application standards reflect a normative judgement regarding an invention's merit. Unlike the novelty and non-obviousness (inventive step) standards, they do not compare the invention to the pre-existing, but are an assessment of the invention itself. This makes the utility and industrial application standards more like the patent-eligible subject matter requirement (discussed below). Yet, while patent-eligible subject matter is the focus of a significant amount of discourse and case law, utility and industrial application likely receive the least attention of all the patentability requirements.

The requirement that an invention has utility or industrial application is meant to assist in preventing patents for basic or fundamental advancements. They do this by delaying the point of patent application to when there is a use or industrial application, to make the protection as narrow as possible.[61] A patent for an invention with no known use would force researchers who later find a use to license the invention. The requirement also historically existed to prevent patents for "frivolous" inventions,[62] or inventions that were not of public benefit.[63] That patentability is limited to inventions with some kind of use makes sense. We do not want patent registers to be cluttered with ideas that have no use. However, the interpretations of "useful" and "industrial application" serve to make patent law gendered.

In the Anglo-American context, one observes this when examining to whom and to what end an invention must be useful, and from what perspective. Historically, knowledge had to be worked in business or industry to be useful.[64] More recent case law refers to the need for a "practical

61 William M Landes and Richard A Posner, *The Economic Structure of Intellectual Property* (The Belknap Press of Harvard University Press, 2003) 302; and Richard P Merges, "Property Rights Theory and the Commons: The Case of Scientific Research" (1996) 13(2) *Social Philosophy & Policy* 145, 165.

62 NS Pierce, "In Re Dane K. Fisher: An Exercise in Utility" (2006) 6 *Journal of High Technology Law* 1, 7.

63 MHM, "Utility as a Factor in Chemical Patentability" (1960) 108(7) *University of Pennsylvania Law Review* 1037, 1042

64 Chris Dent, "New Insights in Patent History: An Application of Evolutionary Theory" (2018) 8(3) *Queen Mary Journal of Intellectual Property* 171, 184, citing *Dolland v Champneys* (1758) 1 CPC 28, 30; and Pierce (n 62) 7 and 72.

Underscoring the close relationship between the utility standard and patent-eligible subject matter, an "invention" constitutes patent-eligible subject matter if it "belongs to a useful art as distinct from a fine art (see *Re Virginia-Carolina Chemical Corporation's Application* (1958) RPC 35, 36) – that its value to the country is in the field of economic endeavour". *NRDC V Commissioner of Patents* (1959) 102 CLR 252, 275.

use".[65] Of course, "business", "industry" or "practical" are constructed masculine. "Business" and "industrial" have been defined according to masculine ideals of work.[66] In addition, males are socially constructed as being more practical than females (though this is evidently untrue).[67]

The typical usages of these terms are not open to women who sell their home remedies, trade their arts, or who create economic value through home-making, childrearing and caregiving. They are also not apt for covering female-dominated professions, such as nursing, care work, education. Business and industry constitute male-dominated domains, such as the mechanical, mass manufacture and, in the twenty-first century, financial markets. If females were and continue to be disproportionately excluded from masculine-constructed business and industry, and do not develop practical knowledge, but are relegated to home-making and caregiving,[68] they are presented fewer opportunities to create "useful" inventions.[69]

65 E.g. *Nelson v Bowler*, 626 F2d 853, 856, 206 USPQ881, 883 (CCPA 1980) ("Practical utility is a shorthand way of attributing 'real-world' value to claimed subject matter. In other words, one skilled in the art can use a claimed discovery in a manner which provides some immediate benefit to the public.") See also *Re Alsop's Patent* (1907) 24 RPC 733, 753; *Apotex Inc v Wellcome Foundation Ltd* [2002] 4 SCR 153, [52]; *AstraZeneca Canada Inc v Apotex Inc* (2017) SCC 36, [57]; *Rehm v Websters Security Systems* (1988) 11 IPR 289, 305 (FCA); *Smale v North Sails* [1991] 3 NZLR 19 (HC), 52–3.

66 Ruth Oldenziel, *Making Technology Masculine: Men, Women, and Modern Machines in America, 1870–1945* (Amsterdam University Press, 1999); Mary Mellor, "Women, Nature and the Social Construction of 'Economic Man'" (1997) 20(2) *Ecological Economy* 129; Sonya O Rose, "'Gender at Work': Sex, Class and Industrial Capitalism" (1986) 21 *History Workshop* 113; Johan Berglund, "The Practical Men of Action. The Construction of Masculinity and Model Leaders in Business Magazines" (1994) Centre for Advanced Studies in Leadership, Research Paper Series No. 4; Vishal K. Gupta et al., "The Role of Gender Stereotypes in Perceptions of Entrepreneurs and Intentions to Become an Entrepreneur" (2009) 33(2) *Entrepreneurship and Practice* 397; Lakshmi Balachandra et al., "Pitch Like a Man: Gender Stereotypes and Entrepreneur itch Success" (2013) 33(8) *Frontiers of Entrepreneurship Research* 1; Connie Hancock, Anna Pérez-Quintana and Esther Hormiga "Stereotypical Notions of the Entrepreneur: An Analysis from a Perspective of Gender" (2014) 20(1) *Journal of Promotion Management* 82.

67 E.g. Roger Lock, "Gender and Practical Skill Performance in Science" (1992) 29(3) *Journal of Research in Science Teaching* 227. See Alison Kelly, "The Construction of Masculine Science" (1985) 6(2) *British Journal of Sociology of Education* 133, 146, who notes that "science changes from a predominantly practical subject in the lower part of the secondary school to an increasingly theoretical activity at higher levels. … in which the activity-based masculinity of science which is established in the early years of secondary school (largely by extending behaviour learned out-of-school into a new context) has to be transformed in later years into a version of masculinity where power is exerted through controlled thought and patient experiments".

68 Maureen Baker, "Choices or Constraints? Family Responsibilities, Gender and Academic Career" (2010) *Journal of Comparative Family Studies* 1, 13–14.

69 Thus, women's careers are taxed because of their biologically and socially assigned role of child bearer and caregiver; Sharmishta Barwa and Shirin M Rai, "Knowledge and/as Power: A Feminist Critique of Trade Related Intellectual Property

Likewise, in Europe, that an invention has to have an *industrial* application under the European Patent Convention (EPC),[70] discriminates against women. Similar terminology appears in the application of the utility and industrial application standards. To have industrial application, an invention must be capable of being made or used in industry, where "'industry' is understood in its broad sense as including any *physical activity* of '*technical* character'".[71] This means that it has to be an activity that "belongs to the useful or *practical* arts as distinct from the aesthetic arts".[72] The aesthetic, presentations of information, and schemes, rules and methods for performing mental acts, are not considered "technical".[73] This understanding leans towards inventions relating to machines or the manufacture of an article, though the Guidelines state that this need not be the case and it would include "a process for dispersing fog or for converting energy from one form to another".[74]

The requirement that patents be useful or embody an industrial application implicates the private/public dichotomy. Generally, the private/public dichotomy categorises women as homemakers, caregivers, creators of "crafts" and preparers of family meals, for example, whereas men are workers, creating "art" and are chefs. Thus, a woman who creates a home remedy is undertaking her private sphere role as a caregiver. Whereas that same home remedy processed through masculine technology undertaken by a scientist is in the public and commercial sphere. Notably, while the feminine is restricted to the private and non-industrial sphere, the masculine may cross freely between the two worlds.

Rights" (2003) 7(1) *Gender, Technology & Development* 91, 107. A woman's socially determined role as caregiver extends not only to children, but also to family members, such as elderly parents. It additionally includes their male partners, as women are more likely make career sacrifices for their male partners than vice versa. This might be vis-à-vis childcare or relocation for a position. Baker (n 68) 12–14.

The caregiver role stereotypically also covers students or junior team members as mentees. Erin Leahey and Amelia Blume, "Elucidating the Process: Why Women Patent Less than Men" in Albert N Link (ed), *Gender and Entrepreneurial Activity* (Edward Elgar, 2017) 159, 155; Waverly L Ding, Fiona Murray and Toby E Stuart "Gender Differences in Patenting in the Academic Life Sciences" (2006) 313 *Science* 665, 666–7; and Sue V Rosser, "The Gender Gap in Patenting: Is Technology Transfer a Feminist Issue?" (2009) 21(2) *National Women's Studies Association Journal* 65, 77.

70 EPC (n 34) art. 57.

71 EPO (n 34) Part G – Chapter III-1 (emphasis added). See also Part G – Chapter I-2 (ii) regarding patent-eligible subject matter, which states that "the invention must be of 'technical character' to the extent that it must relate to a technical field (Rule 42(1)(a) – see F-II, 4.2), must be concerned with a technical problem (Rule 42(1)(c) – see F-II, 4.5) and must have technical features in terms of which the matter for which protection is sought can be defined in the claim (Rule 43(1) – see F-IV, 2.1)".

72 Ibid., Part G – Chapter III-1 (emphasis added).

73 Ibid., Part G – Chapter II-1.

74 Ibid., Part G – Chapter III-1.

A more nuanced way of viewing the divide between the feminine and masculine is that patent law's utility or industrial application requirement discriminates against women according to the care-labour/industrialised-labour binary. Women's labour is typically considered to fall within the former category, as it is labour of the hand, brain and heart, and placed within a social structure that de-commoditises it.[75] Women's labour has generally not been recognised as engendering property or as economically valuable, despite its great benefit to social welfare and, indeed, economic value.[76] Thus, rather than being perceived as business or industry related, or of practical use, women's inventions have often been belittled and considered "make-do" or improvisations. In contrast, men's labour is categorised as industrial, as it generates abstract knowledge in laboratories, research institutes and factories, outside of social relationships, allowing it to be commoditised.[77] It is within the domain of the masculine, situated in the public sphere, that the useful is created.

The embodiment of the private/public dichotomy in the industrial application standard is exemplified in a European Patent Office (EPO) decision regarding a claim for the method of applying a certain amount of a contraceptive ("sperm migration-inhibitory") chemical compound "to the cervix of a female mammal capable of contraception".[78] As noted, an invention is "susceptible of industrial application if it can be made or used in any kind of industry".[79] Regarding the claim at hand, the Board of Appeal found that there was no field of industrial application, as the claim pertained to "private and personal activities".[80] In other words, it is only that which takes place in public in industry that is patentable.

The applicant raised two examples of when the method might be used in industry, by prostitutes and nurses helping disabled women. The Board of Appeal found both unconvincing. Regarding prostitutes, it stated:

> the decisive question is not whether a prostitute's profession is an industry, but whether the application by a prostitute of a contraceptive composition to the cervix is part of an industry. This is not the case. The application of

75 Deborah Halbert, "Feminist Interpretations of Intellectual Property" (2006) 14(3) *American University Journal of Gender, Social Policy & the Law* 431, 439.

76 Both women's intellectual labour and labour of their bodies (such as childbearing, breastfeeding and general caregiving), is undervalued. See e.g. Victoria University of Wellington, "Milk's Billion-dollar GDP Gap" (26 September 2018) *Newsroom*, https://www.newsroom.co.nz/@future-learning/2018/09/25/251486/breast-milks-billion-dollar-gdp-gap; Julie Smith and Nancy Folbre, "New Ways to Measure Economic Activity: Breastfeeding as an Economic Indicator" in Marian Sawer, Fiona Jenkins and Karen Downing (eds), *How Gender Can Transform the Social Sciences* (Palgrave, 2020) 105.

77 Halbert (n 75) 439.

78 *Contraceptive Method/British Technology Group* (1994) T 0074/93 EPO Boards of Appeal.

79 EPC (n 34) art. 57 ("EPC").

80 *Contraceptive Method/British Technology Group* (n 78) [2.2.6].

> a contraceptive composition to the cervix as claimed *is not part of the business relationship between a prostitute and her client, and the contract between them does not cover the question of which means of contraception she may apply to herself.* She has the freedom and responsibility to decide which one to choose, taking into consideration factors such as tolerance or reliability. This holds true at least as long as the client is not affected; if the prostitute applied contraceptive means to her client, their use might become part of the business relationship. As long as she applies them to herself and protects herself outside her contact with the client, the client is in no way involved and the application remains in the private and personal sphere of the prostitute.[81]

The line that the Board of Appeal drew to find a lack of industrial application is strikingly unusual. If the woman is using the method in an industry (and there can no doubt that prostitution is an industry – as the Board of Appeal noted, it is the "oldest industry in the word"),[82] it is unclear why the client is at all relevant. Clients engage with firms all the time without knowing exactly what methods they use (what patented processes or products they license). To illustrate, a client who desires a pharmaceutical compound be made might approach a manufacturing entity. The client might only care about whether the firm will perform the contract well, how it might affect its reputation, whether there are long-term considerations. It might not care that the firm licences and uses a patented process to make an ingredient necessary for the pharmaceutical. However, the examination procedure would never question whether that process has industrial application, simply because a client may not know that the process is being used, indeed may be uninterested in this.

The Board of Appeal appeared to be concerned that the patentee would be able to sue the user of the method (the prostitute) directly. There was no "middle man". Yet, the patentee always has this ability. Let us compare the treatment of this application for the "sperm migration-inhibitory" method with an application for the contraceptive pill. The latter is undoubtedly patentable and susceptible of industrial application under the law. Note that the consumer always has the ability to simply use the invention without the patentee's licence, whether the invention is a method or a product, and the patentee can always sue the user for infringement. This is illustrated in Figure 2.3.

The Board of Appeal continued focusing on the private concerns of the user of the method:

> A prostitute may have a professional interest in not becoming pregnant, in order to remain able to pursue her profession. This is, however, neither her only nor her predominant interest in using a contraceptive. The prostitute has a serious interest in not becoming pregnant from a client for

81 Ibid., [2.2.5.1] (emphasis added).
82 Ibid., [2.2.5.1].

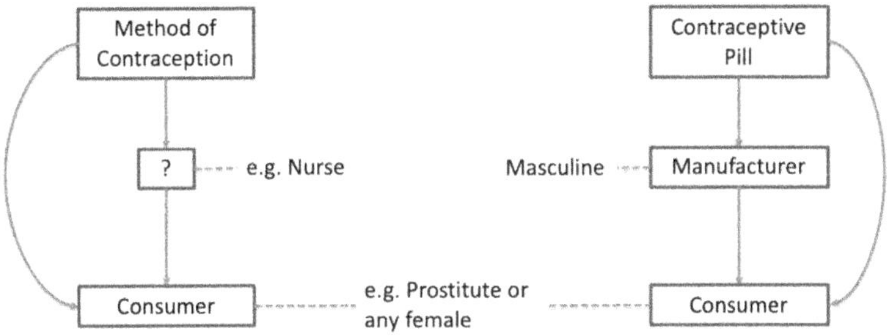

Figure 2.3 Contraceptive method versus product

> purely private and personal reasons, because this could affect her future life to a much higher degree than the temporary inability to practice. Also, a pregnancy arising from a non-professional relationship could damage her professional perspectives. Nevertheless, the use of a contraceptive in a private relationship could hardly be regarded as being of an industrial character. This shows that the mere motive for using a contraceptive is of minor importance for the question of industrial application.[83]

Again, the relevance of this discussion is dubious. When it comes to a contraceptive pill product invention, a patent office would never discuss why women might want to use the pill, how it may or may not affect their private lives or professional perspectives, to decide whether the invention is useful or has an industrial application.

The key difference between these two kinds of invention is the industry of the "middle man". One is female dominated, the other is a masculine mode of production. This is supported by the fact that the EPO allowed a patent for methods of using estrogen to prevent pregnancy.[84] Specifically, the patentee claimed a particular dosage regime and packaging estrogen for that regime. The estrogen and its dosage form still have to be manufactured by a masculine industry. The true defining factor of industrial applicability being the masculine or feminine nature of the "middle man" is also supported by the way the Board of Appeal treated the applicant's argument that nurses could use the "sperm migration-inhibitory" method in industry.

Regarding nurses using the method on disabled patients, the Board of Appeal stated:

> The fact that this person acts professionally is not sufficient to make the application of the contraceptive an industrial activity. The nurse does not offer contraception to the disabled person as an industry but to help her

83 Ibid. [2.2.5.1].
84 EP2305230 "Oral Contraceptives to Prevent Pregnancy and Diminish Premenstrual Symptomatology".

> satisfy her strictly personal needs. It follows from this that the nature of the activity is not changed by the fact that it is not exercised by the disabled woman herself but by her assistant acting according to her instructions. That is the difference between the present case and cases of cosmetic treatment, in which the board has regarded the requirements of [industrial application] as satisfied because there are enterprises whose object is to beautify the human body (T 144/83, OJ EPO 1986, 301).[85]

In other words, there would be no industrial application because the service of applying the "sperm migration-inhibitory" method by a nurse was not offered as "an industry", but rather to satisfy the strictly personal needs of the disabled person at her instruction. The method was purely about the women's "private and personal sphere", not an "industrial activity". Nursing is a female-dominated profession. This decision essentially states that nurses' professional actions on their female patients relate to the "private and personal sphere", not industry. Women, even when in the public sphere, are pushed into the private sphere and presumed to give.

This decision can be contrasted with a patent application for a method of placing a vaginal discharge collector, holding it in place in the vaginal canal of a woman, collecting discharge in the collector, retrieving it and disposing of the collector after a single use.[86] The EPO Board of Appeal held that this method was susceptible of industrial application, because it was imaginable that these steps were to be performed as a paid service and were not exclusively dependent for their execution on the instructions of the woman in question. Unlike the previous "sperm migration-inhibitory" method case, the Board stated, there were "enterprises" that might perform the method, "eg for subsequent visual, chemical or bacterial inspection or for extraction of one or more of its components for use in industrial preparation of pharmaceutical compositions".[87] The Board of Appeal noted that "[w]hether such enterprises [to perform the paid services] actually exist is not relevant … what counts is the possibility that such a service may be offered by an enterprise".[88]

The Board of Appeal distinguished the method of placing a vaginal discharge collector from the application for the "sperm migration-inhibitory" method, stating that:

> In the present case, it can be foreseen that application and retrieval of the discharge collector is performed by a professional in the service of an enterprise. However, in contrast to the case of decision T 74/93 [for the "sperm migration-inhibitory" method], this service is not one satisfying only the strictly personal needs of the woman in question. *Collecting a sample may*

85 *Contraceptive Method/British Technology Group* (n 78) [2.2.5.2]
86 *Feminine Hygiene Device/Ultrafem Inc* (2000) T 1165/97 EPO Boards of Appeal.
87 Ibid. [3.1].
88 Ibid. [3.1].

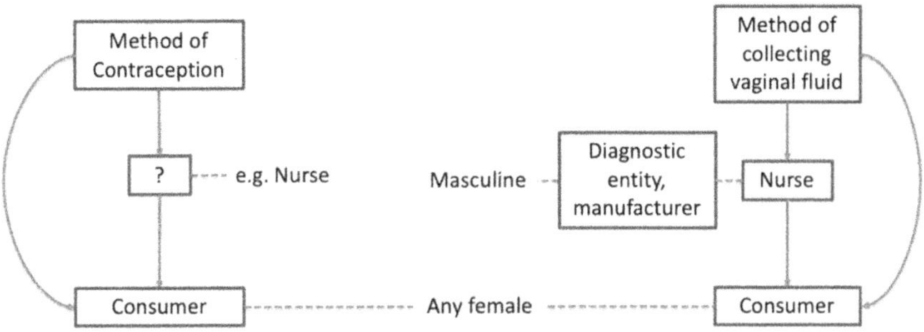

Figure 2.4 Contraceptive method versus method with masculine "middle man" industry

> *be caused by external reasons, e.g. the advice of a medical practitioner to have such a sample taken for further diagnosis. Moreover, in the situation described above, the person taking the sample will generally not be acting on the instructions of the woman in question, but rather on the basis of the instructions supplied with the collector itself, if necessary supplemented by instructions issued by his/her superior.* [89]

In contradistinction to the application for the "sperm migration-inhibitory" method, the middle men entities involved were from masculine industries (see Figure 2.4). Note, however, that these middle men entities are not the ones actually using the patented method. It would likely be nurses actually performing the method. Yet, the fact that masculine entities might somehow be involved and commercially gain is enough to make the invention susceptible of industrial application.

In its "sperm migration-inhibitory" method decision, the Board of Appeal stated that the requirement that there be an industrial application "may be regarded as an expression of the general idea that any natural person has the right to have his or her privacy respected".[90] That is, in this particular case, the industrial application standard protected the private actions of women. This seems noble, but if this were truly the concern at stake, neither of the two method claims (the "sperm migration-inhibitor" nor collecting vaginal fluid) should have been patentable. Instead, the distinction drawn is a mask for the private/public binary that this case law solidifies. What women do "in private" does not belong in the realm of commerce, of "enterprise" and "industry". This is true even if a professional is asked, possibly even paid, to perform the task. However, as soon as there is money to be made by a masculine industry from the female body, as in the application for the method of placing a vaginal discharge collector, that body is pulled into the public sphere – there is "enterprise" and "industry". It is worth reiterating that prostitution and nursing

89 Ibid. [3.2] (emphasis added).
90 *Contraceptive Method/British Technology Group* (n 78) [2.2.6].

are predominantly female professions, whereas manufacturing and diagnostics are masculine industries.

The stark delineation between the masculine–public–industrial = useful/industrial, on the one hand, and the feminine–private–care ≠ useful/industrial, on the other hand, is a reflection of power and domination. It is males who have shaped and made concrete the meaning of useful or industrial. This meaning serves to ascribe social and economic value to the masculine and men, whilst dismissing and not rewarding the feminine and women (see Chapter 4).

Of course, there are females who move in the industrial, public sphere and who patent (though, as outlined in Chapter 1, disproportionately few). However, the point is not that females can work in STEM, or can work in manufacture or diagnostics, and can get patents (though this is contentious, due to the institutionalised biases against women in STEM and the commercial world, discussed in Chapter 3). The point is rather that females (and indeed males) should not be limited to performing masculine in order to gain the power and wealth that patents can endow. Put another way, rather than telling women that they have to perform masculine to create the "useful" and "industrially applicable", our understandings of business, industry and the practically useful should reflect that the feminine is undoubtedly useful, industrial, practical and of economic value.

Overall, women are not placed in environments in order to invent in line with patent law's requirement of utility or industrial application as frequently as men are. When women are in these environments, what is demarcated as useful or industrial is the masculine. The consequence is that, when women have occupied public spaces, their inventions have often been ridiculed (deemed "frivolous"), attributed to males, or not been given the recognition they deserve.[91] This is analysed in the following section.

4.2 Patent-eligible subject matter

The World Trade Organization (WTO) Agreement on Trade-Related Aspects of Intellectual Property Rights (TRIPS) states that "patents shall be available for any inventions, whether products or processes, in all fields of technology".[92] As with all patent law language, this is seemingly gender neutral.[93] However, what constitutes an "invention" and "field of technology" is open to interpretation and it is those who are in power – those who make and interpret national and international laws – who define the terms. That is, it has been (Western) males that have had the power to define, recognise and privilege certain kinds of

91 McDaniel et al. (n 40) 3.

92 *Marrakesh Agreement Establishing the World Trade Organization*, opened for signature 15 April 1994, 1867 UNTS 3 (entered into force 1 January 1995) annex 1C (*Trade Related Aspects of Intellectual Property Rights* (TRIPS)), art 27.1.

93 Dutfield (n 53) 279 and 282, noted that the language of TRIPS does not discriminate between knowledge from different groups. However, the intention was that the rights would be used by certain kinds of entities, namely commercial entities.

knowledge.[94] As discussed in Chapter 3, the everyday understanding of "invention" embodies the masculine, which is reflected in patent law. This, in turn, is a reflection of "science" and the "scientist" being socially constructed as masculine (see Chapter 3). Thus, patent law protects the kind of knowledge that was traditionally considered to be created through masculine modes of production – the "rational", "objective", "systematised" and "made".[95] This knowledge is construed as universalistic. Patent law typically defines "invention" as a manner of manufacture, machine or composition of matter.[96] It is the mechanical, technical and industrial, but not what is "natural" or a "mere discovery".[97]

At the same time, the role of women has been socially constructed as being closer to "nature", "irrational" and "intuitive", rather than rational and scientific.[98] Thus, feminine knowledge is understood as subjective and inherently local and specific. Too close to nature and/or not constructed as abstract and universal, feminine knowledge is invisible to the patent system.

Over time, Western societies have come to see the masculine as the "standard" of knowledge and invention, and as neutral despite being heavily gendered.[99] As stated by Donna Haraway, science "is rhetoric, a series of efforts to

94 Barwa and Rai (n 69) 98. This is similarly true for copyright; see Craig, "Feminist Aesthetics and Copyright Law" (n 12) 16.

95 Evelyn Fox Keller, *Reflections on Gender and Science* (Yale University Press) 43–67 and 75–94. Note that this construction also shows its head in multiple other regimes, such as economic theory on the "rational person" and the legal ideal of the "reasonable person".

96 See e.g. 35 US Code § 101; Patent Act (RSC, 1985, c P-4), s 2 definition of "invention"; Statute of Monopolies 1623, s VI; Patents Act 2013 (NZ), s 14; and Patents Act 1990 (Cth), s 18.

97 The US has doctrines holding that natural products, natural laws and abstract ideas are non-patent-eligible subject matter; e.g. *AMP v Myriad Genetics, Inc* (2013) 133 S Ct 2107; *Mayo Collaborative Services and ors v Prometheus Laboratories Inc* (2012) 132 S Ct 1289; *Alice Corporation v CLS Bank International* (2014) 134 S Ct 2347. The EPC (n 34) art. 52(2) specifically states that the following are not "inventions": discoveries, scientific theories and mathematical methods; aesthetic creations; schemes, rules and methods for performing mental acts, playing games or doing business, and programs for computers; and presentations of information. In Australia and New Zealand, *NRDC v Commissioner of Patents* (n 64) 269 requires that one asks "Is this a proper subject of letters patent according to the principles which have been developed for the application of s 6 of the *Statute of Monopolies?*", which has been used to decline patentability on things too abstract or close to nature. See e.g. *D'Arcy v Myriad Genetics Inc* [2015] HCA 35.

98 Foster, "Situating Feminism, Patent Law, and the Public Domain" (n 44) 285; and Terra L Gearhart-Serna, "Women's Work, Women's Knowing: Intellectual Property and the Recognition of Women's Traditional Knowledge" (2010) 21(2) *Yale Journal of Law & Feminism* 372, 382–4; McDaniel et al. (n 40) 2–3.

99 Halbert (n 75) 436. B Zorina Khan, "'Not for Ornament': Patenting Activity by Nineteenth-Century Women Inventors" (2000) 31(2) *Journal of Interdisciplinary History* 159, 191–2, has pointed out that even women's perception of female "heroes of invention" is marred by the socialised understand of technology. That is, literature on female "heroes of invention" are about those who invented "masculine" inventions.

persuade relevant social actors that one's manufactured knowledge is a route to a desired form of very objective power".[100] Furthermore, as she notes in another article, those in positions of privilege "in the production of science and technology" are the ones who "construct scientific-technical discourses, processes, and objects".[101] That is, science and invention are coded masculine and this generally goes unquestioned, because "[t]he false claims of dominant groups seemed to 'become true' as dominant groups redesigned social relations to fit their vision of an ideal society".[102] Included in this redesign is the embodiment of these constructions in the law, and as Carys Craig has noted in the copyright context, "[l]egal doctrine has a self-perpetuating power: the power to naturalise its constructions, and to solidify its abstractions".[103]

Of course, even if empirically different, feminine knowledge is developed through rational and coherent methodology.[104] Moreover, as discussed in Chapters 3 and 6, all human knowledge is, to some degree, situated and local. In this vein, Evelyn Fox Keller has stated that science's "investment in impersonality, the claim to have escaped the influence of desires, wishes, and beliefs – perhaps even more than the sense of actual accomplishment – that constitutes the special arrogance, even bravura, of modern man, and at the same time reveals his peculiar subjectivity."[105] Nevertheless, Western masculine science only recognises the masculine while ignoring the feminine, and women are consequently not seen as creators or holders of knowledge, or of patentable "inventions".[106] The valorisation of masculine knowledge as rational and

100 Donna Haraway "Situated Knowledges: The Science Question in Feminism and the Privilege of Partial Perspective" (1988) 14(3) *Feminist Studies* 575, 577.

101 Donna Haraway, "A Cyborg Manifesto: Science, Technology, and Socialist-Feminism in the Late 20th Century" in Joel Weiss et al (eds), *The International Handbook of Virtual Learning Environments* (Springer 2016) 117, 136; originally published in (1985) 80 *Socialist Review* 65.

102 Sandra Harding, "A Socially Relevant Philosophy of Science" (2004) 19(1) *Hypatia* 25, 30.

103 Carys J Craig, *Copyright, Communication and Culture: Towards a Relational Theory of Copyright Law* (Edward Elgar, 2011) 11. See also Pierre Bourdieu, *Outline of a Theory of Practice* (Cambridge University Press, 1977) 188, who stated "Law does no more than symbolically consecrate – by recording it in a form which renders it both eternal and universal – the structure of the power relation between groups and classes which is produced and guaranteed practically by the functioning of these mechanisms.... The law thus contributes its own (specifically symbolic) force to the action of the various mechanisms which render it superfluous constantly to reassert power relations by overtly resorting to force".

104 Barwa and Rai (n 69) 108. See also Rosser (n 69) 70. For a parallel discussion on copyright law, gender, African Americans and Indigenous peoples, see Greene (n 12).

105 Fox Keller (n 95) 70.

106 Barwa and Rai (n 69) 92–5. An article by a US Assistant Examiner from 1927, purporting to celebrate women inventors, highlights this perception, stating that in "primitive society" women spent most of their time with their "children or in seeking and preparing food", and "had no occasion to make use of [their] inventive faculty"; Joseph Rossman, "Women Inventors" (1927) 10 *Journal of the Patent and Trademark Office Society* 18, 21. Innovations around childrearing, gathering and food

scientific, over feminine knowledge as intuitive, can be viewed as an iteration of the culture/nature dichotomy,[107] where masculine = culture = made = invention, whereas feminine = nature = non-made = non-invention.

The definitions of invention, discovery, culture and nature, and the invention/discovery and culture/nature dichotomies, are social constructs.[108] Culture and nature have been discussed in the foregoing (see also Chapters 3 and 6).[109] As to the invention and discovery dichotomy, what we understand to be a discovery affects what we perceive to be an invention, and vice versa. The natural and the discovery are co-constructed with the unnatural and the invention. In other words, natural and unnatural, and discovery and invention, are dialectic in that one only has meaning with the other. Helen Longino has stated that the invention and discovery dichotomy puts "blinders" over our eyes, as such "a theory of scientific inquiry that focuses solely on the logic of justification neglects the selection processes occurring in the context of discovery that limit what we get to know about".[110]

Yet, patent law depends on these constructs to legitimise the grant of 20 years of exclusive rights. The distinction between discoveries and inventions creates the veneer of objectivity. That is, a clean black and white line between what is patentable subject matter and what is not, ignoring the socially constructed nature of the dichotomy. Laura Foster has noted that, by doing so, patent law "situat[es] itself as ahistorical and free from challenge by positioning discovery outside of and as separate from invention".[111] As discussed above and in the following, the issue is not only that the masculine is patentable, whereas the feminine is not. It is also that – coded as discoveries of the natural – feminine kinds and sources of knowledge are left in the public domain to be taken and made into inventions through masculine modes of production.

4.2.1 *The "natural"*

An obvious way that the social constructs affect what constitutes patentable subject matter is the way that patent law has dealt with biology and subsequently biotechnology and attempts to find universality in organisms. For a STEM field, biology was traditionally relatively patent poor. This is because it observed and categorised the natural world, rather than create the technical. The local and specific nature of

preparation were not considered of value. In contrast, weapons and feats of engineering are often lauded as the innovations of earlier times. On the transition of inventorship and transfer of technology from females to males, see Stanley (n 40).

107 See e.g. Sherry B Ortner, "Is Female to Male as Nature is to Culture" (1972) 1(2) *Feminist Studies* 5; and Shulamith Firestone, *The Dialectic of Sex: The Case for Feminist Revolution* (William Morrow & Co, 1970) 176–91.

108 See Burk, "Feminism and Dualism in Intellectual Property" (n 12) 194–8.

109 Harding, "Rethinking Standpoint Epistemology" (n 41) 453. See also Helen E Longino, "Subjects, Power, and Knowledge: Description and Prescription in Feminist Philosophies of Science" in Linda Alcoff and Elizabeth Potter (eds), *Feminist Epistemologies* (Taylor & Francis, 1992) 101, 114–117.

110 Longino (n 109) 101.

111 Foster, "Decolonizing Patent Law" (n 6) 157.

biology makes it a difficult field in which to get patents, as it makes it challenging for a patent applicant to describe the invention "sufficiently" so that PHOSITA could make or emulate the invention. In other words, methods in biology are too feminine, whereas a patentable invention must be repeatable – a systematic and rational control of nature[112] – or masculine.

As highlighted in Chapter 1, biology is one of the few STEM fields that sees more gender parity in employment. By restricting patent eligibility for biology and what is closely connected to nature, patent law potentially discriminates against traditionally female-dominated fields of invention. Similarly, women are traditionally the "gatherers" of plants and inventors of traditional medicines. Yet, plant-based knowledge in this feminine form is not patentable. It is not until it is filtered through the masculine – experimented upon by science, perhaps an active ingredient is isolated or the plant is genetically modified (as discussed in the following) – that it becomes patentable. In contrast, inventions relating to the physical tools of agriculture, ploughs, hoes and the machinery in tractors, for example, are undoubtedly patent-eligible subject matter.

It remains the case for many traditional or Indigenous communities that women are the custodians of knowledge pertaining to flora and fauna – the "natural" rather than the "made".[113] Indeed, much knowledge of traditional or Indigenous communities, regardless of gender, is connected to genetic resources. This might include inventions pertaining to methods of harvesting, breeding or cultivation, or a medicinal use of a plant, for example. Patent law favours Western-male-centric modes of invention (machines, industrial manufacture and the "made"), ignoring this knowledge. Such feminine knowledge is, consequently, relegated to being unscientific or not technology,[114] superstition, possibly even as witchcraft.[115] It is "other" and in the public domain, where it can be taken without remuneration.[116] When the knowledge is taken and abstracted through masculine science it becomes "real knowledge" and patentable.[117]

112 Mary Tiles, "A Science of Mars or of Venus" (1987) 62 *Philosophy* 293, 301–2.

113 Gearhart-Serna (n 98); and Harding, "Postcolonial and Feminist Philosophies of Science and Technology" (n 25) 408.

114 E.g. Madrazo (n 52) 487.

115 Barwa and Rai (n 69) 101; and Gearhart-Serna (n 98) 382–3.

Whether women from traditional or Indigenous communities want their knowledge to be protected by the Western paradigm of property is, of course, another matter. This highlights the importance of utilising an intersectional lens, including things like biological sex, race, culture, religion, class and sexuality. Gearhart-Serna (n 98) 395; Foster, "Situating Feminism, Patent Law, and the Public Domain" (n 44); Merritt (n 47) 303–5; Candace West and Sarah Fenstermaker, "Doing Difference" (1995) 9(1) *Gender & Society* 8.

116 Vandana Shiva, "Bioprospecting as Sophisticated Biopiracy" (1997) 32(2) *Signs: Journal of Women in Culture and Society* 307.

117 Landon Schnabel and Lindsey Breitwieser, "Recent Advances in Feminist Science and Technology Studies: Reconceptualizing Subjectivity and Knowledge" (2015) 20(1) *Advances in Gender Research* 43, 55, citing: Londa Schiebinger, "Prospecting for Drugs: European Naturalists in the West Indies" in Sandra Harding (ed.), *The*

The non-patentability of biology has been significantly challenged since the advent of biotechnology in the mid-1980s. No longer about observation and categorisation, but with varying degrees of manipulation, biotechnology does not fit the dichotomy of the cultural and the natural. On the one hand, it results in the existence of things that otherwise would not exist, for example, genetically modified lifeforms. If different enough from that found in nature, it will be a patentable invention.[118] On the other hand, these things seemed quite close to nature.[119] This is illustrated by the discourse around whether merely isolated genes or genetic sequences should be patentable. In some jurisdictions, proponents argued that genes did not exist in their isolated and characterised (sequenced) form, meaning that they were "made".[120] In other jurisdictions, opponents of gene patents successfully argued that isolated genes were mere discoveries or natural products and, thus, not patent-eligible.[121]

It was the introduction of masculine and Western laboratory techniques that appeared to be able to create knowledge in a universalistic (that is, masculine) manner that led to calls for patentability. Colonised by masculine methodology, biotechnology is seemingly less local and specific than biology, making it more like chemistry. To be clear, the kinds of knowledge from classical biology and newer biotechnology are different. However, both are of value. Yet, the law recognises and thereby places more value in one (the more masculine) than the other (the more feminine). In addition, because the "made" in biotechnology (for example, genetically modifying something) is more expensive to create than the identified and isolated, it will be harder for females to invent in biotechnology because they generally have fewer resources.[122]

Postcolonial Science and Technology Studies Reader (Duke University Press, 2011) 110, 114.

118 E.g. *Diamond v Chakrabarty* (1980) 447 US 303 allowed patentability for genetically engineered bacteria; and "Oncomouse", a mouse genetically engineered to have a high susceptibility to cancer, was patented in the US (US Patent No 4,736,866) and was not challenged, and also through the EPO (*Onco-Mouse* (1990) T 0019/90; and *Transgenic Animals/Harvard* (2004) T 0315/03). However, cf. *Harvard College v Canada (Commissioner of Patents)* [2002] 4 SCR 45, which denied patentability for oncomouse as a "higher life form", as they are not "manufactures" or a "composition of matter".

119 Foster, "Situating Feminism, Patent Law, and the Public Domain" (n 44) 287–90.

120 E.g. *Relaxin/Howard Florey Institute* (2002) T 0272/95 EPO Boards of Appeal.

121 E.g. *D'Arcy v Myriad Genetics Inc* (n 97); *AMP v Myriad Genetics, Inc* (n 97). Note that the way that gene patents have been used, especially with respect to women's access to healthcare, has been critiqued. See e.g. E Richard Gold and Julia Carbone, "Myriad Genetics: In the Eye of the Policy Storm" (2010) 12(4) *Genetic Medicine* S39; and Sandra S Park, "The Challenge to Gene Patents as Feminist Patent Litigation" (2018) 19 *Technology and Innovation* 659.

122 Burk, "Feminism and Dualism in Intellectual Property" (n 12) 203.

Notably, invention (and more broadly science) is often described as a mastery of the mind, or control or domination, over nature.[123] In the critical words of Michel Serres, "[m]onopolized by science and by all the technologies associated with property rights, human reason conquered external nature in a combat that has lasted since prehistory, but that sped up relentlessly with the industrial revolution".[124] In other words, the masculine mastering the feminine. It is through this mastery that the feminine becomes patentable. As an illustration of this, Evelyn Fox Keller has examined how biology is slowly being colonised by the masculine fields of chemistry[125] and physics.[126] With respect to the latter, she describes the modern turn to try to rationalise biology, where physicists search for fundamental truths and all-encompassing laws. While the subject matter of biology, life, is traditionally considered to be subjective and local, as opposed to objective and universal, the physicists' colonisation of biology might result in more inventions in biology that appear to be replicate-able and which, thus, can be patented.

4.2.2 "Too abstract"

Modern patent law protects the disembodied invention, not its material reduction to practice. For example, a patent could protect the idea or conceptualisation of a machine, whether or not the machine has ever actually been made, as it is about the intellectual.[127] That is, it focuses on the mental component of the inventive process. This legal favouring of the immaterial thing over the physical instantiation thereof embodies the mind/body binary, and patent law (as well as copyright law) was developed partly on the justification that intellectual labour of the mind was of greater value than mere labour of the body.[128] More specifically, the mind/body dichotomy mirrors the market favouring masculine work in the intellectual (derived from the great male "geniuses"), over feminine labour (derived from nature and the "nurturers"). Thus, patent law idealises an inventor who exists within a capitalist mode of production and "divid[es] subject from object and knower from the known".[129] In contrast, feminine knowledge is

123 Val Plumwood, *Feminism and the Mastery of Nature (Opening Out: Feminism for Today)* (Routledge, 1993); Fox Keller (n 95) 33–42; Genevieve Lloyd, "Reason, Science and the Domination of Matter" in Evelyn Fox Keller and Helen E Longino (eds), *Feminism and Science* (Oxford University Press, 1996) 41; Christine Battersby, *Gender and Genius: Towards a Feminist Aesthetics* (Indiana University Press, 1989).
124 Michel Serres, *The Natural Contract* (Elizabeth MacArthur and William Paulson trans., University of Michigan Press, 1995) 35.
125 Evelyn Fox Keller, *Secrets of Life, Secrets of Death: Essays on Language, Gender and Science* (Routledge, 1992) 113.
126 Evelyn Fox Keller, "A Clash of Two Cultures" (2007) 445 *Nature* 603; and Evelyn Fox Keller, *Making Sense of Life: Explaining Biological Development with Models, Metaphors, and Machines* (Harvard University Press, 2003).
127 Burk, "Feminism and Dualism in Intellectual Property" (n 12) 186–193.
128 Foster, "Situating Feminism, Patent Law, and the Public Domain" (n 44) 319–2.
129 Halbert (n 75) 439.

often physical and typically related to childrearing, caregiving and the domestic.[130]

While patents protect the intellectual, they only protect this with respect to masculine modes of invention (as noted above, the industrial). This is exemplified by the fact that in fields where women do significantly invent the immaterial, patent law has declined patentability on the basis that the inventions are not material enough or are too abstract.[131] Many jurisdictions do not allow patents for abstract method claims, such as business methods, computer-implemented methods, methods of medical treatment (such as surgical and therapeutic methods) and diagnostic methods.[132] Courts have held them to be unpatentable abstract ideas or natural laws.[133] This is in contradistinction to industrial or technical process claims, such as a method to produce a chemical compound, which are patentable.

By excluding certain method claims and abstract ideas from patentability, the patent system potentially excludes fields that are more traditionally (and continually) female dominated, such as education, psychology, social work, caregiving and nursing, where creation is typically in the form of processes rather than products. An analogy can again be made with Indigenous peoples, many of whom have predominantly chosen to invest resources into knowledge that expresses itself in services and processes or "systems maintenance" (such as the ecological system), rather than "technological artefacts", making the application of intellectual property law inappropriate.[134]

As with biology and biotechnology, patent law has been challenged by the encroachment of the masculine into the feminine with respect to method

130 Burk, "Feminism and Dualism in Intellectual Property" (n 12) 191–4.

131 See also Agrawal (n 15) 422–3, who notes that it is untrue that Indigenous peoples only invent that which is tied to immediate physical problems and that, indeed, much of their knowledge is abstract.

132 E.g. *Research Affiliates LLC v Commissioner of Patents* [2014] FCAFC 150; *Grant v Commissioner of Patents* [2006] 69 IPR 221 (Full Court FCA); and *Parker v Flook* (1978) 437 US 584; *Gottschalk v Benson* (1972) 409 US 63; *Diamond v Diehr* (1981) 450 US 175; *Bilski v Kappos* (2010) 561 US 593; *Alice Corporation v CLS Bank International* (n 97); *Mayo Collaborative Services and ors v Prometheus Laboratories Inc* (n 97); *Apotex Pty Ltd v Sanofi-Aventis Australia Pty Ltd* [2013] HCA 50; *Pfizer Inc v Commissioner of Patents* (2004) 60 IPR 624 (CA), upholding *Wellcome Foundation Ltd v Commissioner of Patents* [1983] NZLR 385 (CA).

Note that methods of chemical contraception are typically not considered to be methods of medical treatment (due to the technical definition of medical treatment); e.g. *Schering AG's Application* [1971] RPC 337. This is why the EPO allowed the method for using estrogen (discussed above).

133 See Jessica C Lai, "The Nebulous 'Invention': From 'Idea and Embodiment' to 'Idea/Embodiment and Observable Physical Effects'?" in Jessica C Lai and Antoinette Maget Dominicé (eds), *Intellectual Property and Access to Im/material Goods* (Edward Elgar, 2016) 121.

134 Peter Drahos, "When Cosmology Meets Property: Indigenous People's Innovation and Intellectual Property" (2011) 29(3) *Prometheus* 233, 241–2. Drahos further noted that IPRs "have little relevance to innovators who seek to innovate at the level of systems rather than commodities" (at 243).

claims. Many jurisdictions have long held methods of medical treatment to be unpatentable.[135] This means that nursing and counselling methods, for example, are not patentable. However, the strict non-patentability of methods of medical treatment changed when the pharmaceutical industry sought patents for new uses of known medicaments. The medicaments themselves are not patentable as they are not new. The new uses should not be patentable as a use of a medicament is a method of medical treatment. Nevertheless, many jurisdictions that do not allow patents for methods of medical treatment do allow patents for new uses of known medicaments.[136] That is, methods potentially created by day-to-day healthcare workers, such as nurses, physios, midwives, counsellors and therapists, remain unpatentable. However, methods related to the masculine pharmaceutical industry are patentable.

Once methods enter a masculine realm, non-patentability becomes questioned and exceptions are made. This was also observable with methods relating to financial markets. Until the twenty-first century, most of the English-speaking world did not allow patents for business methods. However, this was challenged by methods to be used in male-dominated financial markets, for example, for hedging against or managing risks in investments, or generating asset indexes.[137] One of these challenges led to the US Supreme Court holding that business methods could be patentable processes, so long as they are not merely abstract ideas.[138] Similarly, other jurisdictions, such as the EPO, allow business method claims if they specify a technical means (such as computers, computer networks or other programmable apparatus) to execute at least some steps of the method.[139]

This leads to the next point, which is that abstract methods are patentable if they are placed in masculine embodiments. For example, let us pretend that a nurse has invented a new way to determine how to speak to patients to keep them calm, based on selected word choice, changed iteratively depending on how a patient reacts. This would not be patentable as it would be an abstract method. However, if the method were filtered through the masculine, and a machine were created using this method, to speak certain words and react to patients based on their behaviour, the machine could be patentable. As would possibly the underlying software. This is elaborated upon in the following.

135 E.g. EPC (n 34) art. 53(c); *Wellcome Foundation Ltd v Commissioner of Patents* (n 132); *Upjohn Company (Robert's) Application* [1977] RPC 94. The US and Australia are exceptions.
136 E.g. EPC (n 34) art. 54(4) and (5); *Pharmaceutical Management Agency Ltd v Commissioner of Patents* [2000] 2 NZLR 529 (CA).
137 E.g. *Bilski v Kappos* (n 132); *Alice Corp v CLS Bank Int'l* (n 97); *Research Affiliates LLC v Commissioner of Patents* (n 132)
138 *Bilski v Kappos* (n 132).
139 EPO (n 34) Part G – Chapter II-3.5.3.

4.2.3 "Too immaterial"

Many jurisdictions do not allow patents for software per se or "as such", because it constitutes mere information or natural laws (composed of algorithms).[140] For example, the EPC explicitly excludes mathematical methods and computer programs.[141] While computer science is now primarily male in the twenty-first century Western world, this was not always the case,[142] and it is not the case everywhere.[143] At its infancy, computing was female dominated, as it was something "soft", non-physical and coded non-industrial.[144] It was not considered to be socially powerful or valuable. Indeed, Augusta Ada King (née Byron), Countess of Lovelace, is recognised as the first computer programmer.[145]

Software is also a feminine field because it requires relatively fewer resources to invent. One does not require a laboratory, chemicals or biological materials. In this sense, it is a field prime for women, who statistically have fewer resources.[146] This is supported by a 2012 study on the information technology sector from the US, which showed that, while males had significantly more patents than females overall, the data (from 1980–2010, a period during which software patents were allowed in the US) revealed that this was less so with

140 E.g. EPC (n 34) art. 52(2)(a); IP Australia, "Manual of Practice and Procedure" (last updated 2 February 2015), s 2.9.2.10; *Grant v Commissioner of Patents* (n 132); *Gottschalk v Benson* (n 132); and *Parker v Flook* (n 132).

141 EPC (n 34) art. 52(2)(a) and (c).

142 See e.g. Margot Lee Shetterly, *Hidden Figures: The American Dream and the Untold Story of the Black Women Who Helped Win the Space Race* (William Morrow and Co, 2016).

143 For example, Malaysia has more females in computer science than males; Ulf Mellström, "The Intersection of Gender, Race and Cultural Boundaries, or Why is Computer Science in Malaysia Dominated by Women?" (2009) 39(6) *Social Studies of Science* 885; and Mazliza Othman and Rodziah Latih, "Women in Computer Science: No Shortage Here!" (2006) 49(3) *Communications of the ACM* 111. India is also experiencing a rapid growth in females in the computer sciences; Namrata Gupta, "Rethinking the Relationship Between Gender and Technology: A Study of the Indian Example" (2015) 29(4) *Work, Employment and Society* 661.

144 These form some of the reasons why computer science is an acceptable profession for women in societies that the Western world would consider less socially progressive, such as India; Roli Varma, "Computing Self-Efficiency Among Women in India" (2010) 16(3) *Journal of Women and Minorities in Science and Engineering* 257.

145 Sarah L Frasier, "In Celebration of Ada Lovelace, the First Computer Programmer" (14 October) *Scientific American*, www.scientificamerican.com/article/in-celebration-of-ada-lovelace-the-first-computer-programmer (accessed 6 December 2019).

146 HM Revenue and Customs, "UK Personal Wealth Statistics 2014 to 2016" (31 January 2019), www.gov.uk/government/statistics/uk-personal-wealth-statistics-2014-to-2016; Nicole Torres, "Closing the Gender Wealth Gap" (3 October 2019) *Harvard Business Review*, https://hbr.org/2019/10/closing-the-gender-wealth-gap; and Margaret Denton and Linda Boos. "The Gender Wealth Gap: Structural and Material Constraints and Implications for Later Life" (2007) 19(3–4) *Journal of Women and Aging* 105; and Anna Fausto-Sterling, "Women and Science" (1981) 4(1) *Women's Studies International Quarterly* 41, 44–5.

software.[147] Catherine Ashcraft and Anthony Breitzman showed that in most subcategories of information technology, 87.4 per cent of patents were attributable to males, 2.1 per cent to females, and 10.5 per cent by mixed teams. However, an exception was computer software, where 82 per cent of the patents had male inventors, 2.9 per cent female inventors, and 15.1 per cent had mixed-sex inventors (Table 2.1).[148] While still heavily weighted towards males, the differences are significant. Ashcraft and Breitzman then fractionalised the mixed-sex patents,[149] and split them between their male and female inventors, which showed that the female contribution to computer software patents for 1980–84 was 3.4 per cent, and for 2006–10 was 9.3 per cent (Table 2.2).[150]

We can compare this to computer hardware patents, where 88.6 per cent of patents were attributable to males, 1.7 per cent to females, and 9.7 per cent to mixed teams. When the mixed-sex patents were fractionalised, this showed that the female contribution to computer hardware patents for 1980–84 was 1.8 per cent, and for 2006–10 was 6.3 per cent.[151] That is, the technical/mechanical field continues to be male dominated more so than the immaterial software

Table 2.1 Percentage of US information technology patents (1980–2010)[152]

	Male-only inventors	*Female-only inventors*	*Mixed-sex patents*
IT generally	87.4	2.1	10.5
Computer software	82.0	2.9	15.1
Computer hardware	88.6	1.7	9.7

Table 2.2 Percentage of US information technology patents (1980–2010), fractionalised[153]

	Fractionalised male		*Fractionalised female*	
	1980–84	*2006–10*	*1980–84*	*2006–10*
Computer software	96.6	90.7	3.4	9.3
Computer hardware	98.2	93.75	1.8	6.25

147 Catherine Ashcraft and Anthony Breitzman, "Who Invents IT? Women's Participation in Information Technology Patenting" (2012) *National Center for Women & Information Technology*, 12.
148 Ibid.
149 E.g. a patent with two males and one female was counted as 2/3 male and 1/3 female.
150 Ashcraft and Breitzman (n 147) 14.
151 Ibid., 12–14.
152 Ibid., 12.
153 Ibid., 14.

field. At the same time, there is no doubt that hardware constitutes patentable subject matter.

Furthermore, the EPO,[154] the US,[155] Australia[156] and New Zealand[157] all (in varying ways) hold that computer programs can constitute an invention as soon as there is any relation to something physical. This includes the computer on which it is run. For example, the EPO Guidelines allow patents for computer programs if they "produce a 'further technical effect' when run on a computer. A 'further technical effect' is a technical effect going beyond the 'normal' physical interactions between the program (software) and the computer (hardware) on which it is run".[158] In practice, simply adding the phrase "computer-implemented" will make software patentable. This is the "any hardware" approach.[159]

In other words, when an invention remains something immaterial and feminine, it is not patentable, as any abstraction pertains to a natural law. However, as soon as the invention becomes more material, the invention moves into the realm of the masculine and is patentable. If we take the new (but unpatentable) method for cooking eggs from above, a machine using this method could be patentable, as could the method embodied in the software tied to the machine.

An exception appears to be mathematics (other than software algorithms) and theoretical physics, which are male-dominated domains, where much research is considered to be mere discoveries of natural laws and not patentable inventions. One could take the exclusion of mathematical and physical discoveries from patentability as evidence that patent law is not gendered, but reflects genuine distinctions between what is upstream and fundamental, on the one hand, and what is downstream and industrially applicable on the other hand. However, this is not correct as feminine knowledge – whether in the form of business methods, methods of medical treatment and diagnostic methods, or processes for cultivation – are potentially directly marketable. It is the law that deems feminine knowledge to be upstream and/or non-industrial, or awaiting filtration through masculine science to become downstream and industrial technology. In contrast, discoveries of mathematics and theoretical physics are

154 EPO (n 34) Part G – Chapter II-3.6. The UK has also distinguished between claims to merely intellectual schemes and information from methods that affect the operation of an apparatus in a physical form; see e.g. *Burroughs* [1974] RPC 147; and *International Business Machines Corp's Application* [1980] FSR 564.

155 *Diamond v Diehr* (n 132).

156 *Grant v Commissioner of Patents* (n 132). IP Australia (n 140) s 2.9.2.7. See also *International Business Machines Corp v Commissioner of Patents* (1991) 22 IPR 41; and *CCOM v Jiejing* (1994) 51 FCR 260, 295.

157 Patents Act 2013 (NZ), s 11.

158 EPO (n 34) Part G – Chapter II-3.6. For examples of patentable computer programs and computer-implemented methods, see Part G – Chapter II-3.6.1.

159 *Auction method/Hitachi* (2004) T 0258/03 EPO Boards of Appeal, which has been cited in over 100 decisions; see www.epo.org/law-practice/case-law-appeals/recent/t030258ep1.html.

not typically directly marketable. They must first be implemented within another invention. In other words, if the line truly is between the fundamental and the industrially applicable, then many discoveries of mathematics and theoretical physics do fall within the former. However, many feminine inventions most certainly fall within the latter and this is not what we observe in the application of patent law.

5 Finding the real problem and solution

This chapter highlights that it is deceptive to make statements that allude to the relationship between patents and STEM as some inherent or objective truth. The creators of patent law designed it to protect the products of their knowledge. STEM is patent heavy because STEM is male heavy. What constitutes patentable subject matter reflects masculine modes of invention and knowing. This is not to say that females have or produce less knowledge. As stated above, masculine and feminine information, knowledge and ways of knowing differ because of gendered socialised roles in society. Feminine knowledge is often in home-technology, childrearing, caregiving and education, reflecting women's gendered roles.[160] This is knowledge that is often not considered scientific or technical, but instead given to the public domain, and is thus not patentable.[161]

Feminine knowledge is invisible until it is filtered through the masculine. This is an important realisation, because it allows us to stop framing the cause of gendered patenting as "not enough women in STEM". As discussed in Chapter 3, that there are not as many women in patent-protected STEM fields naturally means that there are fewer females named as inventors on patents. However, the deeper issue is that women have to be in STEM to patent because the power hegemony at play results in patent law protecting the masculine. Indeed, patent law keeps the feminine free for (mostly) males to take and filter through masculine science and patent (discussed further in Chapter 5).

Until we deconstruct the biases inherent in patent law, we cannot say that anything untoward is occurring. Feminine knowledge and female inventors will remain invisible. The law will retain its veneer of neutrality. And we will not be able to identify what is happening, which is the appropriation of feminine knowledge through its social and legal devaluation, keeping it free for appropriation and filtration through the masculine.

That patent law itself is gendered has consequences beyond the gendered patenting gap. A tool of innovation policy, patent law has bearing upon invention and innovation. This includes what is invented and commercialised, and who invents and innovates. Furthermore, the patent system can affect what information and knowledge is disseminated, built-upon and viewed as valuable. That patent law is gendered is problematic because it incentivises the invention

160 Khan, "Not for Ornament" (n 99) 177; Rosser (n 69) 70 and 76; Gearhart-Serna (n 98) 386.
161 Merritt (n 47) 301.

and commercialisation of the masculine, rather than the feminine, and it valorises masculine knowledge over feminine knowledge. This sustains the social perception that men are scientists and inventors, not women, and that women are supposed to give rather than take. This is examined in depth in Chapter 4, which highlights the importance of having an egalitarian knowledge governance system.

Of course, patent law does not exist in a vacuum, and gendered patenting is also the result of socio-cultural and institutional biases, discussed in the following chapter. These implicate the pre-patenting process, patent law and the use of patents, and are in turn implicated by patent law. Put another way, everything in the patent-related cosmos is interrelated. This means that changing patent law will not be enough to achieve gender (and all) equity in the cosmos. Other changes are necessary, from de-gendering our understandings of science and technology, having more women in our re-constructed STEM in positions of power, to identifying and exorcising deeply ingrained misogyny from society. This is not something that can change overnight. Indeed, it is something that cannot change unless more people are made aware of the socially constructed binaries at play in our understandings of "science" and "invention", what is valuable, and how these binaries are embodied in patent law.

One would think that a good starting point to create an egalitarian knowledge governance system would be to de-gender patent law. However, simply removing the binaries that frame patent law would implicitly broaden patentability. Greater propertisation is not necessarily desirable nor ultimately of benefit to women because it affects access and use of the newly patentable subject matter. For example, while we want our knowledge governance system to be egalitarian, we do not necessarily want methods of contraception to be patented.[162] Similarly we do necessarily want more biotechnology and software to be propertised. In other words, the knowledge governance system should not be gendered, but more patents might not be the answer.

Furthermore, opponents would argue that broadening patentability would negatively affect the public domain and future invention. Nevertheless, as discussed in Chapter 5, the discourse needs to go beyond recognising the importance of the public domain, to asking why the lines that define who has wealth and power are drawn where they are. After all, the patent-protected and propertised versus the public domain is yet another socially constructed binary. More concretely, Chapter 5 addresses whom the public domain serves and argues that the public domain is part of the patent system's framework that benefits the advantaged and harms the disadvantaged. Put another way, the public domain, too, reflects the hegemony and it should not be used as a universalistic argument against women's (and non-Western societies') demands for an egalitarian knowledge governance system.

162 E.g. see the discourse around access to breast and ovarian cancer genetic screening resulting from gene patents (n 121).

We need to break out of the construct of binaries, while avoiding universalistic attempts to govern knowledge (see Chapter 5), to develop a knowledge governance system that recognises and encourages the multiplicity of ways in which invention and innovation can and does occur, and that individuals, groups and communities can behave beyond socially constructed dichotomies. What this knowledge governance system might look like is explored in Chapters 6 and 7.

3 Feeding the cyborg

> … change at the level of substantive rules is not likely in itself to be determinative of redistributive outcomes. Rule change is in itself likely to have little effect because the system is so constructed that changes in the rules can be filtered out unless accompanied by changes at other levels. Programs of equalizing reform which focus on rule-change can be readily absorbed without any change in power relations. The system has the capacity to change a great deal at the level of rules without corresponding changes in everyday patterns of practice or distribution of tangible advantages … Indeed rule-change may become a symbolic substitute for redistribution of advantages.
>
> … breaking the interlocked advantages of the "haves" requires attention not only to the level of rules, but also to institutional facilities, legal services and organization of parties.[1]

1 Introduction

Science, technology, engineering and mathematics (STEM) comprise the patent-heavy fields. The large portion of existing literature focuses on the fact that fewer females in STEM leads to fewer female inventors on patents. Thus, the literature is centred on there not being enough women in STEM. Chapter 2 stepped back from this and analysed how the requirements for patentability are gendered in favour of the masculine to the disadvantage of the feminine. Patent law has been developed around Western-masculine-centric modes of invention and innovation.[2] Because

1 Marc Galanter, "Why the 'Haves' Come Out Ahead: Speculations on the Limits of Legal Change" (1974) 9(1) *Law and Society* 95, 149–50.

2 On the race-dynamic, see Laura A Foster, "Patents, Biopolitics, and Feminisms: Locating Patent Law Struggles over Breast Cancer Genes and the Hoodia Plant" (2012) 19 *International Journal of Cultural Property* 371; Laura A Foster, "Situating Feminism, Patent Law, and the Public Domain" (2011) 20 *Columbia Journal of Gender & Law* 262; and Terra L Gearhart-Serna, "Women's Work, Women's Knowing: Intellectual Property and the Recognition of Women's Traditional Knowledge" 21(2) *Yale Journal of Law & Feminism* 372; Patricia Ive, "Patent and Trademark Innovation of Black Americans and Women" (1980) 62(2) *Journal of the Patent Office Society* 108. See also Jessica C Lai, *Indigenous Cultural Heritage and Intellectual Property Rights* (Springer, 2014) 59–77 on the fundamental disconnects between intellectual property and Indigenous knowledge systems generally.

DOI: 10.4324/9781003128502-4

patentability is skewed towards the masculine, it protects the inventions of masculine industries – STEM. The natural outcome of this is that men do the kinds of inventing that are protected by patents.[3] As stated in Chapter 2, STEM is patent-heavy because STEM is male heavy.

Put another way, the problem is not that there are not enough women in STEM. It is that the gendered nature of patentability requires that women operate in STEM to patent. Yet, STEM represents fields that females have traditionally been socialised away from. Moreover, invention and innovation take place in gendered environments. Thus, when women do enter STEM, they face marginalisation, ostracisation and innumerable biases.

Women can feel "other" in STEM. As discussed in this chapter, women often feel that they have to "play" masculine in order to survive and succeed in STEM. Donna Haraway has used the "cyborg",[4] and Susan Leigh star the "monster",[5] as metaphors for this sense of misplacement. At the crux of this is that women, like cyborgs and Frankenstein's monster, are born into a world with set constructs and relationships, where they constantly feel other. The existing knowledge ecosystem perpetuates the cyborg or monster nature of women in STEM.

This chapter examines the gendered contexts of invention and innovation and how these contribute to the gendered patenting gap.[6] It aims to paint a picture of the patent-regulated knowledge governance system through a gender frame. It comprehensively analyses why there is a gendered patenting gap, and how this affects and is affected by the commercialisation process. The chapter analyses the gendered nature of the Western notions of "science", "invention", the "inventor" and the "entrepreneur". In addition, it examines institutional, structural and organisational biases that impinge upon women's ability to invent, patent and commercialise. It runs through the lifecycle of invention and innovation, from education and industry entry, to performing "science" and "inventing", to patenting one's creation and commercialising it. The chapter shows the circular nature of the problem.

3 Erin Leahey and Amelia Blume, "Elucidating the Process: Why Women Patent Less than Men" in Albert N Link (ed), *Gender and Entrepreneurial Activity* (Edward Elgar, 2017) 159; Sharmishta Barwa and Shirin M Rai, "Knowledge and/as Power: A Feminist Critique of Trade Related Intellectual Property Rights" (2003) 7(1) *Gender, Technology and Development* 91; and Shlomit Yanisky-Ravid, "Eligible Patent Matter – Gender Analysis of Patent Law: International and Comparative Perspectives" (2011) 19(3) *American University Journal of Gender, Social Policy & the Law* 851.

4 Donna Haraway, "A Cyborg Manifesto: Science, Technology, and Socialist-Feminism in the Late 20th Century" in Joel Weiss et al. (eds), *The International Handbook of Virtual Learning Environments* (Springer 2016) 117; originally published in (1985) 80 *Socialist Review* 65.

5 Susan Leigh Star, "Power, Technology and the Phenomenology of Conventions: On Being Allergic to Onions" (1990) 38(S1) *The Sociological Review* 26.

6 This chapter updates and expands upon content from Jessica C Lai, "Patents and Gender: A Contextual Analysis" (2020) 10(3) *Queen Mary Journal of Intellectual Property* 283.

Through the analyses in Chapters 2 and 3, the discourse around women inventors is re-framed by showing that we have to stop focusing on the "women in STEM" narrative, because this focus is a distraction from the underlying problem that the Western knowledge governance system reflects the hegemonic powers at play. The problem is not narrowly that there are not enough women in STEM. It is that the law, and the social constructs it relies upon and sustains, protect the masculine at the sacrifice of the feminine, and that those in power protect those most like themselves and thereby retain their power.

This re-framing is important as giving shape and form to a power dynamic allows us to deconstruct it. This power dynamic needs to be deconstructed, as there are harms of the status quo. Patents are a primary tool used in Western jurisdictions to enhance innovation (whether this eventuates or not) and they can have negative wealth distributing effects through creating "haves" and "have nots".[7] With a knowledge governance system that is gendered, males and those who perform masculine are the haves and females and those who perform feminine are the have nots (analysed in Chapter 4). Furthermore, the re-framing allows us to stop telling women, whether consciously or unconsciously, that they are the problem if they cannot succeed in patenting and commercialisation. When, in reality, the Western knowledge governance system sets women up to fail.

As alluded to in Chapter 2, the consequence of the re-framing is not necessarily that we should de-gender gendered patenting and patent law. This would presume that patents are the ideal innovation policy tool. Instead, the realisation that patenting and patent law are gendered, and the negative consequences thereof, might lead us to re-think the knowledge ecosystem and its governance system. This re-think is imperative to ensure that power does not beget power, leaving the feminine and women progressively behind in the knowledge-driven digital economy.

It is important to note here that the issue is not solely that STEM marginalises and ostracises women. Even if this were not the case, the knowledge system that patent law creates still funnels women and men into masculine modes of production. Yet, diverse experiences and viewpoints, streams of knowledge and approaches are positive factors for innovation. Thus, it would not be ideal to simply have more women trained in STEM, operating within the existing culture and within existing modalities. Instead, the ideal system would maximise innovative potential, beyond socially constructed masculine knowledges. It would do so through offering equal opportunities to create and develop knowledge, and to capture value from it. This equality would ensure

7 Angus C Chu, "Effects of Patent Policy on Income and Consumption Inequality in a R&D Growth Model" (2010) 77(2) *Southern Economics Journal* 336; Angus C Chu and Guido Cozzi, "Effects of Patents versus R&D Subsidies on Income Inequality" (2018) 29 *Review of Economic Dynamics* 68; and Wenkai Tzeng, "Poverty and Patents: Intellectual Property Policy and Economic Inequality" (2017) 5 *Indiana Journal of Law & Social Equality* 313.

that females, as well as males, determine the direction of knowledge and technology generation. It would also result in fairer distribution of wealth.

2 What's my line?[8]

> all [knowledge claims] bear the fingerprints the communities that produce them. All thought by humans starts from socially determinate lives.[9]

Despite the fact that females are generally achieving greater parity in access to and completion of education in many jurisdictions, the STEM fields (whether in industry or academia) continue to be male dominated, especially in mathematics, physics, engineering and the computer sciences.[10] There is a widely held belief that women are inherently less interested in the STEM fields,[11] and innately (that is, biologically) different to males in a way that makes them less suitable for STEM.[12] The biological differences between males and females are highly contentious, with science showing that there is no simplistic binary,

8 This was the name of a US game show from the 1960s and 70s on which four panellists had to determine guests' occupations by asking yes/no questions.

9 Sandra Harding, "Rethinking Standpoint Epistemology: What is 'Strong Objectivity?'" (1992) 36(3) *The Centennial Review* 437, 445.

10 Emma Smith, "Women into Science and Engineering? Gendered Participation in Higher Education STEM Subjects" (2011) 37(6) *British Educational Research Journal* 993; Tessa ES Charlesworth and Mahzarin R Banaji, "Gender in Science, Technology, Engineering, and Mathematics: Issues, Causes, Solutions" (2019) 39(37) *Journal of Neuroscience* 7228; and Stephen J Ceci and Wendy M Williams, "Sex Differences in Math-Intensive Fields" (2010) 19(5) *Current Directions in Psychological Science* 275, 275. Indeed, one study has shown that countries with high levels of gender equality have greater gaps between males and female studying STEM in secondary and tertiary levels; Gijsbert Stoet and David C Geary, "The Gender-Equality Paradox in Science, Technology, Engineering, and Mathematics Education" (2018) 29(4) *Psychol Sci* 581. Stoet and Geary hypothesise that this is due to the "expectancy-value theory", whereby females in countries with lower gender-equality are more likely to undertake the risk of studying STEM to get a higher-paying job.

11 E.g. Rong Su et al., "Men and Things, Women and People: A Meta-Analysis of Sex Differences in Interests" (2009) 135(6) *Psychological Bulletin* 859, found that males are more interested in things, whereas women are people-orientated. However, Su et al. note that the paper did not consider social and environmental factors which result in these varying interests. Educational levels of females in STEM support that women are interested in STEM. On this and why women might not stay in STEM, see Elizabeth M Adamowizc, "Why Aren't Women Choosing STEM Academic Jobs? Observations from a Small-group Discussion at the 2016 American Society for Microbiology Annual Meeting" (2017) 364 *FEMS Microbiology Letters* 1; Abigail Powell, Andrew Dainty and Barbara Bagilhole, "Gender Stereotypes Among Women Engineering and Technology Students in the UK: Lessons from Career Choice Narratives" (2012) 37(6) *European Journal of Engineering Education* 541.

12 For discussion, see Steven Pinker, "Sex Ed. The Science of Difference" (14 February 2005) *New Republic*.

either in terms of sex or sex-dependent characteristics.[13] Ultimately, the debate centres around whether females' empirically lower rate in entering STEM fields is biological or socialised (that is, gender essentialist versus social constructionist), or a mixture of the two.[14]

Not discounting that some differences might be biological,[15] it is without a doubt that the ability to become an inventor is socially determined. Along with gender, it depends on race, socio-economic background, environment, exposure to innovation during one's youth, and role models.[16] Furthermore, women are socialised against studying in STEM fields.[17] They have historically been encouraged to focus on etiquette, culture and the arts; the sciences were

13 Daphna Joel et al., "Analysis of Human Brain Structure Reveals that the Brain 'Types' Typical of Males Are Also Typical of Females, and Vice Versa" (2018) *Frontiers in Human Neuroscience*, https://doi.org/10.3389/fnhum.2018.00399; Daphna Joel et al., "Sex Beyond the Genitalia: The Human Brain Mosaic" (2015) 112(50) *Proceedings of the National Academy of Sciences* 15468; Claire Ainsworth, "Sex Redefined" (2015) 518 *Nature* 288; Jessica Hamzelou, "Scans Prove There's No Such Thing as a 'Male' or 'Female' Brain" (30 November 2015) *New Scientist*; Gina Rippon, "A Welcome Blow to the Myth of Distinct Male and Female Brains" (30 November 2015) *New Scientist*; and Taylor Lorenz, "Are Male and Female Brains Biologically Different?" (25 June 2018) *The Atlantic*.

14 On the falseness of the gender essentialist versus social constructionist dichotomy, see e.g. Anne Fausto-Sterling, "Beyond-Difference: A Biologist's Perspective" (1997) 53(2) *Journal of Social Issues* 233; and Anne Fausto-Sterling, "Against Dichotomy" (2017) 1(1) *Evolutionary Studies in Imaginative Culture* 63.

15 The nature of genetic expression is made further complicated by the relatively nascent field of epigenetics, which studies heritable genomic information/structures that affect the expression of nucleotide sequences. For an introduction to epigenetics, see Virginia Hughes, "Epigenetics: The Sins of the Father" (2014) 507 (7490) *Nature* 22.

16 Alexander M Bell et al., "Who Becomes an Inventor in America? The Importance of Exposure to Innovation" (2019) *The Quarterly Journal of Economics* 647; Holly Fechner and Matthew S Shapanka, "Closing Diversity Gaps in Innovation Gender, Race, and Income Disparities in Patenting and Commercialization of Inventions" (2018) 19 *Technology and Innovation* 727.

17 Campbell Leaper and Christia Brown, "Perceived Experiences with Sexism Among Adolescent Girls" (2008) 79 *Child Development* 685, 694–5; and Annette I Kahler, "Examining Exclusion in Woman-Inventor Patenting: A Comparison of Educational Trends and Patent Data in the Era of Computer Engineer Barbie" (2011) 19 (3) *American University Journal of Gender, Social Policy & the Law* 773, 780. Stoet and Geary have argued that the loss of females in STEM between secondary and tertiary education is in part attributable to females typically scoring higher in reading comprehension than science and mathematics. At the same time, even if males did not score as well as females in science and mathematics, their scores were more likely to reflect personal academic strengths. See Stoet and Geary (n 10). See also Ceci and Williams, "Sex Differences in Math-Intensive Fields" (n 10) 278, who note that "among males and females of comparable outstanding mathematical aptitude, females are more likely to also have outstanding verbal ability. This gives them more career choices than males, who are aware their strength is only maths, whereas females can consider math-orientated fields as well as law, social sciences, humanities and medicine".

considered masculine domains (examined further below).[18] This remains the case, especially in the fields of mathematics, engineering and the computer sciences,[19] and is increasingly more so as a woman advances from undergraduate studies, post-graduate studies and into the work force.[20] Education matters, as "[t]he endowments with which people enter markets and structures of reproduction fundamentally influence market access and, therefore, also influence competition policy".[21]

Sarah-Jane Leslie et al. have shown that, in math-heavy STEM subjects (mathematics, physics and engineering) females are stereotyped as not having the requisite raw, innate talent or brilliance for success.[22] These fields are more likely to endorse the idea that females are less suited for high level scholarly work, rate themselves as less welcoming of females, indeed, have lower female representation, including at the PhD level.[23] The belief that females lack the required innate ability for certain STEM fields permeates through society, including women themselves who might internalise the stereotypes. This can result in women being unable to envisage themselves as engineers, scientists or inventors,[24] and thus believing they cannot study or work in those fields.[25]

If females do enter the STEM fields, they typically find themselves within a primarily masculine culture – a culture that does not change easily. Evelyn Fox Keller explained that this affects "women in STEM":

> Just bringing different kinds of people to the table is not enough, especially when the framework has already been established by a particular subset of the human community with the particular mindsets of that community's culture.[26]

18 Kahler (n 17) 781.
19 Ibid 792–7.
20 Kris de Welde and Sandra L Laursen, "The Glass Obstacle Course: Informal and Formal Barriers for Women PhD Students in STEM Fields" (2011) 3(3) *International Journal of Gender, Science & Technology* 571.
21 Barwa and Rai (n 3) 107. See also Deborah Merritt, "Hypatia in the Patent Office: Women Inventors and the Law, 1865–1900" (1991) 35 *American Journal of Legal History* 235, 293–94, who notes that women not only get less technical training, but also less education about documenting experimentation, patent drafting and model making, in order to apply for patents.
22 Sarah-Jane Leslie et al., "Expectations of Brilliance Underlie Gender Distributions Across Academic Disciplines" (2015) 347(6219) *Science* 262.
23 Ibid.
24 Powell, Dainty and Bagilhole (n 11); and Merritt (n 21) 295.
25 Rachael D Robnett, "Gender Bias in STEM Fields: Variation in Prevalence and Links to STEM Self-Concept" (2016) 40(1) *Psychology of Women Quarterly* 65, 74. See also Allan Wigfield and Jacquelynne S Eccles, "Expectancy–Value Theory of Achievement Motivation" (2000) 25 *Contemporary Educational Psychology* 68, who address how an individual's choice, persistence and performance in an endeavour can be explained by his/her beliefs about how well they will and the extent to which he/she values the activity.
26 Rana Dajani, "What Do We mean When We Talk about Gender and Science? An Interview with Professor Emerita Evelyn Fox Keller (MIT), author of *Reflections on Gender and Science*" (2019) 44(2) *Interdisciplinary Science Reviews* 221, 224.

The culture often excludes or discriminate against women.[27] This includes by both male and female actors.[28] Females also have to work harder to be taken seriously and to achieve the same reputational gains as their male counterparts.[29] While the more overt forms of discrimination may no longer be omnipresent in much of the world, subtle and informal biases remain.[30] Women are often sexualised (objectified as the token woman), are made to feel "unnatural" (for not conforming to traditionally feminine norms) or are treated as being somehow deviant for being in STEM.[31] This is marginalising. More still, the "Old Boys' Club" remains prevalent. The exclusion from this "club" can result in women feeling like outsiders, from the research group, organisation and discipline.[32] Overall, these forms of exclusion and discrimination can decrease a woman's job satisfaction and can make women feel isolated and unwelcome.[33]

As a result, many women do not stay in STEM fields,[34] and attrition is observed from high school, to the undergraduate level, into postgraduate studies and the work place.[35] This is sometimes referred to as the "leaky pipeline".[36] If women do stay in a STEM discipline, women often move away

27 Ulrike Busolt, Kordula Kugele and Iris Tinsel, "European Studies on Gender Aspects of Inventions – Statistical Survey and Analysis of Gender Impact on Inventions (ESGI)" (2008) 2; Dan L Burk, "Do Patents Have Gender?" (2011) 19 *American University Journal of Gender, Social Policy & the Law* 881, 888; and Adamowizc (n 11) 2. Cf Ceci and Williams "Sex Differences in Math-Intensive Fields" (n 10), who conclude that women are not discriminate against with respect to manuscript reviewing, grant funding and interviewing/hiring, when data on these domains are normalised against resources of the individual. However, they note that males have access to more resources than females.

28 Corinne A Moss-Racusin et al., "Science Faculty's Subtle Gender Biases Favor Male Students" (2012) 109(41) *Proceedings of the National Academy of Sciences* 16474; and Robnett (n 25) 74.

29 De Welde and Laursen (n 20) 581.

30 Robnett (n 25) 73; and Kahler (n 17) 777.

31 Naomi C Chesler and Mark A Chesler, "Gender-Informed Mentoring Strategies for Women Engineering Scholars: On Establishing a Caring Community" (2002) *Journal of Engineering Education* 49, 50; and de Welde and Laursen (n 20) 582.

32 De Welde and Laursen (n 20) 579.

33 Isis H Settles et al., "Derogation, Discrimination, and (Dis)satisfaction with Jobs in Science: A Gendered Analysis" (2013) 37 *Psychology of Women Quarterly* 179; and de Welde and Laursen (n 20) 577–83.

34 Leahey and Blume (n 3) 156; Kahler (n 17) 793; and Sue V Rosser, "The Gender Gap in Patenting: Is Technology Transfer a Feminist Issue?" (2009) 21(2) *National Women's Student Association Journal* 65, 67.

35 Helen Shen, "Mind the Gender Gap" (2013) 495 *Nature* 22, 22; Robnett (n 25); Marc J Lerchenmueller and Olav Sorenson, "The Gender Gap in Early Career Transitions in the Life Sciences" (2018) 47 *Research Policy* 1007.

36 Jacob C Blickenstaff, "Women and Science Careers: Leaky Pipeline or Gender Filter" (2005) 17(4) *Gender & Education* 369; and Lerchenmueller and Sorenson (n 35). See also Pooran Wynarczyk and Chloe Renner, "The 'Gender Gap' in the Scientific Labour Market: The Case of Science, Engineering and Technology-Based SMEs in the UK" (2006) 25(8) *Equal Opportunities International* 660. Wynarczyk and Renner conclude that career progression in science, engineering

from research roles, towards marketing and human resources, whether by choice or otherwise.[37]

As noted throughout this book, innovation is served by a diverse array of perspectives and knowledges. There is growing body of literature that evidences the correlation between females in a field and development for women in that field. Female researchers will (more so than male researchers) do research and invent specifically for females and feminine needs.[38] This is particularly true when a research team is female-led.[39] There is some evidence to suggest that this is not due to females choosing fields tending to focus on female and feminine needs, but that their different knowledge, experiences and preferences leads to them inventing for women.[40] The inventive process and what is invented is not ahistorical. It is local and socially contingent.

The confluence of gender stereotypes against women in STEM (which women internalise) and formal (legal) equality in jurisdictions such as the UK or US can lead to women believing that it is their choice not to enter or to stay in STEM.[41] When the reality is that there are social constraints and unconscious biases that affect that "choice".[42] The belief that it is a choice freely made, or that the results are fully in their individual control or a direct result of

and technology were in large part due to "non-gender-related issues", including insufficient resources for training, lack of opportunities for career advancement and lack of encouragement from management. This assessment is lacking in nuance and not backed by their data, which can only be made by a comparison of resources, opportunities and encouragement between men and women.

37 Rosser (n 34) 72; and Ethel L Mickey, "When Gendered Logics Collide: Going Public and Restructuring in a High-Tech Organization" (2019) 33(4) *Gender & Society* 509, 527.

38 See e.g. Mathias Wullum Nielsen et al., "One and a Half Million Medical Papers Reveal a Link between Author Gender and Attention to Gender and Sex Analysis" (2017) 1 *Nature Human Behaviour* 791, who showed a positive correlation between female authorship and the likelihood of a study including gender and sex analysis; and Josh Feng and Xavier Jaravel, "Innovating for People Like Me: Evidence from Female-Founded Consumer Packaged Goods Startups" (2019), https://ssrn.com/abstract=3383703 or http://dx.doi.org/10.2139/ssrn.3383703, who identified a positive link between female consumers and products from startups that were founded by female entrepreneurs, hire female inventors and/or are backed by a female venture capitalist. Feng and Jaravel also showed that, compared to a male-led startup, a female-led startup generates welfare gains for female consumers that are 27 per cent larger than for male consumers.

39 Rembrand Koning, Sampsa Samila and John-Paul Ferguson, "Inventor Gender and the Direction of Invention" (2020) 110 *AEA Papers and Proceedings* 250; Rembrand Koning, Sampsa Samila and John-Paul Ferguson, "Female Inventors and Inventions" (10 June 2019), https://ssrn.com/abstract=3401889.

40 Ibid.

41 Powell, Dainty and Bagilhole (n 11).

42 For critiques of choice feminism, see e.g. Rachel Thwaites, "Making a Choice or Taking a Stand? Choice Feminism, Political Engagement and the Contemporary Feminist Movement" (2017) 18(1) *Feminist Theory* 55; and Shelley Budgeon, "Individualized Femininity and Feminist Politics of Choice" (2015) 22(3) *European Journal of Women's Studies* 303.

their individual efforts, can lead to women internalising their failure when they do not achieve.[43]

To stay in research in STEM, women often feel the need to perform masculine traits in order to fit in (be "normal"), been seen as "legitimate" scientists and gain access to informal networks.[44] In Fox Keller's words:

> For a long time, many people expected that women would bring, with their bodies as it were, a feminine point of view, a different perspective on science, a more caring perspective, a more intuitive perspective. I don't think women bring these traits with their bodies. If they bring them, they bring them with their culture. And culture can be changed. Those women who have been drawn to science in the past and have become successful scientists have been obligated to reject any prior acculturation into a traditional feminine culture; if so enculturated, they have needed to remake themselves to better conform to traditional scientific values. So I don't expect women to change science just by their presence. The pressure on any newcomers is to conform, and that pressure can be enormous. So I doubt the arrival of more women, by itself, has changed science.[45]

That is, the context will not change, thus, women are forced to engage on masculine terms.[46] This may be through dressing a certain way (less feminine) and acting and speaking in a more masculine manner (more assertively and self-promoting).[47] This rearticulates socialised constructions of scientists and inventors as masculine (discussed below), reifies the masculine, and reinforces the binary between the masculine and feminine. Furthermore, that women are forced to morph their subjectivity to fit the existing mould homogenises possibilities;[48] "it cripples our ability to imagine and create new ways of relating to

43 See e.g. Grainne Fitzsimons, Aaron Kay and Jae Yun Kim, "'Lean In' Messages and the Illusion of Control" (30 July 2018) *Harvard Business Review*, https://hbr.org/2018/07/lean-in-messages-and-the-illusion-of-control.

44 De Welde and Laursen (n 20) 578; Mickey (n 37) 519; Susan A McDaniel, Helene Cummins and Rachelle Sender Beauchamp, "Mothers of Invention? Meshing the Roles of Inventor, Mother, and Worker" (1988) 11(1) *Women's Studies International Forum* 1, 3; and Anna Fausto-Sterling, "Women and Science" (1981) 4(1) *Women's Studies International Quarterly* 41, 46–7; Dajani (n 26) 222–3.

45 In an Interview by Dajani (n 26), 223.

46 Deborah Halbert, "Feminist Interpretations of Intellectual Property" (2006) 14(3) *American University Journal of Gender, Social Policy & the Law* 431, 436.

47 De Welde and Laursen (n 20) 578–79; Mickey (n 37) 525–26; Fausto-Sterling, "Women and Science" (n 44) 46; and Dajani (n 26) 223–4.

48 Dianna Taylor, "Toward a Feminist 'Politics of Ourselves'" in Christopher Falzon, Timothy O'Leary and Jana Sawicki (eds), *A Companion to Foucault* (Blackwell Publishing, 2013) 403, 407–8: "Asserting subjectivity is normalizing. Such an approach reinforces the prevailing view of subjectivity as both positive and given, thereby reproducing the obedience and subjugation to which it is bound, effectively masking its self-sacrificing character, and making critique appear at best unnecessary and at worst destructive. To the extent that subjectivity continues to be

ourselves, other people, and the world".[49] This homogenisation negatively affects innovation.

That it is predominantly males who hold senior positions in STEM also makes culture change difficult. As Sandra Harding has noted, "the activities of those at the top both organize and set limits on what persons who perform such activities can understand about themselves and the world around them".[50] In other words, it is men who set the scene and define what it means to be a scientist and inventor. Multiple females in senior positions are required to "erode the meaning of traditional gender labels in the very domain in which they worked, and for everyone working in that domain."[51] Yet, even then, women who make it through a masculine space into a leadership position might "assimilate" and go on to reflect gender discrimination against junior women.[52] Even if this is not the case, it is questionable if one ever feels safe enough to be herself or to push back against macro and micro aggressions, and women often feel that they need to compete with one another.[53] Furthermore, those in senior positions might not see the need for change if women are simply conforming to masculine expectations.

After all, gender is socially constructed behaviour, such that women can (and, as noted, do) perform masculine. However, most women are socialised into adulthood to be feminine. Some (possibly not all) feminine attributes form part of their identity. No one, men or women, should have to behave in a way that makes them uncomfortable or that is contrary to their identity. This is particularly true in light of the fact that women are already being forced to engage on masculine terms in masculine spaces (that is, against their socialisation) in order to patent. Another way to view is that it is one thing to know intellectually that gender is constructed, it is another thing to live contrary to one's constructed life. The perceived need to perform can result in an internal conflict in an individual's identities (or "identity interference") between the woman and the scientist.[54] That is, the identity as a woman is felt to be

considered what we are and must be, on the one hand, and as the sole mechanism for the exercise of our freedom, on the other, over time we become increasingly efficient at constituting, understanding, and relating to ourselves exclusively as subjects. We therefore find ourselves caught in a self-destructive cycle in which increasingly more effective enactment of our own subjugation is experienced as emancipatory."

49 Ibid., 411.

50 Harding (n 9) 442.

51 Fox Keller in an interview by Dajani (n 26) 223.

52 Belle Derksa, Colette Van Laarb and Naomi Ellemers, "The Queen Bee Phenomenon: Why Women Leaders Distance Themselves from Junior Women" (2016) 27 (3) *The Leadership Quarterly* 456.

53 Robin J Ely, "The Effects of Organizational Demographics and Social Identity on Relationships among Professional Women" (1994) 39(2) *Administrative Science Quarterly* 203.

54 Isis Settles et al., "Climate Perceptions and Identity Interference Among Undergraduate Women in STEM: The Protective Role of Gender Identity" (2016) 40(4) *Psychology of Women Quarterly* 488.

incompatible with the identity as a scientist. This results in poorer psychological wellbeing for the individual.[55]

Moreover, as noted above, invention and innovation do not benefit from everyone performing masculine. It benefits from diversity. But, more importantly, expecting women to act masculine in order to operate in STEM places the entire burden on women. Implicit in the expectation is that women should change themselves to conform and then, perhaps once there and promoted into senior positions, they can change the system from within. However, simply having a seat at the table is not enough. It matters how she got that seat (for example, did she have to sacrifice her psychological wellbeing?). And it is questionable why women are expected to do even more emotional work once in that seat. It should not be on women alone to survive in a hostile environment, reach a position of power and then use that power (social and political capital, time and resources) to support other women.[56] Men should equally be part of the solution of achieving egalitarian knowledge generation. After all, gender normative roles are just as binding on men as they are on women.

Overall: (1) there is not a critical mass of women to change the cultures or research direction of most STEM fields; (2) fewer women end up in senior positions – positions of power to more significantly effect change; (3) those who do end up staying and who rise to senior positions have often assimilated, so will not have a proportionate effect on changing culture or broadening the development of knowledge through diversity; and (4) there are disproportionately fewer inventions created for females to address feminine needs. Women in STEM can only gradually affect the culture by gradually changing the social perception of women and science.[57] However, this is slowed down by women performing masculine, as the women do not proportionately effect change through their presence and behaviour. This represents a further reason why the "women in STEM" discourse is a diversion.

3 Constructions of creation and creators

> scientific and technological projects are co-constituted with their social orders … That is, no sciences and technologies are or could be autonomous and value-free …[58]

As noted above, much of the research and discourse around women in STEM focuses on whether exhibited differences between how men and women

55 Ibid.

56 Sharon Mavin, "Queen Bees, Wannabees and Afraid to Bees: No More 'Best Enemies' for Women in Management?" (2008) 19(1) *British Journal of Management* S75.

57 Evelyn Fox Keller, "What Impact, if Any, Has Feminism Had on Science?" (2004) 29(1) *Journal of Biosciences* 7, 12.

58 Sandra Harding, "Postcolonial and Feminist Philosophies of Science and Technology: Convergence and Dissonances" (2009) 12(4) *Postcolonial Studies* 401, 403.

behave in STEM are biological or socialised. The debate is set up in binary, when the truth is likely that they are both. While gender and what is masculine or feminine is socially constructed, we cannot discount that sex and biology affect our physical expression and our behaviour, which in turn affects social perceptions of power and value. But this debate is a red herring, as regardless of the source of the differences, their empirical existence is used to discriminate against female inventors and their inventions. The conceptualisations of "science", the production of knowledge and the inventive process are gendered.[59] In these domains, what are considered to be "male" or "masculine" traits are viewed as the norm and given value, and "female" or "feminine" traits are viewed as inferior.[60]

3.1 "Science" and the "scientist"

> science is politics by other means...[61]

> in talking of the central modern institutions of science and technology, we are talking of moral and political order.[62]

One of the main reasons why more "women in science" is the wrong focus is that it ignores that Western science has been constructed as masculine. As noted by Fox Keller,

> If we restrict our focus to bringing more women to the table then we ignore the ways in which the prevailing framework that dominates the discussion has already been established by a long patriarchal tradition, imaged by a particularly gendered relationship.[63]

Indeed, one can expand this to say that the general international understanding of science is dominated by Western notions and is, therefore, also masculine. This is not surprising when Western science has been developed within a culture almost free of women and the women present were invisible, and the

59 See e.g. Evelyn Fox Keller, *Reflections on Gender and Science* (Yale University Press, 1985); Evelyn Fox Keller "Feminism and Science" (1982) 7(3) *Signs* 589; Mary F Fox, "Gender, Knowledge, and Scientific Styles" (1999) 869(1) *Annals of the New York Academy of Sciences* 89; Judy Wajcman, "Feminist Theories of Technology" (2010) 34 *Cambridge Journal of Economics* 143; and Judy Wajcman, "Gender and Technology" in *International Encyclopedia of the Social & Behavioral Sciences* (Pergamon, 2001, Vol. 9) 5976.

60 Yanisky-Ravid (n 3) 855; Rosser (n 34) 76; and Kara W Swanson, "Getting a Grip on the Corset: Gender, Sexuality, and Patent Law" (2011) 23(1) *Yale Journal of Law & Feminism* 57, 64–5.

61 Bruno Latour, *The Pasteurization of French Society, with Irreductions* (Harvard University Press,1987) 229.

62 Star (n 5) 31.

63 In an interview by Dajani (n 26) 223.

Western world has colonised the international domain. The masculine construction of science affects what is understood as being scientific.

Science is understood as being the rational, objective, dispassionate, systematised, and gained through reason.[64] It is what is classified, with defined nomenclature, able to be replicated and published in the correct language in the rights spaces. This is, in turn, coded masculine and Western:[65]

> subjectivity came to be associated with the making of scientific knowledge through reason and rationality following the Enlightenment … Normative constructions of scientific knowledge, as well as the subjects that produce such knowledge, have been historically associated with reason and rationality aligned with white, male norms … Western white men have thus fashioned themselves as subjects worthy of cultivating, controlling, and disseminating knowledge.[66]

It is when knowledge is created through this construct that it is deemed to result in "made" inventions, which affects what constitutes patentable subject matter (examined in Chapter 2). It is Western males who have subjectivity – they are scientists,[67] which is legitimated by the patent system.

In opposite to the masculine, the feminine and the non-Western are categorised as irrational, subjective, emotional and intuitive, "what Reason supposedly left behind"[68] – that is, not scientific.[69] Furthermore, feminine knowledge is coded as relating to the natural rather than the made.[70] This

64 Genevieve Lloyd, "Reason, Science and the Domination of Matter" in Evelyn Fox Keller and Helen E Longino (eds), *Feminism and Science* (Oxford University Press, 1996) 41, 42.

65 See e.g. Fox (n 59) 91; Genevieve Lloyd, *The Man of Reason: "Male" and "Female" in Western Philosophy* (2nd edn, Routledge, 1993); and Arun Agrawal, "Dismantling the Divide between Indigenous and Scientific Knowledge" (1995) 26 *Development and Change* 413. This continues to be the case; see e.g. Charlesworth and Banaji (n 10) 7234–6 on implicit bias.

66 Landon Schnabel and Lindsey Breitwieser, "Recent Advances in Feminist Science and Technology Studies: Reconceptualizing Subjectivity and Knowledge" (2015) 20(1) *Advances in Gender Research* 43, 47.

67 Fox Keller (n 59) 43–67 and 75–94.

68 Genevieve Lloyd, "Reason, Science and the Domination of Matter" (n 64) 42.

69 Susan T Fiske, "Stereotype Content: Warmth and Competence Endure" (2018) 27 *Current Directions in Psychological Science* 67; and Nikhil Garg et al., "Word Embeddings Quantify 100 years of Gender and Ethnic Stereotypes" (2018) 115 *Proceedings of the National Academy of Sciences* E3635. Christine Battersby, *Gender and Genius: Towards a Feminist Aesthetics* (Women's Press, 1989), has generally argued that these traits, which are considered feminine and a natural imperfection in women, become accomplished perfection when executed by a man for the purposes of creation and the "romantic author".

See also Kathy Bowrey and Jane Anderson, "The Politics of Global Information Sharing: Whose Cultural Agendas are Being Advanced?" (2009) 18(4) *Social & Legal Studies* 479, 489–90.

70 Sherry B Ortner, "Is Female to Male as Nature is to Culture?" (1972) 1(2) *Feminist Studies* 5.

means that women must engage in masculine fields on masculine terms if they are to be considered scientists and they wish to patent (as discussed in Chapter 2). Women and non-Western peoples have no subjectivity. Instead:

> women's and indigenous peoples' contributions to science have been erased, positioning them as simply consumers of refined products, as instruments/laborers that provide raw materials or "unscientific" knowledge, or as curious objects of study.[71]

Women and non-Western peoples are not constructed as scientists,[72] which the patent system confirms. They give to the public domain and then consume the products of masculine science, often created from their knowledge.

The issue runs deeper than the traits of science being constructed masculine. The traits themselves are constructs. There is arguably no such thing as "objective" science and universalistic knowledge, as all observations are interpreted through the lens of the social biases of the observer.[73] No knowledge is wholly autonomous, neutral or impartial; cast solely by cognitive values – truth, empirical robustness, explanatory power and predictive success.[74] As Catharine MacKinnon has stated, "to look at the world objectively is to objectify it".[75] Or, in Harding's words, "[i]t is a delusion – and a historically identifiable one – to think that human thought could completely erase the fingerprints that reveal its production process".[76] All knowledge is dyed by non-cognitive values – the social, cultural and political. For example, any piece of knowledge is analysed, interpreted and understood within the context of its generation, evaluated against historically contingent background assumptions. Indeed, Mary Tiles noted that the conceptualisation that science is the control and domination of nature (discussed in Chapter 2) exemplifies the fact that knowledge is not neutral, disinterested and value-free.[77]

71 Schnabel and Breitwieser (n 66) 47. See also Madhavi Sunder, "The Invention of Traditional Knowledge" (2006) 70 *Law and Contemporary Problems* 97.

72 Helen E Longino, "Subjects, Power, and Knowledge: Description and Prescription in Feminist Philosophies of Science" in Linda Alcoff and Elizabeth Potter (eds), *Feminist Epistemologies* (Taylor & Francis, 1992) 101, 104, stated: "Although the sciences have increased human power over natural processes, they have, according to this analysis, done so in a lop-sided way, systematically perpetuating women's cognitive and political dis-empowerment (as well as that of other groups marginalized in relation to the Euro-American drama)."

73 Dan L Burk, "Feminism and Dualism in Intellectual Property" (2007) 15(2) *American University Journal of Gender, Social Policy & the Law* 195, 193–94 and 201; and Burk, "Do Patents Have Gender?" (n 27) 896–903.

74 Hugh Lacey, *Is Science Value Free? Values and Scientific Understanding* (Routledge, 1999).

75 Catharine A MacKinnon, *Feminism Unmodified* (Harvard University Press, 1987) 50.

76 Harding, "Rethinking Standpoint Epistemology" (n 9) 446.

77 Mary Tiles, "A Science of Mars or of Venus" (1987) 62 *Philosophy* 293, 306.

The social, cultural and political limit of what can be known and how it is known.[78] Objects of observation are not the same as nature "out there", but

> nature-as-an-object-of knowledge. Trees, rocks, planetary orbits, and electrons always appear to natural scientists only as they are already socially constituted in some of the ways that humans and their social groups are already socially constituted for the social scientist. Such objects are already effectively "removed from pure nature" into social life – they are social objects – by, first of all, the contemporary general cultural meanings that these objects have for everyone, including the entire scientific community. They also become socially constituted objects of know ledge through the shapes and meanings they gain for scientists because of earlier generations of scientific discussion about them. Scientists never observe nature apart from such traditions; even when they criticize some aspects of them they must assume others in order to carry on the criticism. They could not do science if they did not both borrow from and also criticize these traditions. Their assumptions about what they see are always shaped by "conversations" they carry on with scientists of the past. Finally, their own interactions with such objects also culturally constitute them: to treat a piece of nature with respect, violence, degradation, curiosity, or indifference is to participate in culturally constituting such an object of knowledge.[79]

In other words, the social, cultural and political that define a subject of knowledge are also used by that subject to define the objects they observe.[80]

Jane Flax has noted that claims to objective and universalistic knowledge "reflect and reify the experience of a few persons – mostly white, Western males."[81] Thus, the production of knowledge is not devoid of the social, cultural and political, but is "territorialized, and entrance is based upon gender".[82] Moreover, the patent system is a "political construct that privileges one way of thinking and doing over another".[83] This is problematic as, regardless of whether different ways of thinking and doing are attributable to biology or socialisation, differential treatment should not be discriminatory based on gender or race/ethnicity, for example. Such treatment reflects power and domination.[84]

78 Ibid., 299.
79 Harding, "Rethinking Standpoint Epistemology" (n 9) 453.
80 See also Michel Foucault, *Discipline and Punish: 1970–1975* (2nd edn, Vintage Books, 1995) 27; Michel Foucault, *The History of Sexuality* (Pantheon Books, 1978, vol. I) 93–5. For a commentary on power/knowledge, see Joseph Rouse, "Power/ Knowledge" in Gary Gutting (ed), *The Cambridge Companion to Foucault* (2nd edn, Cambridge University Press, 2005) 95.
81 Jane Flax, "Postmodernism and Gender Relations in Feminist Theory" (1987) 12(4) *Signs: Journal of Women in Culture and Society* 621, 626.
82 Halbert (n 46) 436.
83 Ibid 440.
84 Ibid.

3.2 The "inventor"

The social construction of the "invention" and the reflection thereof in patent law is explored in depth in Chapter 2. Here we look at the related construction of the inventor and its consequences.

The archetype of the "inventor" of patentable inventions is a man.[85] It is men who can create culture. This intellectual "creative genius" was developed in the Age of Enlightenment, which constructed the act of discovery (of adventure), pursuit and creativity as masculine.[86] This construct is decidedly European and not only casts women as tied to nature, but also non-Western peoples. In the words of Kathy Bowrey and Jane Anderson:

> The modern notion of invention leaves Indigenous people as unindividuated subjects within Nature. Like the plants, animals and minerals of the Natural world, they too can become objects of discovery through specific fact-finding endeavours – through the gaze of specifically targeted disciplines on the "study of man" and specifically targeted fact-finding missions … But Indigenous peoples are not credited with agency in relation to either discovery or invention. The construction of the "indigenous" is antithetical to the subject position of science and applied knowledge.[87]

Furthermore, the Enlightenment framed the individual as the subject of genius.[88] Patent law idealises the constructed lone genius inventor.[89] In order to get a patent, each person who contributed to the conception of an invention must be named as an inventor. It is not possible to grant a patent to a community of unlisted individuals. This is despite the fact that invention is communal and cumulative (building on the work that came before), as explored in Chapter 5.[90] In addition, there is an explicit and implicit stereotype that women work communally and are group-serving.[91] Knowledge created in a communal environment is often inseparable from what has come before and from its knowers. This

85 Battersby (n 69); Kara W Swanson, "Intellectual Property and Gender: Reflections on Accomplishments and Methodology" (2015) 24(1) *American University Journal of Gender, Social Policy & the Law* 175, 185; and Gearhart-Serna (n 2) 377.

This is similarly true for the "author" in copyright law; see Carys J Craig, "Reconstructing the Author-Self: Some Feminist Lessons for Copyright Law" (2007) 15(2) *American University Journal of Gender, Social Policy & the Law* 207; Carys J Craig, "Feminist Aesthetics and Copyright Law: Genius, Value, and Gendered Visions of the Creative Self" (2014) 10(1) *Osgoode Legal Studies Research Paper* No. 42, 8–15; and Halbert (n 46) 447–59.

86 Yanisky-Ravid (n 3) 856; and Charlesworth and Banaji (n 10) 7234.

87 Bowrey and Anderson (n 69) 490.

88 Craig "Feminist Aesthetics and Copyright Law" (n 85) 9–10.

89 Fausto-Sterling, "Women and Science" (n 44) 45–6.

90 Burk, "Do Patents Have Gender?" (n 27) 909–12. Burk suggests that acknowledging that invention is communal and cumulative might results in a broadening of patentable subject matter.

91 Charlesworth and Banaji (n 10) 7234.

ostensibly does not sit well with modern patent law requiring that all inventors can be named.[92] Of course, many patented inventions are created within research entities, which are also collectives of individuals. This led Graham Dutfield to note that it is not communal production that results in non-patentability, but rather politics and power that allow for the patentability of "collective corporate discoveries".[93] In other words, masculine communities are accepted as capable of owning patents, but not feminine communities.

In light of the masculine construction of the inventor, women have historically been portrayed as incapable of invention. Their inventions were habitually attributed to males (often their husbands),[94] and they were not taken seriously as inventors, often even receiving derision for their inventions.[95] For example, in interviews with Canadian women inventors in the mid-1980s, Susan McDaniel, Helene Cummins and Rachelle Sender Beauchamp reported that they were often made to feel "silly", like they were wasting time on "nonsense" and that their husbands were perhaps worried that their neighbours would think they were "strange".[96] Annette Kahler stated:

> Unflattering stereotypes of women inventors were pervasive, and prevailing cultural norms reinforced them. Inventing and patenting were simply not considered appropriate activities for women, and women were not encouraged to explore opportunities in science and technology. The fear of ridicule and of becoming a social outcast prevented some women from pursuing patents for their inventions. Society strongly reinforced the concept that women belonged at home taking care of household duties, and inventions for household and personal use were commonly trivialized.[97]

It should, thus, come as no surprise that male inventors might prefer to work with other male inventors. A study of US granted patents from 1976–2018 confirms this to be the case, with the vast majority of collaborations being male-male.[98] This is problematic when the majority of actors in STEM are male and is

92 Malla Pollack, "Towards a Feminist Theory of the Public Domain, or Rejecting the Gendered Scope of United States Copyrightable and Patentable Subject Matter" (2006) 12 *William & Mary Journal of Women and the Law* 603, 615–6.

93 Graham Dutfield, "The Public and Private Domains" (2000) 21(3) *Science Communication* 274, 282.

94 Margaret W Rossiter, "The ~~Matthew~~ Matilda Effect in Science" (1993) 23 *Social Studies of Science* 325.

95 Merritt (n 21) 295–98.

96 McDaniel, Cummins and Sender Beauchamp (n 44) 8.

97 Kahler (n 17) 780. See also McDaniel, Cummins and Sender Beauchamp (n 44) 9–10, who discuss how female inventors often hid that they invented, often even denying that they were inventors, reflecting internalised understandings of the "inventor" as male, working outside the home on the technical.

98 Yukai Wang et al., "Gender Bias in Patenting Process" (2019) 14 *Journal of Infometrics* 101046

exacerbated by senior positions being male dominated. It perpetuates the notion the women are not inventors and inhibits their ability to achieve seniority.

In addition, patent examiners historically showed prejudice against female inventors.[99] Undertaking an analysis of nineteenth-century patent application decisions in the US, Deborah Merritt uncovered biases in the way the Commissioner of patents and patent examiners treated inventions by women for women compared to similar inventions for men.[100] For example, a women's safety belt designed to hold sanitary napkins was pronounced to be "necessarily somewhat trifling", while a minor improvement for a men's undergarment was enthusiastically described as "graceful", "making not only a genteel, but comfortable fitting garment" and "a very great improvement".[101] The Commissioner of patents and patent examiners furthermore prejudiced inventions related to feminine hygiene, childrearing and housekeeping, which were predominantly invented by women.[102]

Indeed, it appears to still be the case that patent offices discriminate against women, with Kyle Jensen, Balázs Kovács and Olav Sorenson finding that, between 2001 and 2014 in the US, female patent applicants were more likely to be rejected than male applicants.[103] Those applicants who were granted patents had fewer of their claims allowed and had more words added to reduce the scope of patented subject matter.[104] Similarly, Jessica Milli et al. analysed US data from 2000–2016 to show that 67.2 per cent of patent applications from females were accepted in contrast to 70 per cent of applications from males.[105]

Milli et al. postulated that women's poorer ability to sell their inventions and negotiate with patent examiners might contribute to the lower acceptance rates of patent applications from females than males.[106] This is exemplified in the patent battle that arose around CRISPR/Cas9, a protein and ribonucleic acid (RNA) found naturally in bacteria (prokaryotes), but not plants or animals (eukaryotes). It is a revolutionary gene-editing technology, identified by Jennifer Doudna and Emmanuelle Charpentier.[107] Doudna and Charpentier applied for patents for their invention. The patent battle pertained to Feng Zhang and his later patent

99 Merritt (n 21) 289–90 and 300–305; Kara W Swanson, "Rubbing Elbows and Blowing Smoke: Gender, Class, and Science in the Nineteenth Century Patent Office" (2017) 108(1) *ISIS* 40; Kahler (n 17) 782; and Foster, "Situating Feminism, Patent Law, and the Public Domain" (n 2) 316.

100 Merritt (n 21) 300–301.

101 Ibid., 301.

102 Ibid.

103 Kyle Jensen, Balázs Kovács and Olav Sorenson. "Gender Difference in Obtaining and Maintaining Patent Rights" (2018) 36(4) *Nature Biotechnology* 307.

104 Ibid.

105 Jessica Milli et al., "Equity in Innovation: Women Inventors and Patents" (2016) *Institute for Women's Policy Research*, 12.

106 Ibid.

107 Martin Jinek et al., "A Programmable Dual-RNA–Guided DNA Endonuclease in Adaptive Bacterial Immunity" (2012) 337 *Science* 816; Jennifer Doudna and Emmanuelle Charpentier "The New Frontier of Genome Engineering with CRISPR-Cas9" (2014) 346(6213) *Science* 1258096

applications for CRISPR/Cas9 for editing eukaryotic cells. In the United States, the dispute centred on whether Zhang's inventions embodied an inventive step over and above Doudna and Charpentier's invention. In 2017, the US Patent Trial and Appeal Board found for Zhang, holding that his invention was non-obvious, as researchers skilled in the art would not have had a "reasonable expectation of success" that CRISPR/Cas9 would work in eukaryote cells. This decision, in part, turned on statements from Doudna that "she had experienced 'many frustrations' getting CRISPR to work in human cells and that she knew that if she succeeded, CRISPR would be 'a profound discovery'".[108] The Court took this as indicating "an eagerness to learn the results of experiments in eukaryotic cells and the importance of such results", but not an expression of an "expectation that such results would be successful".[109] In other words, had Doudna and Charpentier been more confident about their invention and its potential, Zhang's development would have been obvious, as he would have had a "reasonable expectation of success".[110] At least, this is what can be inferred from the Court's decision. Gender role incongruity theory (examined in Chapter 4) tells us that, in fact, had Doudna and Charpentier been more confident about their invention and its potential, they may have been punished for this display because it would have been incongruent with their gender normative roles.

Gendered differences in the way patent offices treat applications are likely also partially attributable to the fact that, even in the twenty-first century, most patent examiners and patent attorneys are male.[111] This is unsurprising, as having a STEM background is often a prerequisite to become a patent attorney or examiner, and fewer females than males are educated in

108 *The Broad Institute, MIT and President and Fellows of Harvard College v The Regents of the University of California, University of Vienna and Emmanuelle Charpentier* (15 February 2017) 37 CFR § 41.125(a), 15. Thank you to Rochelle Dreyfuss for pointing this example out to me. See also Jacob S Sherkow "Inventive Steps: The CRISPR Patent Dispute and Scientific Progress" (2017) 18(7) *EMBO Reports* 1047, 1049.

109 *The Broad Institute, MIT and President and Fellows of Harvard College v The Regents of the University of California, University of Vienna and Emmanuelle Charpentier* (n 108) 17.

110 That being said, to be seen as confident, women must show competence and warmth, whereas men must only exhibit competence; Margarita Mayo, "To Seem Confident, Women Have to Be Seen as Warm" (8 July 2016) *Harvard Business Review*, https://hbr.org/2016/07/to-seem-confident-women-have-to-be-seen-as-warm.

111 This is true in the US, Kahler (n 17) 773 and Elaine Spector, "Ensuring Women and Diverse Candidates in the Patent Bar: We Must Address the Root of the Problem" (15 March 2021) *IP Watchdog*, www.ipwatchdog.com/2021/03/15/ensuring-women-diverse-candidates-patent-bar-must-address-root-problem/id=130896; UK, Hayleigh Bosher, "Females and Felines in Intellectual Property Law" (3 December 2017) *IP Kat*, http://ipkitten.blogspot.com/2017/12/females-and-felines-in-intellectual.html; and Australia and New Zealand, see Mark Summerfield, "A Profile of Australian and New Zealand Patent Attorneys" (7 January 2018) *Patentology*, https://blog.patentology.com.au/2018/01/a-profile-of-australian-and-new-zealand.html.

STEM.[112] Just as patent examiners are not neutral administrators, patent attorneys are not mere vessels who only translate their clients' inventions into "patentese" (patent language) and apply their legal skills in the patenting process. As Jessica Silbey has highlighted, patent attorneys "harvest" intellectual property, advising their clients at what point there is a patentable invention and when to pursue a patent.[113] They likely do so with their socialised gendered understandings of science, invention and the inventor. The institutions around patenting, thus, remain masculine and likely reflect related biases.[114]

Even if there were gender parity in patent-related professions – including researchers in STEM, patent attorneys and patent examiners – this would not fully or even proportionately reduce the gender patenting gap. This is because patent law itself is gendered, as shown in Chapter 2.

4 Constructions of the "entrepreneur" and collaboration partner

As elaborated upon in Chapter 4, that females have fewer patents than males impacts who commercialises in favour of males. More males will be able to raise finance to commercialise their inventions,[115] and use patents to signal both

112 J Shontavia Johnson et al., "Diversifying Intellectual Property Law: Why Women of Color Remain 'Invisible' and How to Provide More Seats at the Table" (2018) 10(4) *Landslide*, www.americanbar.org/groups/intellectual_property_law/publications/landslide/2017-18/march-april.

113 Jessica Silbey, *The Eureka Myth* (Stanford University Press, 2015), ch 5. On the importance of contextualising inventors, law, lawyers and the legal system, see also Kara W Swanson, "'Great Men,' Law, and the Social Construction of Technology" (2018) 43(3) *Law & Social Inquiry* 1093.

114 It is worth noting that until relatively recently, females could not own property, such that they could not own patents. See B Zorina Khan, "Married Women's Property Laws and Female Commercial Activity: Evidence from US Patent Records, 1790–1895" (1996) 56 *Journal Economic History* 356; and Merritt (n 21) 290, who additionally notes that historically in the US women could not enter into contracts, so could not license out their patents (if they could obtain them). Because their husbands controlled all real property, women could not get mortgages to finance commercialisations.

115 F Scott Kieff, "Property Rights and Property Rules for Commercializing Inventions" (2001) 85 *Minnesota Law Review* 697, 747–8; Peter S Menell, "Intellectual Property: General Theories" in B Boudewijn Bouckaert and Gerrit de Geest (eds), *Encyclopedia of Law and Economics, Volume I. The History and Methodology of Law and Economics* (Edward Elgar, 2000) 129, 146–7; Jessica Silbey, "Patent Variation: Discerning Diversity Among Patent Functions" (2013) 45 *Loyola University Chicago Law Journal* 441, 475; Report of the President's Commission on the Patent System, "To Promote the Progress of…Useful Arts: In an Age of Exploding Technology" (1966) 2; and Dietmar Harhoff, "The Role of Patents and Licenses in Securing External Finance for Innovation" (2009) 14(2) EIB Papers, 74–95. On small inventors, see James Bessen and Michael J Meurer, *Patent Failure: How Judges, Bureaucrats, and Lawyers Put Innovators at Risk* (Princeton University Press, 2008) 177–9.

the presence of their invention and their competence.[116] Furthermore, more males will be able to use patents to legally transact around their inventions and facilitate coordination and technology transfer.[117] More still, that what is patentable is principally masculine results in the masculine being commercialised more than the feminine.

Even if women patented as much as men, they would not commercialise their inventions as successfully as men do, as the commercialisation process has been constructed as masculine.[118] The archetype of the entrepreneur, the start-up genius or the market-savvy scientist, is a man.[119] This person has agentic characteristics, such as being assertive or aggressive, confident, dominant, controlling, self-confident and leading. In contrast, women are constructed as communal, kind, helpful, giving, nurturing and gentle.[120]

Lisa Marovich has noted that the masculine construction of the entrepreneur, historically, led to women inventors performing in unusual ways in trying to commercialise their inventions:

> Many of the most notable women inventors were flamboyant, socially deviant, idiosyncratic, or just plain "crazy" by contemporary standards. They typically masked their economic ambitions and profit motives by claiming that their inventive activities were the products of good will, divine intervention, or fervent patriotism. Since women inventors were less likely to realise substantial returns on their inventive activities as compared to their male counterparts, they had to be exceptionally protective of their ideas and even more strategic in their plans for patent commercialization.

116 Harhoff (n 115) 80–2; Bronwyn H Hall and Dietmar Harhoff, "Recent Research on the Economics of Patents" (2012) 4 *Annual Review of Economics* 541, 542; and Silbey (n 115) 454–6.

117 Bessen and Meurer (n 115) 31, 35–6; Edmund W Kitch, "Elementary and Persistent Errors in the Economic Analysis of Intellectual Property" (2000) 53 *Vanderbilt Law Review* 1727, 1740; Edmund W Kitch, "The Nature and Function of the Patent System" (1977) 20(2) *Journal of Law and Economics* 265. Cf. Robert P Merges and Richard R Nelson, "On the Complex Economics of Patent Scope" (1990) 90 *Columbia Law Review* 839; Donald G McFetridge and Douglas A Smith, "Patents, Prospects, and Economic Surplus" (1980) 23 *Journal of Law and Economics* 197; and John F Duffy, "Rethinking the Prospect Theory of Patents" (2004) 71 *U Chi L Rev* 439; Kieff (n 115) 732–6; Richard A Posner, "Intellectual Property: The Law and Economics Approach" (2005) 19(2) *Journal of Economic Perspectives* 57, 68; and Christine Godt, *Eigentum an Information* (Mohr Siebeck, 2007) 262, 402–5 and 449.

118 Francisco J Santos, Muhammad Azam Roomi and Francisco Liñán, "About Gender Differences and the Social Environment in the Development of Entrepreneurial Intentions" (2016) 54(1) *Small Business Management* 49; and Rosser (n 34) 76.

119 Malin Malmström, Jeaneth Johansson and Joakim Wincent, "Gender Stereotypes and Venture Support Decisions: How Governmental Venture Capitalists Socially Construct Entrepreneurs' Potential" (2017) 41(5) *Entrepreneurship Theory and Practice* 833.

120 Alice H Eagly, *Sex Differences in Social Behavior: A Social-Role Interpretation* (Erlbaum, 1987).

> Moreover, those women inventors who crossed traditional gender boundaries or defied pervasive cultural expectations were easier to label as social deviants.[121]

Implicit in this is that the masculine construction of the innovator can have negative implications for whether women are supported to commercialise their inventions.[122] After all, most individual inventors cannot bring a product or service to market alone. Commercialisation requires multiple resources, from manufacturing and distribution capability to human capital, all of which requires financial capital. Those who hold the purse strings are gatekeepers. Most gatekeepers (for example, venture capitalists)[123] are male and this affects whether women can raise capital and support to commercialise their inventions.

Homophily bias is implicated. This bias explains the tendency for people to associate with those with similar backgrounds or experiences because communication is more effective – the receiver understands the source.[124] A successful homophilous communication leads to further interaction.[125] Put another way, male gatekeepers are used to dealing with male inventors, associate market-worthy inventions with male inventors, so will continue to interact with male inventors.[126] Along these lines, venture capitalists will be unfamiliar with feminine products/services, making it difficult for them to judge their market value.[127] There is indeed evidence that male venture capitalists do not know how to evaluate female-led start-ups.[128] As a result, female entrepreneurs have

121 Lisa A Marovich, "'Let Her Have Brains Too': Commercial Networks, Public Relations, and the Business of Invention" (1998) 27(1) *Business & Economic History* 140, 144.

122 See e.g. Christina Constantinidis, Annie Cornet and Simona Asandei, "Financing of Women-Owned Ventures: The Impact of Gender and Other Owner- and Firm-Related Variables" (2006) 8(2) *Venture Capital* 133.

123 Paula E Stephan and Asmaa El-Ganainy, "The Entrepreneurial Puzzle: Explaining the Gender Gap" (2007) 32 *Journal of Technology Transfer* 475, 484. For a summary of research on raising venture capital, see Will Drover et al., "A Review and Road Map of Entrepreneurial Equity Financing Research: Venture Capital, Corporate Venture Capital, Angel Investment, Crowdfunding, and Accelerators" (2017) 43(6) *Journal of Management* 1820.

124 Everett M Rogers and Dilip K Bhowmik, "Homophily-Heterophily: Relational Concepts for Communication Research" (1970) 34(4) *The Public Opinion Quarterly* 523; Candida Brush et al., "The Gender Gap in Venture Capital – Progress, Problems, and Perspectives" (2018) 20(2) *Venture Capital* 115, 131; Everett M Rogers and Dilip K Bhowmik, "Homophily-Heterophily: Relational Concepts for Communication Research" (1970) 34(4) *The Public Opinion Quarterly* 523.

125 Rogers and Bhowmik (n 124) 529.

126 Rosser (n 34) 79.

127 Gry Agnete Alsos and Elsbet Ljunggren, "The Role of Gender in Entrepreneur-Investor Relationships: A Signaling Theory Approach" (2016) 41(4) *Enterpreneurship Theory and Practice* 567, 584.

128 Sahil Raina, "VCs, Founders, and the Performance Gender Gap" (10 December 2019), https://dx.doi.org/10.2139/ssrn.2846047.

to more strongly communicate their legitimacy and the legitimacy of their venture.[129]

Negative gender stereotypes against women also play a role in promoting male entrepreneurs.[130] For example, one study showed that bias affects the questions that investors ask female entrepreneurs.[131] Males were asked promotion-focused questions (i.e. how would they succeed), whereas females were asked prevention-focused questions (i.e. how would they prevent failure). This affected what the entrepreneurs said and negatively affected female entrepreneurs obtaining investment.

Furthermore, gender discounting (where, all else being equal, the accomplishments of women are viewed differently from men)[132] likely results in women not being asked to participate in commercialisation,[133] not being funded or receiving less funding under less favourable conditions.[134] Monica Biernal and Diane Kobrynowicz showed that women have more "hoops" to jump through than men to evidence ability, but even so they are judged on a different spectrum, e.g. "good" for a woman is different from "good for a man".[135] As a further illustration, in a study on registered start-ups in California and Massachusetts from 1995–2011, Jorge Guzman and Aleksandra Kacperczyk found that female-led ventures are 63 per cent less likely to get venture capital funding than male-led ventures.[136] The authors attributed 65 per cent of this to the growth orientation of the venture – the greater the growth potential, the more likely to get venture capital, and more males than females had ventures with high growth potential.[137] Guzman and Kacperczyk also found that, where the growth orientation was the same, less sophisticated venture capitalists were less likely to invest in female-led ventures, due to a reliance on gender

129 Alsos and Lljunggren (n 127) 585.

130 Malin Malmström et al., "When Stereotypical Gender Notions See the Light of Day, Will They Burst? Venture Capitalists' Gender Constructions versus Venturing Performing Facts" (2018) 9 *Journal of Business Venturing Insights* 32.

131 Dana Kanze et al., "We Ask Men to Win and Women Not to Lose: Closing the Gender Gap in Startup Funding" (2018) 61(2) *Academy of Management Journal* 586.

132 Madeline E Heilman, "Description and Prescription: How Gender Stereotypes Prevent Women's Ascent Up the Organizational Ladder" (2001) 57(4) *Journal of Social Issues* 657, 662.

133 Stephan and El-Ganainy (n 123) 482; and Rosser (n 34) 79.

134 Zhenyu Wu and Jess H Chua, "Second-order Gender Effects: The Case of US Small Business Borrowing Cost" (2012) 36 *Entrepreneurship Theory and Practice* 443, showed that women had to pay higher interest rates for loans.

135 Monica Biernal and Diane Kobrynowicz, "Gender- and Race-Based Standards of Competence: Lower Minimum Standards but Higher Ability Standard for Devalued Groups" (1997) 72(3) *Journal of Personality and Social Psychology* 544.

136 Jorge Guzman and Aleksandra Kacperczyk, "Gender Gap in Entrepreneurship" (2019) 48 *Research Policy* 1666, 1672–1673.

137 The authors (at 1677) note that women are less likely to found and run start-ups with "appropriable and differentiated technology (as evidenced by patents), in biotechnology, IT or semiconductors. They are more likely to start ventures for local business activity".

stereotypes to evaluate the potential of a venture.[138] That is, unless there was strong growth orientation, less sophisticated venture capitalists were less likely to invest in female-led ventures, due to bias against female entrepreneurs.

Fiona Murray and Leigh Graham's interviews with faculty in the life sciences in the US showed that women also face these biases in academia.[139] They identified a "dominant narrative" that women felt explicitly excluded from commercialisation and ignored by industry because of their gender. One academic stated "what I say doesn't count … if [a male colleague] got up and said it, it might count".[140] Women did not feel that they were taken seriously. Indeed, they felt that their male colleagues were approached more than they were, even if those colleagues did not specialise in the topic at issue and they did. Furthermore, senior female academics "noted that 'below the surface' there exists a different 'comfort level' where men interact".[141]

The inventing, patenting and commercialisation stages of innovation are not in exclusive silos. This means that the construction of the entrepreneur as male can correspondingly affect whether women patent, because being viewed as a commercialisation partner, or innovator to invest in, can lead to collaboration and subsequently patents. In other words, that the stereotypical entrepreneur is a man results in women being disproportionately left out of the commercial space and, thus, negatively affects their patenting rates as well as their ability to bring products or services to market. Participation in the inventive process and market access are, thus, socially determined.[142] To illustrate this, Albert N Link and Martijn van Hasselt showed that, in the US, women-owned small entrepreneurial firms were less likely to patent compared to similarly sized and funded male-owned firms.[143]

In a similar vein, females may not have the necessary social, political or commercial (legal, business and financial) networks to patent and market their inventions.[144] This is often due to females generally not having the same networking opportunities provided to them in college or university and the workplace.[145] "The male dominated social locations in which networking takes place are difficult for women to access."[146] This is partly attributable to the

138 Guzman and Kacperczyk (n 136) 1674.
139 Fiona Murray and Leigh Graham, "Buying Science and Selling Science: Gender Differences in the Market for Commercial Science" (2007) 16(4) *Industrial and Corporate Change* 657, 672–4.
140 Ibid, 674.
141 Ibid.
142 Barwa and Rai (n 3) 106.
143 Albert N Link and Martijn van Hasselt, "Exploring the Impact of R&D on Patenting Activity in Small Women-Owned and Minority-Owned Entrepreneurial Firms" (2020) 54 *Small Business Economics* 1061.
144 See e.g. Marovich (n 121).
145 Clare O'Hagan et al., "Perpetuating Academic Capitalism and Maintaining Gender Orders Through Career Practices in STEM in Universities" (2019) 60(2) *Critical Studies in Education* 205, 211–212.
146 Ibid., 212.

exclusion of women from the "Old Boys' Club", an informal cultural mechanism that serves to keep women as outsiders.[147] This not only denies networking opportunities, but also access to useful information and guidance,[148] such as funding sources and the best way to seek out funding, or reputable legal advice.[149]

If at a university, female academics typically have smaller networks for collaboration and commercialisation because they have fewer graduate and post-doctoral students, receive fewer opportunities to consult with industry or government, serve less frequently on science advisory boards, and interact less with industry.[150] Women are not as exposed to knowledge about the commercialisation process and lack the institutional support for patenting.[151] The result is that females are not socialised to patent or commercialise their inventions.

Related to this, Kjersten Bunker Whittington and Laurel Smith-Doerr discussed the fact that the patent gap in the life sciences in the US is larger in universities compared to industry. Among other things, they suggested that the lower female patenting rates at universities are due to: academics having more freedom to choose their research subject matter at universities and females focusing on subject matter that does not lend itself to commercial application; and fewer females being interested in commercialisation.[152] That is, they postulated that, even if working in a STEM field, females are not driven by the idea of commercialisation. As the foregoing illustrates and as discussed further below, it is incorrect to say that females innately do not research subject matter that has no commercial application or do not wish to enter the commercialisation space.[153] What is considered to be industrial and patentable has been drawn from the masculine. Moreover, there are biases stacked against women to patent and commercialise their inventions, ranging from being socially constructed as givers (see Chapter 2) and not as entrepreneurs, to being made to feel "other" and discriminated against when they engage in masculine fields on masculine terms.

147 De Welde and Laursen (n 20) 577–80.

148 Ibid 578.

149 Merritt (n 21) 299.

150 Rosser (n 34) 78; Waverly L Ding, Fiona Murray and Toby E Stuart, "Gender Differences in Patenting in the Academic Life Sciences" (2006) 313 *Science* 665, 666; Waverly W Ding, Fiona Murray and Toby E Stuart, "From Bench to Board: Gender Differences in University Scientists' Participation in Corporate Scientific Advisory Boards" (2013) 56(5) *Academy of Management Journal* 1443; and Kahler (n 17) 781.

151 Kjersten Bunker Whittington and Laurel Smith-Doerr, "Gender and Commercial Science: Women's Patenting in the Life Sciences" (2005) 30 *Journal of Technology Transfer* 366. See also Rosser (n 34) 78.

152 Ibid.

153 Khan has quantitatively shown a positive correlation between laws granting women property rights separate from their husbands, and rights to contract and enforce these, on female patents. Khan concluded that women were generally incentivised in the same way as men; namely, to benefit economically from their inventions, by selling or commercialising them, and responding to market demand in fields where they had comparative advantage (such as household appliances). Khan (n 114) 371.

5 A focus on academia

This chapter has picked up on numerous institutional, structural or organisational biases against females in the processes of inventing, patenting and commercialising. Given all of these biases against women in science, Anne Fausto-Sterling stated that the question is not why there are not more women scientists, "but rather 'why, given the strictures, were there any at all?'"[154] This section focuses on ingrained biases in academia, in part because much of the literature on women's experiences in STEM is based on academic environments. In addition, certain issues are particularly pertinent to academia because of an academic's multiple concurrent roles as lecturer, administrator, service-provider, mentor, supervisor, researcher and author. It is only the latter three of these that directly contribute to invention and innovation.

Women who work in universities tend to not be at research universities, have teaching-intensive positions and/or hold temporary, part-time or adjunct positions. For example, in the UK in the academic year 2016/2017, only 59.7 per cent of female academic staff were full-time, in comparison to 73.0 per cent of male academic staff.[155] Similarly, while 68.2 per cent of male academic staff had permanent contracts, this was only 63.9 per cent for female academic staff.[156] In the UK, 31.1 per cent of female academics had teaching only positions, whereas only 23.8 per cent of their male counterparts had such positions.[157]

Furthermore, constructed as nurturing and giving, women are often disproportionately burdened with service or administration tasks and advising or counselling students.[158] These factors reduce women's access to resources and their productivity and, thereby, also negatively affect women's application and success rates for journal article publications, research funding applications[159] and ultimately women's ability to advance in their careers. Notably, the move towards the neo-liberal university favours men, as research is valued more greatly than teaching and service.[160]

154 Fausto-Sterling, "Women and Science" (n 44) 42.

155 Equality Challenge Unit, "Equality in Higher Education: Statistical Report 2018" (6 September 2018) 204. See also Miriam E David, "Women and Gender Equality in Higher Education?" (2015) 15(1) *Education Sciences* 10; Women and Work Commission, "A Fair Deal for Women in the Workplace: An Interim Statement" (March 2005); and Maria Smith, "Gender, Pay and Work Satisfaction at a UK University" (2009) 16(5) *Gender, Work and Organization* 621, 625.

156 Equality Challenge Unit (n 155) 205.

157 Ibid., 216.

158 Leahey and Blume (n 3) 155; Ding, Murray and Stuart, "Gender Differences in Patenting in the Academic Life Sciences" (n 150) 666–7; Stephan and El-Ganainy (n 123) 477–8; and Rosser (n 34) 77.

159 Ceci and Williams, "Sex Differences in Math-Intensive Fields" (n 10); and Lerchenmueller and Sorenson (n 35) 1010–11.

160 O' Hagan et al. (n 145).

Empirical studies show that women have generally received less government funding than men.[161] Statistics from private funding organisations would probably reflect an even larger gender gap. The gender gap in funding is likely in part due to most gatekeepers to such funding being middle-aged males, including "members of national science and technology councils, funding organisation directors and managers, funding organisation board members, research council and sub-council members, staff members of funding organisations, individuals involved in evaluation committees and panels, and reviewers."[162]

Having more female gatekeepers might not proportionately increase the number of successful funding applications from women. However, there are indirect benefits of having more female gatekeepers. Namely, it normalises the presence of women in STEM, which could potentially change the social constructions of the "scientist" and "inventor". It could also have a "seed effect", whereby it allows for the growth of more women into such roles. In addition, having women in gatekeeping roles gives women inside knowledge on the funding application process and gives them access to networks of senior researchers and potentially also industry.[163] This would have a positive effect on women's ability to collaborate and to innovate. Furthermore, it can result in a "signal shock", where a woman who is appointed to high profile administrative position subsequently experiences a rapid increase in invitations to collaborate in a commercial space.[164]

One of the reasons why there are few female gatekeepers is that women generally tend not to hold senior positions, particularly in STEM.[165] This is true in industry as well as the academic realm. The latter might have more significance as academics need to actively seek out commercialisation opportunities, more so than those working in industry. In comparison to male academics, female academics lack the requisite "title" to woo industry partners and venture capitalists, and therefore find it more difficult to commercialise their inventions.[166]

161 See e.g. European Commission, *The Gender Challenge in Research Funding – Assessing the European National Scenes* (European Commission, 2009); Susan D Hosek et al., *Gender Differences in Major Federal External Grant Programs* (RAND, 2005); and Shen (n 35) 24. This appears to be changing in the US in certain fields, though disparities remain, see Charlesworth and Banaji (n 10) 7232–3.

162 Liisa Husu and Suzanne de Cheveigné, "Gender and Gatekeeping of Excellence in Research Funding: European Perspectives" in Birgit Riegraf (ed), *Gender Change in Academia: Re-Mapping the Fields of Work, Knowledge, and Politics from a Gender Perspective* (VS Verlag, 2010) 43, 49.

163 Ibid 50.

164 Murray and Graham (n 139) 681. On collaboration, gender and seniority, see Monica Gaughan and Barry Bozeman, "Using the Prisms of Gender and Rank to Interpret Research Collaboration Power Dynamics" (2016) 46(4) *Social Studies of Science* 536.

165 See e.g. Equality Challenge Unit (155) 226 and 242.

166 Rosser (n 34) 78; and Gaughan and Bozeman (n 164).

A further consequence of there being fewer females in senior positions is that there are insufficient numbers of women available to undertake mentoring responsibilities.[167] There is some evidence that cultural homogeneity in the mentor-mentee relationship is beneficial for career progression in the long run.[168] This is in part due to homophily bias, which results in greater interpersonal attraction and liking of people who are demographically similar.[169] The similarity is theorised to allow individuals to interact more easily, because they have shared experiences and values.

Furthermore, junior researchers require formal and informal mentoring to fulfil their technical and psychosocial needs. Technical guidance might be on research, funding applications, research proposals and unwritten rules of the industry and organisation. In contrast, psychosocial mentoring includes how to deal with interpersonal relationships, work and life/family balance, and discrimination. Naomi Chesler and Mark Chesler have outlined a multitude of related reasons why it is important that women have women as mentors.[170] This includes that women are socialised to value interpersonal satisfaction and integration, group affiliation, egalitarianism, community, collaboration and diversity, which they are more likely to get from, and find in, a female mentor, who is similarly so socialised. In contrast, men are socialised to mentor on the technical and often have a "boot camp" style, testing the steel of individuals, rather than fostering integration and collaboration. In addition, mentees need mentors who have gone through similar experiences, difficulties and challenges, which they are most likely to find in someone of the same gender. The lack of female mentorship can result in women in STEM feeling isolated and abnormal. Finally, the dearth of multiple female role models means that female mentees are not shown the various ways that women can succeed in the industry. Junior women need to see that having a successful career in STEM is possible and they need different approaches modelled for them to emulate.[171]

While junior women might benefit from female mentorship, they might not seek it out if there are only a small number of women in senior positions.[172] This is because they might believe that they will gain little social capital from doing so, because the senior women might themselves be marginalised and,

167 Maureen Baker, "Choices or Constraints? Family Responsibilities, Gender and Academic Career" (2010) *J Journal of Comparative Family Studies* 1, 6.

168 Ward Ooms, Claudia Werker and Christian Hopp, "Moving up the Ladder: Heterogeneity Influencing Academic Careers Through Research Orientation, Gender, and Mentors" (2019) 44(7) *Studies in Higher Education* 1268.

169 Katherine Y Williams and Charles A O'Reilly, "Demography and Diversity in Organizations: A Review of 40 Years of Research" (1998) 20 *Research in Organizational Behavior* 77.

170 Chesler and Chesler (n 31) 50–1. See also de Welde and Laursen (n 20) 583–5.

171 Jane G Nilanjana Dasgupta, Matthew Hunsinger and Melissa A McManus, "STEMing the Tide: Using Ingroup Experts to Inoculate Women's Self-Concept in Science, Technology, Engineering, and Mathematics (STEM)" (2011) 100 *Journal of Personality and Social Psychology* 255.

172 Chesler and Chesler (n 31) 51.

thus, have little power and influence, making them less effective mentors. Furthermore, women might not be able to offer mentorship around either skills relating to commercialisation, or valuable networks.[173] On top of this, senior women might not want to take on mentees, because (as implied above) this is a role that women are stereotypically considered to fit into due to the gendered presumption that women are more nurturing, patient and sympathetic.[174] Already disproportionately burdened with administrative tasks, senior women might avoid the additional work of mentoring.[175]

This is particularly understandable when one factors in that a woman's ability to invent, patent and commercialise is impacted by the fact that it is females who bear children and, due to gendered expectations, typically act as the primary caregiver.[176] Childbearing and caregiving are the chief reasons why women, more so than men, have short-term or part-time positions. These positions are often framed as being ideal for women, because women "choose" these positions so that they can continue their caregiver role. While these women may "choose" such roles, we should look at the options that they are given and the social constraints that lead to their choice. Coded as caregivers and socially expected to sacrifice their careers for their male partners (discussed further below), it is socially determined that women "choose" part-time and short-term contracts.[177]

In such positions, women usually have less time than men to undertake research, go to conferences and network.[178] Furthermore, the stress of childbearing and caring might negatively impact the time that a woman does have to research – they are never free from distraction.[179] This may mean that female researchers predominantly invent in smaller ways, which is not as easily patentable, as it is more likely to be obvious or not constitute an inventive step. Such inventing is also likely to gain women fewer reputational benefits. The role as caregiver might additionally impact women's ability to invent through tinkering or playing.[180]

173 Murray and Graham (n 139) 679. See Kjersten Bunker Whittington, "'A Tie is a Tie?' Gender and Network Positioning in Life Science Inventor Collaboration" (2018) 48 *Research Policy* 511, who notes that women tend to collaborate with other women, which is problematic when there are fewer women in science.

174 Yun Ling Li and Anthony A Peguero, "Professional Women's Dilemna Between Work and Family: An Examination of the Advance Program" (2015) 19(2) *Gender, Technology & Development* 119, 122.

175 Chesler and Chesler (n 31) 51.

176 Kjersten Bunker Whittington, "Mothers of Invention? Gender, Motherhood, and New Dimensions of Productivity in the Science Profession" (2011) 38(3) *Work & Occupations* 417; Nancy Folbre "Who Cares? A Feminist Critique of the Care Economy" (2014) Rosa Luxemburg Stiftung; Rosser (n 34) 780; and Baker (n 167) 12–13.

177 Julia Astegiano, Esther Sebasián-González and Camia de Toledo Castanho, "Unravelling the Gender Productivity Gap in Science: A Meta-Analytical Review" (2019) 6 *Royal Society Open Science* 181566, 9–10.

178 Ibid.

179 Li and Peguero (n 174) 124.

180 Autumn Stanley, "Once and Future Power: Women as Inventors" (1992) 15(2) *Women's Studies International Forum* 193, 198–200.

Caregiving may not sit well with the traditionally male-centred career-progression path, or may prevent a woman from attending events important for knowledge acquisition and networking, such as social events, evening seminars and conferences.[181] Kris de Welde and Sandra Laursen have referred to this as "competing clocks"; career versus biological.[182] Childbearing years also coincide with the early and vital period of a STEM-related career, where a researcher would build her name and reputation. As stated by Stephen Ceci and Wendy Williams in relation to the academic career:

> The tenure structure in academe demands that women having children make their greatest intellectual contributions contemporaneously with their greatest physical and emotional achievements, a feat not expected of men. When women opt out of full-time careers to have and rear children, this is a choice – constrained by biology – that men are not required to make.[183]

Thus, women's careers are taxed because of their biologically and socially assigned roles of child bearer and caregiver.[184] It is worth noting that a woman's socially constructed role as caregiver extends to family members, such as elderly parents.[185] Male partners are also included, as women are more likely make career sacrifices for their male partners than vice versa. This might be vis-à-vis childcare or relocation for a position.[186] As examined in the foregoing, the caregiver role stereotypically also covers taking care of the mental and emotional wellbeing of students and junior team members.

On the caregiving work of women, Harding stated:

> women are assigned the work that men do not want to do for themselves, especially the care of everyone's bodies – the bodies of men, of babies and children, of old people, of the sick, and of their own bodies. And they are assigned responsibility for the local places where those bodies exist as they clean and care for their own and others' houses and work places. This kind of "women's work" frees men in the ruling groups to immerse the selves in the world of abstract concepts. The more successful women are at this concrete work, the more invisible it becomes to men as distinctively social labor. Caring for bodies and the places bodies exist disappears into "nature," as, for example, in sociobiological claims about the naturalness of "altruistic" behavior for females and its un naturalness for males, or in the systematic reticence of many prefeminist marxists actually to analyze who

181 Baker (n 167) 9; and O'Hagan et al. (n 145) 214–15.
182 De Welde and Laursen (n 20) 585.
183 Ceci and Williams, "Sex Differences in Math-Intensive Fields" (n 10) 278.
184 Barwa and Rai (n 3) 107.
185 McDaniel, Cummins and Sender Beauchamp (n 44) 8 (noting that "women's first responsibilities are to be back-up staff to men"); Baker (n 167) 12–13.
186 Baker (n 167) 13–14.

> does what in everyday sexual, emotional, and domestic work, and to integrate such analyses into their accounts of "working class labor."[187]

Women must care for others and their households.[188] As discussed in Chapter 2, this is the invisible work of women.[189] More still, it is work that subsidises the efforts of the men,[190] who then have more time and energy to be creative. This has a cyclic effect.[191]

While motherhood undoubtedly harms a woman's career, there is a "fatherhood premium". Bunker Whittington has shown that, in the US, in both academia and industry, males with children patent more than males without children, and females generally.[192] This is consistent with studies on publication rates.[193] Of particular note, in academia, fathers are almost twice as likely to patent than mothers. The least likely to patent are mothers in academia. In academia, there is a "motherhood penalty".[194] The author hypothesises that academic mothers are affected more than mothers in industry because (whilst viewed positively) patenting is still considered optional in academia, whereas it is part of commercial life in industry. Bunker Whittington pointed out that the "fatherhood premium" is consistent with the gendered constructions of the "ideal worker" and "ideal parent", which are compatible and indeed symbiotic for males, but viewed as contradictory for females, resulting in the "motherhood penalty".[195]

Finally, invention, patenting and commercialisation require education, money and resources.[196] These are all things that females have historically had

187 Harding, "Rethinking Standpoint Epistemology" (n 9) 443.

188 See also Jennifer L Hook, "Gender Inequality in the Welfare State: Sex Segregation in Housework, 1965–2003" (2010) 115(5) *American Journal of Sociology* 1480; Janeen Baxter, "Gender Equality and Participation in Housework: A Cross-National Perspective" (1997) 28(3) *Journal of Comparative Family Studies* 220.

189 Drucilla K Barker, "What is Feminist Economics?" in Jill Steans and Daniela Tepe-Belfrage (eds), *Handbook on Gender in World Politics* (Edward Elgar, 2016) 414.

190 See e.g. Heidi I Hartmann, "The Unhappy Marriage of Marxism and Feminism" (1979) 3(2) *Capital and Class* 1, 14–22.

191 See e.g. Shirin M Rai and Catherine Joskyns, "Social Reproduction – The Achilles Heel of Feminist Transformation" in Jill Steans and Daniela Tepe-Belfrage (eds), *Handbook on Gender in World Politics* (Edward Elgar, 2016) 394.

192 Bunker Whittington "Mothers of Invention?" (n 176) 442.

193 See e.g. Jacques Mairesse, Michele Pezzoni and Fabiana Visentin, "Impact of Family Characteristics on the Gender Publication Gap: Evidence for Physicists in France" (2019) 44(2) *Interdisciplinary Science Reviews* 204. Cf. Mary Frank Fox, "Gender, Family Characteristics, and Publication Productivity among Scientists" (2005) 35(1) *Social Studies of Science* 131, whose data indicates that female scientists with one preschool child might publish more, which Fox attributes to a certain kind of female scientists who "have especially strong stamina for and commitment to research" and are particularly disciplined (at 142).

194 Bunker Whittington, "Mothers of Invention?" (n 176) 448.

195 Ibid., 442.

196 Barwa and Rai (n 3) 98–9 and 105–6; Merritt (n 21) 290–300; and Kahler (n 17) 779.
Due to the prohibitive cost of patenting, Susan Corbett has discussed alternatives for women, such as using copyright and trade secrecy; Susan Corbett "The Female

less access to than males.[197] While the socio-economic status of women has generally progressed, this continues to be the case. Undertaking a review of empirical literature, Ceci and Williams concluded that the underrepresentation of women in science (particularly mathematics) is not due to discrimination with respect to the review of manuscript submissions, grant funding or interviewing/hiring.[198] When data was normalised against available resources, differences in these areas between males and females diminished. However, Ceci and Williams noted that the real problem is the uneven distribution of resources. That is, that males have more resources than females (through having more senior, fixed or full-time roles and research-based positions rather than teaching-focused ones). Importantly, Ceci and Williams recognised that the differences in resources are in part due to choices made that are "constrained by biology and society".[199] This includes a woman's choice to have and raise children, sacrificing their career for their male partners, being more focused on a work-life balance, or caring for elderly parents.

Overall, the institutional, structural or organisational biases against females in the processes of inventing, patenting and commercialising are self-perpetuating. The patent system tells women that they have to be in STEM, working on the masculine in a masculine-coded manner, to achieve success. Yet, the number of women in most STEM disciplines has not reached critical mass and it cannot do so under current conditions. When women remain a minority in a discipline, men continue to be able to behave badly (retain misogynistic culture, maintain Old Boys' Clubs, practice overt or subtle sexual discrimination or harassment with impunity), women continue to feel marginalised and "abnormal", there are not enough senior women to be mentors, junior women researchers feel isolated and dissatisfied, the "leaky pipeline" persists in STEM fields, there are fewer women in patent-heavy STEM disciplines, biases result in those women who remain not being supported to patent or commercialise their inventions, few progress to senior roles, and the myth continues that women are not suitable for invention and innovation. Thus, the patent-based knowledge governance system continues to chiefly benefit its creators, Western males.

6 An incumbency bias

> These accounts of hurt and fear describe a system without balance, plagued by incumbency bias, and whose civility norms have broken down.
>
> By "without balance," I mean disproportionate outcomes given the quality and quantity of inputs by different participants. And by "incumbency bias," I mean the perpetuation of exclusivity and exclusion through past successes,

Inventor: What Price Intellectual Capital?" (2002) *New Zealand Intellectual Property Journal* 91, 94–7.

197 Kahler (n 17) 780–1; and Fausto-Sterling, "Women and Science" (n 44) 44–5.

198 Stephen Ceci and Wendy M Williams, "Understanding Current Causes of Women's Underrepresentation in Science" (2011) 108(8) *Proceedings of the National Academy of Sciences* 3157.

199 Ibid., 3158.

> whether justified or not. The latter has been analyzed in the sociolegal literature in terms of "the 'Haves' come out ahead." The critical factor in the interview accounts is not, however, that the repeat players succeed because they have learned to play the game, but that repeat players succeed because their relative wealth and influence from past successes accumulates to assure their dominance and future successes. Both a lack of proportionality and a rigged system that maintains existing power and privilege predominate in the accounts of everyday creativity and innovation.[200]

This chapter has highlighted the gendered nature of the different stages of invention that lead to patents, the patenting process and commercialisation. Together with the fact that patent law itself is gendered (as analysed in Chapter 2), the current knowledge governance framework favours the masculine over the feminine, and benefits men over women. The immediate reaction to this is either to push for more women in STEM, or to adjust patent law to account for different kinds of knowledge and modes of invention.

However, as alluded to in the Introduction, both of these potential solutions miss the point. If we frame the problem narrowly as too few women in STEM, this runs the risk of telling women that they are the problem. For example, they are not good or resilient enough. It takes responsibility away from men and from society, who are then absolved from having to acknowledge and address the socialised and institutionalised biases stacked-up against women to invent, patent and commercialise. In addition, focusing on STEM valorises it, while under-valuing feminine knowledge. Women (and men) should not have to operate in STEM in a masculine-coded manner in order to be viewed as inventors, and supported to invent, patent and commercialise their inventions. Women are not the problem. The knowledge ecosystem and its governance system constitute the problem. Furthermore, as elaborated upon in Chapter 5, patent law is by no means an otherwise perfect knowledge governance system.

Therefore, we need to stop the "women in STEM" rhetoric and focus instead of the system that requires that women be in STEM and that marginalises them when they are. Only changing the system can we change social relations. As stated by Judith Butler:

> There are social contexts and conventions within which certain acts not only become possible but become conceivable as acts at all. The transformation of social relations becomes a matter, then, of transforming hegemonic social conditions rather than the individual acts that are spawned by those conditions.[201]

200 Jessica Silbey, "Intellectual Property Harms: A Paradigm for the Twenty-First Century" (2019) 99 *Boston University Law Review* 2447, 2460.

201 Judith Butler, "Performative Acts and Gender Constitution: An Essay in Phenomenology and Feminist Theory" (1988) 40(4) *Theatre Journal* 519, 525.

And there must be change as patents affect what knowledge is generated, developed and commercialised, and who gets financial, reputational and career benefits from this. This is examined further in Chapter 4 to highlight that, while the answer to gendered patenting and patent law is by no means easy to discern, seeking an answer is imperative. The status quo is that it is the masculine that is incentivised, brought to market, built-upon and valorised. It is chiefly males who get the financial and reputational gains of patenting. That is, there is an incumbency bias, as noted by Jessica Silbey in the quote above. In Silbey's words, "[t]hose already with significant wealth or economy of scale control the welfare and opportunities of others, even if the new entrants or everyday artists and innovators provide essential fodder for those on the top".[202]

202 Silbey (n 200) 2464.

4 The consequences of gendered patent law and patenting

> Male power is real; it is just not what it claims to be, namely, the only reality. Male power is a myth that makes itself true. What it is to raise consciousness is to confront male power in this duality: as total on one side and a delusion on the other. In consciousness raising, women learn they have *learned* that men are everything, women their negation, but that the sexes are equal.[1]

1 Introduction

So far, this book has addressed the exact ways that patenting is gendered and how this, in part, is due to patent law itself being gendered. The logical question to ask is, "Does this matter?" It does and this chapter explains why. It shows that male power is real and has significant consequences. The chapter analyses the consequences of patent law and patenting being gendered in light of patent law theory. Patents are theorised to serve multiple roles relating to the development of an invention, the dissemination of knowledge relating to the invention, and the commercialisation or marketing of the invention. As analysed in the following, each of these roles is affected by patent law and patenting being gendered.[2] The chapter is organised into two main sections, looking first at the roles of patents relating to the process of invention, before turning to the roles of patents pertaining to the commercialisation of inventions. The chapter ends with some thoughts on how patent law and patenting being gendered sustains existing power relations.

1 Catharine A MacKinnon, "Feminism, Marxism, Method, and the State: An Agenda for Theory" (1982) 7(3) *Journal of Women in Culture and Society* 515, 542.
2 This chapter updates and expands upon content from Jessica C Lai, "The Role of Patents as a Gendered Chameleon" (2021) 30(2) *Social & Legal Studies* 203.

DOI: 10.4324/9781003128502-5

2 Invention

2.1 What do patents incentivise?

Modern patent law[3] is justified via the "incentive theory".[4] This theory holds that, without the incentive of the patent (embodied in the 20 years of property or exclusive rights), there would be fewer inventions.[5] This is because the products of intellectual endeavours are "public goods". Public goods are non-rivalrous (more than one person can consume them at the same time) and non-excludible (the creator cannot exclude others from consuming it).[6] In the absence of intellectual property, there would be free-riding, where a third party benefits from the actions and efforts of the innovator without paying or sharing the costs. In other words, third parties would free-ride on the innovator's investment. Free-riding can reduce the incentive to create intellectual goods, resulting in underproduction.[7] That is, people would be less willing to invest in invention if their competitors would be able to copy the product or service as soon as it is marketed, and offer it at a lower price because they would not have to make up the costs of invention.[8] In theory, patents prevent free-riding and thereby ensure an incentive to invent.

That patent-eligible subject matter predominantly reflects masculine forms of invention potentially results in the incentive role of patents being stronger for men than for women. This could have the effect of excluding women from the "patent as an incentive to invent" paradigm. Alternatively, the patent system could incentivise women to inhabit traditionally masculine ways and fields of inventing and knowing, as only by doing so can they obtain patents and better partake in the knowledge economy. Masculine institutions of knowledge are embodied in science, technology, engineering and mathematics (STEM). As noted throughout this book, there is indeed a "women in STEM" narrative that tells women (and society at large) that they must be in STEM in order to actively engage in the knowledge economy.

3 Defined as 1850 to present; Brad Sherman and Lionel Bently, *The Making of Modern Intellectual Property Law: The British Experience, 1760–1911* (Cambridge University Press, 1999).

4 William Cornish, David Llewelyn and Tanya Aplin, *Intellectual Property: Patents, Copyright, Trade Marks and Allied Rights* (7th edn, Sweet & Maxwell, 2010) [3–36]–[3–48].

5 Peter S Menell, "Intellectual Property: General Theories" in B Boudewijn Bouckaert and Gerrit de Geest (eds), *Encyclopedia of Law and Economics, Volume I. The History and Methodology of Law and Economics* (Edward Elgar, 2000) 129, 146–7.

6 On the reality of whether intellectual products are public goods, see Dan L Burk, "Copyright and the New Materialism" in Jessica C Lai and Antoinette Maget Dominicé (eds), *Intellectual Property and Access to Im/material Goods* (Edward Elgar, 2016) 44, 50–3.

7 See e.g. William Landes and Richard Posner, "An Economic Analysis of Copyright Law" (1989) 18 *Journal of Legal Studies* 325; and William Landes and Richard Posner, *The Economic Structure of Intellectual Property Law* (Belknap Press, 2003).

8 Kenneth W Dam, "The Economic Underpinnings of Patent Law" (1994) 23 *Journal of Legal Studies* 247, 247.

While the patent system incentivises women (as well as men) to research what could become patent-eligible subject matter, men are not incentivised to move into traditionally feminine fields.[9] Gendered constructs and roles constrict both women and men. As stated by Jane Flax:

> From the perspective of social relations, men and women are both prisoners of gender, although in highly differentiated but interrelated ways. That men appear to be and (in many cases) are the wardens, or at least the trustees within a social whole, should not blind us to the extent to which they, too, are governed by the rules of gender. (This is not to deny that it matters a great deal – to individual men, to the women and children sometimes connected to them, and to those concerned about justice – where men as well as women are distributed within social hierarchies.)[10]

Men are just as bound by gender constructions as women, though they are generally placed higher on the social hierarchy. They are also directed towards masculine modes and fields of production. More specifically, the patent system affects the behaviour of both men and women by silently dictating what and how they should invent. In this sense, "[b]oth women and men are alienated within such a system because the framework itself remains invisible".[11]

In the twenty-first century, it is predominantly entities rather than individuals that decide upon the direction of invention. That is to say that it is not only individual inventors who are affected by the patent incentive, but also universities, small start-ups, or large corporate companies, for example. These entities are also affected by the patent system and incentivised to invent in masculine fields. This affects both the men and women within those entities, who will research towards patent-eligible subject matter if they wish to be successful.

In addition, that patentable subject matter is primarily masculine means that the patent system incentivises the creation of masculine inventions. This may be to the detriment of feminine modes and kinds of invention. This is especially true if women shift into masculine fields (which the "women in STEM" rhetoric would indicate is occurring) and men do not move into feminine fields. As elaborated upon below, this is negative for women and for traditionally feminine industries, which require feminine inventions. To illustrate, society benefits from inventions within the preschool industry, which is female dominated and feminine. However, while the existing patent system incentivises inventions such as new game consoles, it does not incentivise methods relating to teaching or social development. This is not good for pre-schoolers, parents or society at large.

9 Dan L Burk, "Do Patents Have Gender?" (2011) 19 *American University Journal of Gender, Social Policy & the Law* 881, 889.

10 Jane Flax, "Postmodernism and Gender Relations in Feminist Theory" (1987) 12(4) *Signs: Journal of Women in Culture and Society* 621, 629.

11 Debora Halbert, "Feminist Interpretations of Intellectual Property" (2006) 14(3) *American University Journal of Gender, Social Policy & the Law* 431, 446.

That patentable subject matter is masculine, and this has led to women moving into STEM fields, could have the effect of homogenising knowledge. This is negative for knowledge production and invention, which benefits from diversity. Gender diversity is associated with higher innovative performance.[12] It can allow for new perspectives and ways of thinking.[13] This includes identifying new problems[14] and defining the problems to be solved,[15] as well as finding solutions. It can also include developing new hypotheses and methods for testing them. This is exemplified in studies showing that patents (normalised for age and technology) from mixed-gender-team inventors get more citations than patents from male-team inventors, which in turn get more citations than patents from female-team inventors.[16] The same trend is observed with respect to patent assignment (also a proxy for invention quality).[17] This indicates that gender diversity leads to higher quality research and innovation, because the team can draw on more diverse knowledge. One can imagine that the diversity and the benefits therefrom would be even greater if the patent system were not confined to masculine knowledge.

One could argue that perhaps males are more driven by external motivations than females, and this is why they created a system that gives external validation and reward for masculine forms of invention. If females are less moved by external motivations, as indicated by their tendency to focus on non-commercial

12 Juan Fernández Sastre, "The Impact of R&D Teams' Gender Diversity on Innovation Outputs" (2015) 24(1) *International Journal of Entrepreneurship and Small Business* 142; and Daniela Ritter-Hayashi, Patrick Vermeulen and Joris Knoben, "Is This a Man's World? The Effect of Gender Diversity and Gender Equality on Firm Innovativeness" (2019) 14(9) *PLoS ONE* e0222443. Note that the gains of diversity can be counteracted by heterophily; Katherine Y Williams and Charles A O'Reilly, "Demography and Diversity in Organizations: A Review of 40 Years of Research" (1998) 29 *Research in Organizational Behavior* 77. This is because heterophily can lead to ineffective communication. Thus, in order for diversity to be effective, the possibility of communication failures must be directly addressed by empathy (projecting oneself into the situation of another), the receiver giving feedback and the source addressing that feedback, which can allow for more empathy; Everett M Rogers and Dilip K Bhowmik, "Homophily-Heterophily: Relational Concepts for Communication Research" (1970) 34(4) *The Public Opinion Quarterly* 523, 5356.

13 Anna Fausto-Sterling, "Women and Science" (1981) 4(1) *Women's Studies International Quarterly* 41, 48; and J Shontavia Johnson et al., "Diversifying Intellectual Property Law: Why Women of Color Remain 'Invisible' and How to Provide More Seats at the Table" (2018) 10(4) *Landslide*, www.americanbar.org/groups/intellectual_property_law/publications/landslide/2017-18/march-april.

14 Sandra Harding, "Rethinking Standpoint Epistemology: What is 'Strong Objectivity?'" (1992) 36(3) *The Centennial Review* 437,

15 Sandra Harding, "A Socially Relevant Philosophy of Science" (2004) 19(1) *Hypatia* 25, 32–4.

16 Catherine Ashcraft and Anthony Breitzman, "Who Invents IT? Women's Participation in Information Technology Patenting" (2012) National Center for Women & Information Technology, 16–17.

17 Lisa D Cook and Chaleampong Kongcharoen, "The Idea Gap in Pink and Black" (September 2010) *NBER Working Paper* No. 16331, 9, www.nber.org/papers/w16331.

endeavours, they do not need the patent system to incentivise them to invent in traditionally female fields. This polarised conceptualisation is flawed for several reasons.

First, it ignores the power dynamics involved in law and policymaking. The reasons why the definition of patentable subject matter reflects traditionally male modes of invention are multiple, but include that it has been males who historically have had the power to create, apply and enforce law and policy. Power begets power. As stated by Dan Burk, "the patent system may not only be overlooking 'feminine' technologies, but also actively promoting technologies that facilitate and reinforce current social hierarchies, including gender hierarchies".[18]

Second, females have traditionally invented in non-commercial arenas because their spaces have been constructed as being non-commercial. They are not inherently non-commercial. Chapter 2 highlighted the way that the work of women has been cast as private and non-industrial. It is socially invisible. This is in contrast to the spaces of men, which have been constructed as public, and within those spaces exist the masculine constructions of science, invention and industry.[19] Furthermore, women were only permitted to operate within the private sphere. They were (and continue to be) marginalised and ostracised (cast as deviants) when they deigned to enter the public and industrial sphere.

Third, even if it were empirically correct that women are less motivated by external rewards than men are, this would be a reflection of socialisation. Women have historically neither moved within the commercial sphere nor been encouraged to do so. Women are not socialised to take. Instead they are socialised to give, as homemakers and caregivers.

Finally, there is no evidence that females are inherently uninterested in the commercial. Qualitative studies of women in science point to the opposite. These indicate that women are inhibited from patenting and commercialisation because of lack of legal, financial and business networks, and institutional support.[20] B Zorina Khan has quantitatively shown a positive correlation between

18 Burk, "Do Patents Have Gender?" (n 9) 906.

19 See e.g. Shlomit Yanisky-Ravid, "Eligible Patent Matter – Gender Analysis of Patent Law: International and Comparative Perspectives" (2011) 19(3) *American University Journal of Gender, Social Policy & the Law* 851, 855; Sue V Rosser, "The Gender Gap in Patenting: Is Technology Transfer a Feminist Issue?" (2009) 21(2) *National Women's Studies Association Journal* 65, 76; and Kara W Swanson, "Getting a Grip on the Corset: Gender, Sexuality, and Patent Law" (2011) 23(1) *Yale Journal of Law and Feminism* 57, 64–5.

20 See e.g. Lisa A Marovich. "'Let Her Have Brains Too': Commercial Networks, Public Relations, and the Business of Invention" (1998) 27(1) *Business and Economic History* 140; Kris de Welde and Sandra L Laursen, "The Glass Obstacle Course: Informal and Formal Barriers for Women PhD Students in STEM Fields" (2011) 3 (3) *International Journal of Gender, Science and Technology* 571, 578; Deborah Merritt, "Hypatia in the Patent Office: Women Inventors and the Law, 1865–1900" (1991) 35 *American Journal of Legal History* 235, 299; Kjersten Bunker Whittington and Laurel Smith-Doerr, "Women Inventors in Context: Disparities in Patenting Across Academia and Industry" (2008) 22(2) *Gender & Society* 194, 366. See also Rosser (n 19) 78.

laws granting women property rights separate from their husbands, and rights to contract and enforce these, and female patenting.[21] Khan concluded that women were generally incentivised in the same way as men; namely, to benefit economically from their inventions, by selling or commercialising them, and responding to market demand in fields where they had comparative advantage (such as household appliances).[22]

2.2 What is being disseminated?

As well as incentivising invention, patents are also theorised to incentivise the publication and dissemination of knowledge.[23] In the absence of patents (and the 20 years of exclusive rights they represent), inventors (and the entities that invest in invention) would be motivated to keep their inventions secret rather than publishing them. This would be negative for further invention and the overall production of knowledge, as invention does not occur in a vacuum, but cumulatively off the back of existing information/knowledge.[24] Patent rights are, thus, granted in exchange for patentees disclosing their inventions to the public.[25] Patent applications are technical documents. They are accompanied by a "specification", which must be "sufficient" for the person skilled in the art to replicate the invention, or to "enable" this person to "work" the invention.[26] Patent documents are publicly available. The exchange of exclusive rights for the disclosure of the invention is the quid pro quo or social contract of patents.[27]

21 B Zorina Khan, "Married Women's Property Laws and Female Commercial Activity: Evidence from US Patent Records, 1790–1895" (1996) 56 *Journal of Economic History* 356.
22 Ibid., 371.
23 Sherman and Bently (n 3) 142–57; Landes and Posner, *The Economic Structure of Intellectual Property* (n 7) 294 and 326–32; Bronwyn H Hall and Dietmar Harhoff, "Recent Research on the Economics of Patents" (2012) 4 *Annual Review of Economics* 541, 542.
24 Mark A Lemley, "The Myth of the Sole Inventor" (2012) 110 *Michigan Law Review* 709, 712–33, who discusses the social (rather than individual) phenomenon of invention and the consequential prevalence of simultaneous invention; and Gregory S Alexander and Eduardo M Peñalver, *An Introduction to Property Theory* (University Press, 2012) 194–5.
25 *Pope Appliance Corporation v Spanish River Pulp & Paper Mill Ltd* (1929) 46 RPC 23, 55 (Viscount Dunedin); Peter Drahos, *The Global Governance of Knowledge: Patent Offices and Their Clients* (Cambridge University Press, 2010) 27–32; Hector L MacQueen, Charlotte Waelde and Graeme T Laurie, *Contemporary Intellectual Property: Law and Policy* (Oxford University Press, 2008) [10.15]–[10.16].
26 *Liardet v Johnson* (1778) 1 WPC 53. See also *Turner v Winter* (1787) 99 ER 1274 (KB). For commentary, see Christine MacLeod, *Inventing the Industrial Revolution. The English Patent System, 1660–1800* (Cambridge University Press, 1988) 49l; Klaus Boehm, *The British Patent System, Vol. I: Administration* (Cambridge University Press, 1967) 20–1; Justine Pila, "Inherent Patentability in Anglo-Australian Law: A History" (2003) 14 *Australian Intellectual Property Journal* 111, 113.
27 Donald S Chisum et al., *Principles of Patent Law* (Foundation Press, 2nd ed, 2001) 6; Cornish, Llewelyn and Aplin (n 3) [3–05]–[3–06], [3–49]–[3–51].

If what is patentable is primarily masculine, patent documents chiefly disseminate masculine information and knowledge. In turn, it is masculine knowledge that is diffused through society rather than feminine knowledge. Furthermore, it is masculine knowledge that is cited by others, built upon and developed. Even if we do not think about knowledge as being gendered, the fact that more males than females patent means that men are influencing the direction of knowledge development more than women. This is worrying when we consider the evidence that women tend to work in a more interdisciplinary manner,[28] and interdisciplinarity is considered to be central for future innovation in an ever-increasingly complex world.[29] Related to this, there is a positive correlation between gender diversity and innovation,[30] innovation efficiency,[31] as well as radical invention/innovation.[32]

That it is the masculine that is disseminated and developed is compounded by evidence that men publish more than women generally and in more affluent journals.[33] In addition, men's publications and patents tend to be cited more

28 Yu Meng and Philip Shapira, "Women and Patenting in Nanotechnology: Scale Scope and Equity" in Susan E Cozens and Jameson M Wetmore (eds), *Nanotechnology and the Challenges of Equity: Equality and Development* (Springer, 2011) 23, 38–9; Cassidy R Sugimoto et al., "The Academic Advantage: Gender Disparities in Patenting" (2015) 10(5) *PLoS ONE* e0128000, 7.

29 See e.g. Frank Kessel, Patricia L Rosenfeld and Norman B Anderson, *Expanding the Boundaries of Health and Social Science: Case Studies from Health and Social Science* (Oxford University Press, 2008); Alan F Blackwell et al., "Radical Innovation: Crossing Knowledge Boundaries with Interdisciplinary Teams" (November 2009) University of Cambridge Computer Laboratory Technical Report No. 760, www.cl.cam.ac.uk/techreports/UCAM-CL-TR-760.pdf; B Taebi et al., "Responsible Innovation as an Endorsement of Public Values: the Need for Interdisciplinary Research" (2014) 1(1) *Journal of Responsible Innovation* 118; Diana Rhoten and Andrew Parker, "Risks and Rewards of an Interdisciplinary Research Path" (2004) 306(5704) *Science* 2046; Dries Faems and Annapoornima M Subramanian, "R&D Manpower and Technological Performance: The Impact of Demographic and Task-related Diversity" (2013) 42(9) *Research Policy* 1624.

30 Fernández Sastre (n 12) 142; and Ritter-Hayashi, Vermeulen and Knoben (n 12).

31 Luqun Xie et al., "Gender Diversity in R&D Teams and Innovation Efficiency: Role of the Innovation Context" (2020 49 *Research Policy* 103885.

32 Cristina Díaz-García et al., "Gender Diversity within R&D Teams: Its Impact on Radicalness of Innovation" (2013) 15(2) *Innovation: Management, Policy & Practice* 149, Christian R Østergaard, Bram Timmermans and Kari Kristinsson, "Does a Different View Create Something New? The Effect of Employee Diversity on Innovation" (2011) 40 *Research Policy* 500; Martina Schraudner and Helga Lukoschat (eds), *Gender als Innovationspotenzial in Forschung und Entwicklung* (Fraunhofer Verlag, 2006); and Mathias Wullum Nielsen, Carter Walter Bloch and Londa Schiebinger, "Making Gender Diversity Work for Scientific Discovery and Innovation" (2018) 2(10) *Nature Human Behaviour* 726.

33 Julia Astegiano, Esther Sebasián-González and Camia de Toledo Castanho, "Unravelling the Gender Productivity Gap in Science: A Meta-Analytical Review" (2019) 6 *Royal Society Open Science* 181566, 7; Steven Stack, "Gender and Scholarly Productivity: 1970–2000" (2002) 35(3) *Sociological Focus* 285; J. Scott Long, "Measures of Sex Differences in Scientific Productivity" (1992) 71(1) *Social Forces* 159; Chris Brooks, Evelyn M Fenton and James T Walker, "Gender and the Evaluation of Research" (2014) 43 *Research Policy* 990; Carolin Lerchenmüller, Marc J

frequently than those of women are.[34] This is significantly affected by males self-citing more than females do.[35] That males achieve more impact for their publications is true even for co-authored articles. This is partly because men tend to be the lead authors on co-authorships with women.[36] However, when women are named in a lead-authorship position, their publications have fewer citations.[37] That is, placing a male name in a lead-authorship position would statistically raise the number of citations.

Regarding patents, a study of US granted patents from 1976–2018 analogously showed that females are seldom named as the lead inventor.[38] Cumulatively within that period, females were lead inventors on only 11 per cent of granted patents.[39] Furthermore, the impact gap between male-inventor patents compared to female-inventor patents is larger for patents owned by universities than by firms.[40] This is concerning given that the gender patenting gap is narrower in universities than firms (see Chapter 1). It implies that, even when women's inventions result in patents, this does not translate into proportionate impact.

The problem extends beyond the patent system predominantly disseminating masculine knowledge. Protected by property law and granted by the state, patents are seen as a state-endorsement of inventions that are new, inventive and useful (see Chapter 2). As discussed further below, patents have a signal

Lerchenmueller and Olav Sorenson, "Long-Term Analysis of Sex Differences in Prestigious Authorships in Cardiovascular Research Supported by the National Institutes of Health" (2018) 137(8) *Circulation* 880.

34 Vincent Larivière et al., "Global Gender Disparities in Science" (2013) 504 *Nature* 211, 212; Sugimoto et al. (n 28) 7; see also Kyle Jensen, Balázs Kovács and Olav Sorenson, "Gender Difference in Obtaining and Maintaining Patent Rights" (2018) 36(4) *Nature Biotechnology* 307. Though looking at citations of US patents, controlling for technology and year of publication, Cook and Kongcharoen found that citations of female-inventor patents are just as high as the overall US median in most technologies; Cook and Kongcharoen (n 18) 9

35 Astegiano, Sebasián-González and de Toledo Castanho (n 33) 7.

36 Francesco Lissoni, Fabio Montobbio and Lorenzo Zirulia, "Inventorship and Authorship as Attribution Rights: An Enquiry into the Economics of Scientific Credit" (2013) 95 *Journal of Economic Behavior & Organization* 49, 59–61. These authors also found that women are significantly more likely to be listed as an author in a publication, but not as an inventor on the patent for the related invention (at 63).

37 Jevin D West et al., "The Role of Gender in Scholarly Authorship" (2013) 8(7) *PLoS ONE* e0066212; Giovanni Filardo et al., "Trends and Comparison of Female First Authorship in High Impact Medical Journals: Observational Study (1994–2014)" (2016) 352 *British Medical Journal* 1; Larivière et al. (n 34) 213. Note that this does vary across disciplines, and there is evidence that disciplines that require more risk for success (and, thus, self-select outstanding females) have more gender equity in citation rates; Jordi Duch et al., "The Possible Role of Resource Requirements and Academic Career-Choice Risk on Gender Differences in Publication Rate and Impact" (2012) 7(12) *PLoS ONE* e51332, 5–7.

38 Yukai Wang et al., "Gender Bias in Patenting Process" (2019) 14 *Journal of Infometrics* 101046.

39 Ibid., 7.

40 Sugimoto et al. (n 28) 7.

effect. By imputing value to the masculine, the patent system subordinates feminine knowledge. Burk has noted that:

> If patents are intended to encourage new ideas, new knowledge, and innovation, a standard that implicitly valorizes only certain types of knowledge might cause the system to either completely overlook other types of knowledge that might be beneficial, or to simply place too little value on developing types of knowledge that do not fit the profile of objectivity.[41]

Thus, the grant of patents for predominantly masculine information and knowledge serves to perpetuate the notion that this is of greater value than feminine information and knowledge. The devaluation of women's work and inventions allows for the continued subordination of women to men.[42]

In reality, both feminine and masculine knowledge are valuable and – as noted by Catharine MacKinnon in the quote at the beginning of this chapter – the sexes are equal. Much feminine knowledge and women's work is simply invisible – not considered "scientific", unrecognised by the patent system and not disseminated in patent documents. Yet, the invisible knowledge and work is of value. If this were not the case, it would not be taken from the public domain, filtered through the masculine and patented in masculine form (examined in Chapters 2 and 5). To give value to the feminine, some have called for broadening patentable subject matter to include fields that are traditionally female dominated, to incentivise more invention in those fields.[43] The questionability of this is examined in Chapter 5.

2.3 Who is rewarded?

Patents act as an incentive to invent by ensuring that inventors (or investors) are rewarded for their efforts with up to 20 years of exclusive rights and the potential supra-competitive prices that these can represent. The idea that property can be a reward for work stems primarily from John Locke's labour

41 Burk, "Do Patents Have Gender?" (n 9) 904.

42 Terra L Gearhart-Serna, "Women's Work, Women's Knowing: Intellectual Property and the Recognition of Women's Traditional Knowledge" 21(2) *Yale Journal of Law and Feminism* 372, 388. Note that this is similarly true in other areas of cultural production, such as copyright law, where failure to acknowledge women as authors (or "creative geniuses"), has resulted in their works being devalued, while simultaneously perpetuating masculine ideologies; B Courtney Doagoo, "Feminist Anthropology and Copyright: Gauging the Application and Limitations of Oppositions Models" in B Courtney Doagoo et al. (eds), *Intellectual Property for the 21st Century: Interdisciplinary Approaches* (Publisher Irwin Law, 2014) 193.

43 Rosser (n 19) 70; Yanisky-Ravid (n 19) 863–70 and 873; Sharmishta Barwa and Shirin M Rai, "Knowledge and/as Power: A Feminist Critique of Trade Related Intellectual Property Rights" (2003) 7(1) *Gender, Technology and Development* 91, 104–5.

theory.[44] A natural-rights theory, Lockean labour theory holds that it is a moral imperative that labour be met with property.[45]

Whether patents actually incentivise invention or are an effective means of dissemination of knowledge is highly contentious. One could, hence, argue that the gendered nature of patent law and patenting does not affect the inventive process or the information that is built upon. However, those who patent can most certainly reap financial and reputational benefits. If patents are a reward for invention, then the gendered law is rewarding masculine forms of invention over feminine forms. Moreover, patent law rewards males more than it rewards females, a fact supported by the statistics around patent application and ownership (Chapter 1).

Patents can represent financial value because, as property, they can be commercialised, licensed or sold.[46] It is males who mainly capture this value, which, as noted by Sharmishta Barwa and Shirin Rai, causes females to "fall progressively behind in the race for ring-fencing products for monopoly exploitation".[47] This is true even if it is mostly institutes that own patents and not the inventors of inventions. Firstly, patent-rich STEM fields are male dominated. Secondly, most named inventors are male and named inventors on a patent often get royalties if the patent is commercialised. There are also reputational gains (discussed further below) and possibly even financial bonuses for patenting.[48] That females patent less, thus, has implications for financial equality and economic power, where females already have fewer resources than males in general.[49]

The issue is cyclical, as invention, patenting and commercialisation require education, money and resources.[50] The underrepresentation of women in

44 John Locke, *Two Treatises of Government* (Peter Laslett ed., 2nd edn, Cambridge University Press, 1960), s 27. Sherman and Bently (n 3) 23–4. In Continental Europe copyright protection was and continues – to some degree – to be grounded in Kantian and Hegelian natural-rights theories related to personality and individuality. See Immanuel Kant, "On the Injustice of Counterfeiting Books" (1785), reprinted in JAL Sterling, *World Copyright Law* (2nd edn, Sweet & Maxwell, 2003); Georg WF Hegel, *Philosophy of Right* (Thomas M Knox Eng trans., Oxford University Press, 1967).

45 Sigrid Sterckx, "The Ethics of Patenting – Uneasy Justifications" in Peter Drahos (ed.), *Death of Patents* (Lawtext Publishing and Queen Mary Intellectual Property Research Institute, 2005), 186.

46 Rosser (n 19) 65.

47 Barwa and Rai (n 43) 97.

48 Annette I Kahler, "Examining Exclusion in Woman-Inventor Patenting: A Comparison of Educational Trends and Patent Data in the Era of Computer Engineer Barbie" (2011) 19(3) *American University Journal of Gender, Social Policy & the Law* 773, 797; and Rosser (n 19) 65.

49 Malla Pollack, "Towards a Feminist Theory of the Public Domain, or Rejecting the Gendered Scope of United States Copyrightable and Patentable Subject Matter" (2006) 12 *William and Mary Journal of Women and the Law* 603, 606; Autumn Stanley, "Once and Future Power: Women as Inventors" (1992) 15(2) *Women's Studies International Forum* 193, 199; Kahler (n 48) 780–1.

50 Barwa and Rai (n 43) 98–9 and 105–6; Merritt (n 20) 290–300; and Kahler (n 48) 779.

It is without a doubt that the ability to become an inventor is socially determined. Along with gender, it depends on race, socio-economic background, environment, exposure to innovation growing up, and role models. See Alexander

science (particularly mathematics) is due to the uneven distribution of resources.[51] These might be financial resources or organisational support, for example. Males have more resources than females (through having more senior, fixed or full-time roles and research-based positions rather than teaching-focused ones). Women in fields that require more resources, such as physical sciences, publish less.[52] Women patenting less and, thus, being less likely to obtain the associated reward serves to ensure that women continue to have fewer resources than men. This negatively impacts their ability to invent and innovate.

Another way to view this is that women are taxed for the fact that there are historical, cultural, social and institutional reasons why they invent and create value in a different way and in different fields. Barwa and Rai stated that the World Trade Organization (WTO) Agreement on Trade-Related Aspects of Intellectual Property Rights (TRIPS) (one of the core international agreements on intellectual property):

> does not recognize that women take different risks as compared to men, but these are not recognized as such and, therefore, not rewarded. Nor that they contribute significantly towards enhancing household security through food production, processing, and marketing on a daily basis. TRIPS further does not reflect the inequality that women experience in the communication of information and skills, education, and selection due to the socially embedded nature of national policymaking; and thus women use, adapt, and adopt technology very differently from men.[53]

Lockean labour theory does not justify patent law's distinction between masculine and feminine kinds of invention. The theory requires that labour (particularly physical labour) that adds value be met with property. Of course, not all labour is met with property. As Locke was theorising private property in land, the application of his theory to patents can be viewed with scepticism. However, the literature is replete with Lockean justifications for patents regarding masculine intellectual creations. Yet, women's labour, especially the labour of their bodies (such as childbearing, breastfeeding and general caregiving), has not been recognised as property (or even as economically valuable), despite its great benefit to

M Bell et al., "Who Becomes an Inventor in America? The Importance of Exposure to Innovation" (January 2019) *NBER Working Paper* No. 24062.

Due to the prohibitive cost of patenting, Corbett has discussed alternatives for women, such as using copyright and trade secrecy; Susan Corbett, "The Female Inventor: What Price Intellectual Capital?" (2002) *New Zealand Intellectual Property Journal* 91, 94–7.

51 Stephen J Ceci and Wendy M Williams, "Sex Differences in Math-Intensive Fields" (2010) 19(5) *Current Directions in Psychological Science* 275, who conclude that women are not discriminated against with respect to manuscript reviewing, grant funding and interviewing/hiring, when data on these domains are normalised against resources of the individual, However, they note that males have access to more resources than females.

52 Duch et al. (n 37) 4.

53 Barwa and Rai (n 43) 108.

social welfare (and indeed economic value).[54] Analogously, women's intellectual labour has not been recognised as patentable subject matter, though it indisputably increases social wealth. For example, intellectual labour in education, caregiving and mental health. Given the obvious value to society of feminine forms and modes of invention, the valorisation of male-socialised forms of invention over feminine ones also cannot be based on utilitarian theory.

If women can only gain recognition and reward for their inventions if they conform to traditionally masculine modes and spaces of invention, this serves to reinforce the belief that domains that have been more female dominated do not generate knowledge or worthy inventions. Women's knowledge and status as inventors is further ignored and devalued.[55] Furthermore, the devaluation of feminine knowledge is reinforced if men are not incentivised to invent in traditionally female-dominated fields. Overall, the existing patent system serves to make starker the socialised understanding and dichotomisation of masculine and feminine knowledge, and to valorise the former over the latter.

3 Innovation

Patents are theorised as playing a role, not only in incentivising invention, but also ensuring that innovation can take place; that is, patents have a role in commercialisation and bringing a product or service to market.[56] Simply inventing something – no matter how inventive and potentially desirable – does not ensure market success. There is often a long and resource-intensive road between the steps of invention and successfully bringing something to market. This can mean that smaller or non-practising entities (such as universities or publicly funded research institutes) and start-ups cannot commercialise their inventions, as they have no manufacturing capability, existing customer-base, distribution network, or business acumen (including understanding business strategies, marketing, financial, tax and accounting systems, and basic commercial law).[57] An important aspect of the innovation phase is, thus, securing finance or external investment. Patents can play a pivotal role towards this, for the patentees themselves and also potential investors (whether they

54 Julie Smith and Nancy Folbre, "New Ways to Measure Economic Activity: Breastfeeding as an Economic Indicator" in Marian Sawer, Fiona Jenkins and Karen Downing (eds), *How Gender Can Transform the Social Sciences* Palgrave, 2020) 105; and "Breast Milk's Billion-dollar GDP Gap" (26 September 2018) *Newsroom* at www.newsroom.co.nz/@future-learning/2018/09/25/251486/breast-milks-billion-dollar-gdp-gap.

55 Gearhart-Serna (n 42) 380.

56 F Scott Kieff, "Property Rights and Property Rules for Commercializing Inventions" (2001) 85 *Minnesota Law Review* 697, 747–8; Menell (n 5) 146–7; Jessica Silbey, "Patent Variation: Discerning Diversity Among Patent Functions" (2013) 45 *Loyola University Chicago Law Journal* 441, 475; Sam Ricketson, Megan Richardon and Mark Davison, *Intellectual Property: Cases, Materials and Commentary* (LexisNexis Butterworths Australia, 2013) 705–7; Report of the President's Commission on the Patent System, "To Promote the Progress of… Useful Arts: In an Age of Exploding Technology" (1966) 2.

57 On small inventors, see James Bessen and Michael J Meurer, *Patent Failure: How Judges, Bureaucrats, and Lawyers Put Innovators at Risk* (Princeton University Press, 2008) 177–9.

be banks, venture capitalists, securities investors and even "friends and family").[58] Patents can play this role because of what they signal and also because of their nature as property. These two functions of patents are discussed in the following.

3.1 What gets signalled and who benefits from this?

Ideally, decisions are made with perfect information. Such situations are, however, rare (if at all existent). In the absence of perfect information, decision-makers use "signals" as a proxy to infer the information they require to make decisions. Michael Spence developed signal theory around hiring decisions, viewing such decisions as investments made with imperfect information, which must be supplemented by the signals that applicants give.[59] One can view the decision of whether or not to invest in or purchase an invention as similarly made under imperfect conditions, where signals will play an important role.

Given the intricate relationship between gender and behaviour, and the stereotypes that society builds around sex, it should come as no surprise that sex and gender have signal effects.[60] Gender role congruity theory dictates that behavioural signals will only work to one's benefit if they are congruous with one's gender (i.e. with societal expectations and stereotypes).[61] If signals are incongruent, they will be disregarded or interpreted negatively. This is because the interpreter might not be able to deal with the dissonance between the incongruence and their cognitive biases, which will widen any information asymmetry.

In the context of venture funding, the commercialisation process has been constructed as masculine (examined in Chapter 3).[62] The archetype of the entrepreneur, the start-up genius or the market-savvy scientist, is a man.[63] Most venture capitalists are male,[64] are used to dealing with male inventors and

58 Stuart JH Graham et al., "High Technology Entrepreneurs and the Patent System: Results of the 2008 Berkeley Patent Survey" (2009) 24(4) *Berkeley Technology Law Journal* 1255, 1303–9.

59 Michael Spence, "Job Market Signalling" (1973) 87(3) *The Quarterly Journal of Economics* 355; and Michael Spence, "Signaling in Retrospect and the Informational Structure of Markets" (2002) 92 *American Economic Review* 434. See also Brian L Connelly et al., "Signaling Theory: A Review and Assessment" (2011) 37(1) *Journal of Management* 39.

60 Malin Malmström, Jeaneth Johansson and Joakim Wincent, "Gender Stereotypes and Venture Support Decisions: How Governmental Venture Capitalists Socially Construct Entrepreneurs' Potential" (2017) 41(5) *Entrepreneurship Theory and Practice* 833, 852; and Jorge Guzman and Aleksandra Kacperczyk, "Gender Gap in Entrepreneurship" (2019) 48 *Research Policy* 1666, 1678.

61 Alice H Eagly and Steven J Karau, "Role Congruity Theory of Prejudice Towards Female Leaders" (2002) 109(3) *Psychological Review* 573; and Will Drover, Matthew S Wood and Andrew C Corbett, "Toward a Cognitive View of Signalling Theory: Individual Attention and Signal Set Interpretation" (2018) 55(2) *Journal of Management Studies* 209.

62 Rosser (n 19) 76.

63 Marovich (n 20) 144.

64 Paula E Stephan and Asmaa El-Ganainy, "The Entrepreneurial Puzzle: Explaining the Gender Gap" (2007) 32 *Journal of Technology Transfer* 475, 484.

associate market-worthy inventions with male inventors.[65] This means that it is masculine traits – such as leadership, determination and competitiveness – that signal that someone is worth investing in. However, studies show that gender role congruity means that exhibiting these traits predominantly benefits males.[66] Conversely, gender role incongruity can be disadvantageous and females may be punished for exhibiting masculine attributes.[67] That is, women are in a "lose lose situation". If they behave feminine, they will not be viewed as entrepreneurs and innovators and might encounter negative gender stereotypes.[68] However, if women exhibit masculine traits, this might also be to their detriment.

This is illustrated by evidence suggesting that men are better at "selling" their research than women – talking about it in grander terms and indicating broader implications, whereas women use smaller terms and focus on details.[69] Men are also more comfortable with selling their research and themselves.[70] In a similar vein, even when publication rates are similar between women and men, men are more likely to indicate that they have an invention of commercial potential.[71] This is because men are socialised to be self-promoting, assertive, forceful or confident. When men exhibit these masculine traits, they gain from gender congruity. In contrast, women are unlikely to gain from exhibiting these traits. Indeed, they possibly do not confidently sell their inventions and themselves (even if they observe their male colleagues successfully doing so), as gender role incongruity can result in penalties.[72] Men may be confident, but women should be demure.

There is some evidence that gender role congruity can benefit women if a venture is more socially orientated and funding is aimed at such ventures. This is because women may benefit from the gender stereotype that they are more

65 Rosser (n 19) 79.

66 Eagly and Karau (n 61); Kimberly A Eddleston et al., "Do You See What I See? Signaling Effects of Gender and Firm Characteristics on Financing Entrepreneurial Ventures" (2016) 40(3) *Entrepreneurship Theory and Practice* 489; and Malmström, Johansson and Wincent (n 60) 833.

67 Eagly and Karau (n 61); Madeline E Heilman, "Description and Prescription: How Gender Stereotypes Prevent Women's Ascent Up the Organizational Ladder" (2001) 57(4) *Journal of Social Issues* 657, 661; and Shu Wang, Romi Kher and Scott L Newbert, "What Signals Matter for Startups? It Depends: The Influence of Gender Role Congruity on Social Impact Accelerator Selection Decisions" (2020) 35(2) *Journal of Business Venturing*, https://doi.org/10.1016/j.jbusvent.2019.03.001.

68 Malin Malmström et al., "When Stereotypical Gender Notions See the Light of Day, Will They Burst? Venture Capitalists' Gender Constructions versus Venturing Performing Facts" (2018) 9 *Journal of Business Venturing Insights* 32.

69 Fiona Murray and Leigh Graham, "Buying Science and Selling Science: Gender Differences in the Market for Commercial Science" (2007) 16(4) *Industrial and Corporate Change* 657, 670–1.

70 Ibid. 678.

71 Jerry G Thursby and Marie C Thursby, "Gender Patterns of Research and Licensing Activity of Science and Engineering Faculty" (2005) 30 *Journal of Technology Transfer* 343.

72 Heilman (n 67) 661 and 666–7.

trustworthy, compassionate, community orientated and giving.[73] With respect to socially orientated projects and funding sources, one would think that males might face gender role incongruity. However, there is some evidence that men can benefit from incongruous signals (e.g. reflecting social signals) to obtain funding targeted at socially conscious projects.[74]

Another way to view this literature is that women need external signals to overcome the signals that their gender emits or fails to emit.[75] That is, to signal that they are potential and capable commercialisation partners, and/or they have something worthy of investing in. One external signal is one's title. Fiona Murray and Leigh Graham have referred to "signal shocks", where women were appointed to high profile administrative positions and subsequently experienced a rapid increase in invitations to collaborate in a commercial space.[76] Rather problematically, few women hold senior positions in STEM, whether in industry or academia.[77]

Patents are another source of external signal.[78] They communicate or evidence the potential of an invention – after all, the existence of a patent means that a patent office has deemed the invention to be new, non-obvious and as having utility or industrial application.[79] Because patents are property, they also signal appropriability.[80] That is, something that can be bought, sold and traded. Patents additionally signal that the patentee is competent, as they invented something able to be granted a patent.[81] Furthermore, they signal "industriousness and a well-

73 See e.g. Matthew Lee and Laura Huang, "Gender Bias, Social Impact Framing, and Evaluation of Entrepreneurial Ventures" (2018) 29(1) *Organization Science* 1; Jason Greenberg and Ethan Mollick, "Activist Choice Homophily and the Crowdfunding of Female Founders" (2017) 62(2) *Administrative Science Quarterly* 341; and Michael A Johnson, Regan M Stevenson and Chaim R Letwin, "A Woman's Place is in the… Startup! Crowdfunder Judgments, Implicit Bias, and the Stereotype Content Model" (2018) 33 *Journal of Business Venturing* 813.

74 Wang, Kher and Newbert (n 67).

75 Gry Agnete Alsos and Elsbet Lljunggren, "The Role of Gender in Entrepreneur-Investor Relationships: A Signaling Theory Approach" (2016) 41(4) *Enterpreneurship Theory and Practice* 567, 584–5.

76 Murray and Graham (n 69) 681.

77 Rosser (n 19) 78; and Astegiano, Sebasián-González and de Toledo Castanho (n 32) 7.

78 Existing literature on patents as signals for investors is predominantly about small companies or start-ups, which often do not have other observable measures of success. For such entities, the reputational gain and signal effects from having patents is vital for securing financing and improving liquidity. Hall and Harhoff (n 23) 552–3; Graham et al. (n 58) 1298–1302 and 1303–9.

79 Carolin Haeussler, Dietmar Harhoff and Elisabeth Mueller, "How Patenting Informs VC Investors – The Case of Biotechnology" (2014) 43 *Research Policy* 1286.

80 David B Audretsch, Werner Bönteb, Prashanth Mahagaonkar, "Financial Signaling by Innovative Nascent Ventures: The Relevance of Patents and Prototypes" (2012) 41 *Research Policy* 1407.

81 Dietmar Harhoff "The Role of Patents and Licenses in Securing External Finance for Innovation" (2009) 14(2) *EIB Papers*, 80–2; Hall and Harhoff (n 23) 542; Silbey, "Patent Variation" (n 56) 454–6.

See also Graham Dutfield and Uma Suthersanen, *Global Intellectual Property Law* (Edward Elgar, 2008) 51, who discuss the stakeholder analysis of intellectual

functioning organization" or "managerial sophistication" of a company.[82] For example, they reflect that the patentee or organisation had the business acumen to obtain a patent. There is evidence that venture capitalists look upon patents favourably when deciding whether to invest.[83] Yet, while women need the signal effect of patents more than men, the majority of patents name male inventors, which means that more males than females will be able to use patents to signal the quality of their inventions, or their competence, industriousness or managerial sophistication.

Even if females patented at the same rates as males, it is possible that they would not be able to use the signal as effectively. Because patents are something viewed as neutral (something to be traded) rather than behavioural, one could presume that there should not be any incongruity when women have and seek to exploit patents. However, evidence suggests that seemingly neutral signals benefit males more than females. For example, with respect to getting bank financing in the US, Kimberly Eddleston et al. showed that venture viability signals from firm age and past performance contributed positively to the amount of bank financing for males, but not females.[84]

Further exemplifying women's struggle to use the patent signal, women do not assign their patents to the same degree as men. The assignment of patents is a proxy for commercialisation, as it indicates that another person or entity is interested in the patented invention.[85] Patent assignment is only a weak proxy because many patents are automatically assigned to an inventor's employer (not reflecting commercialisation). Nonetheless, studies from the US show that patents for inventions with male primary inventors are significantly more likely to be assigned.[86] Patents with only female inventors are the least likely to be assigned.[87] Of patents that are

property and note that the three main stakeholders are the author/inventor, the producer/investor and the consumer.

82 Silbey, "Patent Variation" (n 56) 460.

83 E.g. Graham et al. (n 58) 1279–83; and Harhoff (n 81); and Pierre Nadeau, "Venture Capital Investment Selection: Do Patents Attract Investors?" (2010) 19 *Strategic Change* 325.

84 Eddleston et al. (n 66).

85 See e.g. B Zorina Khan, "'Not for Ornament': Patenting Activity by Nineteenth-Century Women Inventors" (2000) 31(2) *Journal of Interdisciplinary History* 159, 187, who used assignment contracts in late-nineteenth century United States to show that women with more than one patent were more likely to have assigned their patents. Khan suggested that this was likely because these women had a greater reputation, having been issued more than one patent.

86 Jessica Milli et al., "Equity in Innovation: Women Inventors and Patents" (2016) *Institute for Women's Policy Research*; and Jennifer Hunt et al., "Why Don't Women Patent?" (2012) *NBER Working Paper* No. 17888, 833–4, www.nber.org/papers/w17888. This true even for universities and hospitals; USPTO, "Progress and Potential: A Profile of Women Inventors on US Patents" (February 2019) Office of the Chief Economist, *IP Data Highlights* No. 2, 9.

87 Cook and Kongcharoen (n 17)

assigned, those stemming from male inventors are more likely to be maintained (renewed) than those from female inventors.[88]

As noted in Chapter 1, when women are named as inventors on patents, this is predominantly together with male inventors. Very few patents name solely female inventors. Heather Sarsons has shown that, when women co-author with men and the actual individuals' contributions are unclear, women receive less credit.[89] Presuming the same applies for patents, the implication is that – even when females patent – the majority of the time, they will neither receive the same reputational gains as their male co-inventors, nor will they benefit from the same degree of signal effect.

The consequence of women having fewer patents and not being able to use their signal effect as successfully as men is that fewer females will be able to commercialise their inventions, or launch, build or sell-off start-ups, as they will struggle to get investors. This is supported by data that indeed shows that women are less likely to form start-ups and they receive less funding when they do.[90] This is not only concerning because women are less likely to have funding to commercialise, but is also detrimental for female entrepreneurs because venture capitalists offer valuable coaching as well as capital.[91]

The impact of lower patenting rates for females than males reaches into career progression. There is a certain level of prestige that comes with being an "inventor" and owning a patent, which can facilitate career advancement.[92] As noted by Annette Kahler, "[p]rolific inventors, whose credentials are more favorable due to patent-inventor status, find it easier to obtain competitive positions in the job market in their field of invention".[93] Because patented inventions are by definition novel and inventive, they signal that their inventors are at the forefront of their field. Patents are also markers of success the way that publications are. Women having fewer patents means they are not seen as leaders in their field.[94] Thus, the patenting gap can inhibit the upward mobility of women,[95] and women continue to be unequal participants in the development of science and technology.[96] One could view this as discriminating

88 Jensen, Kovács and Sorenson (n 34) 308.
89 Heather Sarsons, "Recognition for Group Work: Gender Differences in Academia" (2017) 107(5) *American Economic Review: Papers & Procedures* 141.
90 Guzman and Kacperczyk (n 60); Alicia M Robb and Susan Coleman, "Sources of Financing for New Technology Firms: A Comparison by Gender" (July 2009) The Ewing Marion Kauffman Foundation.
91 Joel AC Baum and Brian S Silverman, "Picking Winners or Building Them? Alliance, Intellectual, and Human Capital as Selection Criteria in Venture Financing and Performance of Biotechnology Startups" (2004) 19 *Journal of Business Venturing* 411.
92 Kahler (n 48) 797.
93 Ibid.
94 Rosser (n 19) 65.
95 Ibid.; and Yanisky-Ravid (n 19) 874.
96 Rosser (n 19) 65.

against females because they invent in fields that do not produce patent-eligible subject matter, despite often creating welfare-promoting inventions.[97]

The impacts of fewer females having patents with which to signal can correspondingly be observed in academia, where universities are increasingly trying to get a piece of the commercialisation pie. That is, being a named inventor on a patent can also positively affect an academic's professional visibility and reputation, and thereby his/her career progression.[98] If an academic patents and commercialises, he/she might gain access to better equipment, become more attractive as a postgraduate supervisor and collaborator.[99] This precipitates more success. Furthermore, as in industry, academics can use patents as bargaining chips to progress their careers with their employers or prospective employers.[100] If female academics patent less, they do not get these benefits, which negatively impacts their careers.[101]

Continuing within the academic setting, it appears that collaborating with industry increases the chances that women will patent.[102] There is a "chicken-and-the-egg" situation: women need patents to signal to industry their presence and ability, inventions and the commercial potential thereof, yet they are less likely to have patents without that collaboration in the first place. They do not have those collaborations because women do not have the same opportunities as men to form industry (business and financial) networks.[103] Women generally do not have the same networking opportunities provided to them in college or university, which is partly attributable to the exclusion of women from the "Old Boys' Club" (see Chapter 3). Female academics typically have smaller networks because they have fewer graduate and postdoctoral students, receive fewer opportunities to consult with industry or government, serve less frequently on science advisory boards and interact less with industry.[104]

97 Yanisky-Ravid (n 19) 873.
98 Kahler (n 48) 797. Whether patents are a good measure of academic prowess is another matter; see Immaculada de Melo-Martín, "Patenting and the Gender Gap: Should Women Be Encouraged to Patent More?" (2013) 19 *Science and Engineering Ethics* 491, 495–7. Citing a strong body of literature, de Melo-Martín also questions whether patents are in fact good for society and, thus, perhaps we should not be encouraging female academics to patent. However, any problems created by academic patenting should be used to argue against academic patenting. To raise such arguments with respect to the gender patenting gap ignores the social and financial inequities that arise when it is predominantly males who are named as inventors on patents.
99 Bunker Whittington and Smith-Doerr (n 20) 366–7. See also Kahler (n 48) 797; Erin Leahey and Amelia Blume, "Elucidating the Process: Why Women Patent Less than Men" in Albert N Link (ed.), *Gender and Entrepreneurial Activity* (Edward Elgar, 2017) 151, 152; Yanisky-Ravid (n 19) 859; and Rosser (n 19) 71.
100 Kahler (n 48) 797.
101 Ibid.
102 Yu Meng, "Collaboration Patterns and Patenting: Exploring Gender Distinctions" (2016) 45 *Research Policy* 56.
103 See e.g. Marovich (n 20); and Murray and Graham (n 69).
104 Rosser (n 19) 76 and 78; Waverly L Ding, Fiona Murray and Toby E Stuart, "Gender Differences in Patenting in the Academic Life Sciences" (2006) 313 *Science* 665, 666; and Kahler (n 48) 781.

The issue is clearly cyclical. Women struggle to patent because they do not collaborate with industry as much as men do. This continues to be the case because exclusion from the commercial space means that women neither gain experience in it nor develop networks,[105] and they patent less and then cannot use patents to signal their inventive and business capabilities. The cycle is potentially made stronger by the fact that women generally act as primary caregivers of their children. The fact that motherhood might divert women's time and resources could negatively affect industry's perception of women as potential collaborators.[106]

3.1 What gets commercialised?

Having exclusive rights can mean that a patent owner can charge supra-competitive (possibly even monopolistic) prices for their products and services. Patents can also be sold and licensed, offering income streams. The ability to monetise patents can function as an incentive to invest in innovation and bring a product to market. Utilitarian theory states that commercialisation would not be undertaken in the absence of patents.[107] Companies will often only invest in setting up manufacturing processes, hiring necessary staff and developing know-how to formulate marketable forms of the invention, for example, if they have the security of a patent, which offers a certain degree of exclusivity and promise of low market competition.[108]

That patents are physical documents that describe the invention also helps, as investors have something tangible that allows them to understand something that is otherwise intellectual and potentially inaccessible.[109] The fact that patents are a form of property is also important, as property is something well defined to contract around.[110] It allows for the division and transfer of rights, thereby facilitating transactions.[111] This is particularly important with patents

105 Murray and Graham (n 69) 676–7.

106 Kjersten Bunker Whittington, "Mothers of Invention? Gender, Motherhood, and New Dimensions of Productivity in the Science Profession" (2011) 38(3) *Work and Organisations* 417, 448.

107 Sterckx (n 45) 195; and Kieff (n 56) 726.

108 Harhoff (n 81) 74–95.

109 Silbey, "Patent Variation" (n 56) 459.

110 Kieff (n 56) 732–36; and Richard A Posner, "Intellectual Property: The Law and Economics Approach" (2005) 19(2) *Journal of Economic Perspectives* 57, 68.

111 Bessen and Meurer (n 57) 31 and 35–6; and Edmund W Kitch, "Elementary and Persistent Errors in the Economic Analysis of Intellectual Property" (2000) *53 Vanderbilt Law Review* 1727, 1740.

The ability of property to structure transactions forms the basis of the "prospect theory", which states that we should allow for early, broad patents in order to ensure coordinated development of a technology and minimise duplication of research; see Edmund W Kitch, "The Nature and Function of the Patent System" (1977) 20(2) *Journal of Law and Economics* 265. The prospect theory has been challenged; Robert P. Merges and Richard R Nelson, "On the Complex Economics of Patent Scope" (1990) 90 *Columbia Law Review* 839; Donald G McFetridge and

that pertain to complementary knowledge and that are associated with "sticky" knowledge (sticky to a particular inventor or group of inventors), as the presence of patents may promote coordination between different patentees to ensure that innovation can take place.[112] Patents might do so through signalling to others that the information or knowledge exists and by structuring interactions between different entities.[113] Patents can, thus, enable technology transfer.[114] Furthermore, as property, patents can be securitised and act as security for debt.

If patent law is gendered in favour of masculine forms and fields of invention, these are more likely to have the structural support offered by patent law (and property law) to secure financing and achieve commercialisation. Masculine forms of inventions are then more likely to go through the entire process of innovation and result in a marketed product or service. This means that technologies that are feminine forms and fields of invention – for the home, caregiving, education, psychology and social work, for example – are less likely to be developed into marketable form. This is negative because inventions in these fields often have great social and welfare value.[115]

Furthermore, if inventions created by women and/or for women are not incentivised, disseminated and commercialised, this harms women.[116] This is exacerbated by the fact that what is commercialised typically reflects market demand. If females generally have lower financial means and, thus, less buying power, fewer inventions will be created for them, even if the patent system were truly gender neutral. Therefore, masculine inventions will continue to

Douglas A Smith, "Patents, Prospects, and Economic Surplus" (1980) 23 *Journal of Law and Economics* 197. See also John F Duffy, "Rethinking the Prospect Theory of Patents" (2004) 71 *University of Chicago Law Review* 439.

For a critique on centring economic analysis on property's function of facilitating contractual transfer, see Thomas W Merrill and Henry E Smith, "What Happened to Property in Law and Economics?" (2001) 111 *Yale Law Journal* 357, 360–6. See also Lemley (n 24) 748, who suggests that licenses for patents do not facilitate the ongoing exchange of technological knowledge or know-how, but are predominantly cross-licences.

112 Julien Pénin and Jean-Pierre Wack, "Research Tool Patents and Free-Libre Biotechnology: A Suggested Unified Framework" (2008) 37 *Research Policy* 1909, 1917–18.

113 Silbey, "Patent Variation" (n 56) 466–7. There is, of course, a fine line between patents acting as a means of signalling and coordination, on the one hand, and patents hindering cooperation and the downstream application of the different pieces of information, on the other hand (at 470).

114 Christine Godt has gone as far as to say that patents are no longer about an incentive or reward for innovation or the dissemination of information, but the private organisation of information (technology transfer via commodification) and the protection of the production process rather than the product itself. Christine Godt, *Eigentum an Information* (Mohr Siebeck, 2007), 262, 402–5 and 449.

115 Rosser (n 19) 70.

116 See Josh Feng and Xavier Jaravel, "Innovating for People Like Me: Evidence from Female-Founded Consumer Packaged Goods Startups" (2019), https://ssrn.com/abstract=3383703 or http://dx.doi.org/10.2139/ssrn.3383703; and Caroline Criado Perez, *Invisible Women: Exposing Data Bias in a World Designed for Men* (Vintage Publishing, 2020); and Leslie Kern, *Feminist City* (Verso, 2020).

shape the world and social development, and men will continue to have stronger commercial networks.[117]

If masculine inventions are more likely to hit the market, this reinforces the idea that masculine information and knowledge have more value (whether financial or social) than feminine ways of knowing and fields traditionally dominated by females. Yet, Kjersten Bunker Whittington and Laurel Smith-Doerr have shown that female-owned patents have an equal or higher degree of applicability and quality (based on citation rates and originality) as male-owned patents.[118] They found this to be consistent across generational cohorts across two decades, and stronger in academia.[119] Bunker Whittington and Smith-Doerr suggest that this means that science and society are losing out with the current patent system.[120]

Of course, there could be a variety of reasons why female patents are of equal or higher quality. For example, it could be because women must feel more certain of the quality of their inventions before they seek patents. As discussed above, women are socialised to be less confident and less assertive than men. It is nevertheless possible to state that science and society are losing out because there is likely much more knowledge that women do not seek patents for. This knowledge is, in turn, not disseminated through patent documents and not brought to market. Furthermore, entities (and possibly even states and nations) are potentially missing the opportunity to gain the competitive advantage that feminine inventions might produce.[121] Put another way, the knowledge-based economy is being deprived of a significant resource.[122]

4 Power begets power

> Th[e] hegemonic story [of capitalistic creation and innovation] goes like this: we work hard to make something valuable, and law – like the laws of patents, copyrights, and so on – gives us a way to prevent someone from taking it away without paying. *In this story of law and capital, equality is achieved when law treats alike all who create and innovate according to the same standards, and freedom is realized by making and selling valuable things that enable us to move between socioeconomic classes.* Notice how in this story of capitalism, law and the state's authority to protect it assume a precarity of power and self-determination in the very activity of producing art and science. We require the state to protect that which we make and value. This generates a discursive circularity and produces further insecurity in the person's relationship to the state by demanding more laws that facilitate more individual control, ownership, and thus also division.[123]

117 Stanley (n 49) 200.

118 Bunker Whittington and Smith-Doerr (n 20) 365. See also Ding, Murray and Stuart (n 104) 666, who find that there is no difference in quality of scholarship between males and females.

119 Bunker Whittington and Smith-Doerr (n 20) 365.

120 Ibid. 367.

121 Ibid.; and Rosser (n 19) 65.

122 USPTO (n 86) 3.

123 Jessica Silbey, "Intellectual Property Harms: A Paradigm for the Twenty-First Century" (2019) 99 *Boston University Law Review* 2447, 2455 (emphasis added).

I would take this quote from Jessica Silbey a step further and say that, when the law does not treat alike all who create and innovate according to *equitable* (ungendered and unracialised) standards, freedom is not realised equally and consequently neither is movement between socio-economic classes. Patent law protects according to masculine standards. This results in there being more men whose freedom is realised making and selling valuable things and who are able to move between socio-economic classes.

Chapters 2, 3 and 4 of this book have shown how patent law protects masculine knowledge, embodied in STEM. This forces females into this masculine understanding of STEM if they wish to patent and to gain economic and political power. Yet, when they enter STEM spaces, they are often marginalised and ostracised. As a result, STEM sees a high attrition rate of females. As a result of the "women in STEM" rhetoric, women feel like they are failures when they do not succeed in STEM, despite all the biases running against them. Moreover, women leaving STEM perpetuates: (1) the construction of women as non-scientists or inventors; and (2) that men are scientists and inventors. That men in STEM patent then preserves the stereotype that it is the masculine and STEM that is valuable, and it is men who are entrepreneurs. Furthermore, it is men who are rewarded financially and reputationally, and who are dictating the future direction of technology through dissemination of knowledge and commercialisation of products and services. In this book, I have focused on the patent system. However, there are many legal systems that have similar effects. For example, tax credits for research and development where what qualifies for the tax benefit conforms to masculine constructions of technology. This is illustrated in Figure 4.1.

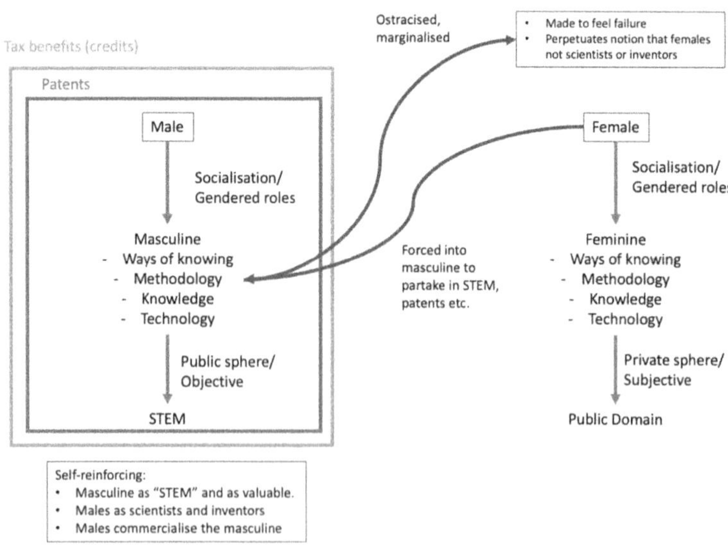

Figure 4.1 The gendered knowledge system created by patent law

One might argue that, if women behave differently than men, as underlies much of the discussion in Chapters 2, 3 and 4, and their invention generally differ from those of men, then perhaps there is a justification for the knowledge governance system treating women and the feminine differently from men and the masculine. There are two things to remember here. First, gendered behaviour is socialised. It is not inherent and a gendered knowledge governance system perpetuates gender normative roles to the detriment of women. It is also restricting on males, who must also behave a certain way to fit into society as "real men". Second, equity does not necessarily require that groups must be identical in order to have equal treatment. As Joan Scott has noted, the political notion of equality is based on difference – there would be no need to demand equal treatment if all were identical.[124] In other words, simply that women empirically behave differently from men is not grounds to treat their inventions differently.

The knee-jerk reaction to the patent-created knowledge governance system favouring the masculine would be to expand patentability to include the feminine. As Silbey notes in the quote beginning this section, the story of capitalism dictates that those feeling insecure will demand more protection from the state. However, as discussed in Chapter 5, this would not be ideal. The patent system is flawed beyond it being gendered. After explaining why it is that the "master's tools will never dismantle the master's house"[125] in Chapter 5, I discuss alternative ways of viewing knowledge in Chapter 6, before attempting to develop a more equitable and egalitarian knowledge governance system in Chapter 7.

124 Joan W Scott, "Deconstructing Equality-versus-Difference: Or, the Uses of Post-structuralist Theory for Feminism" (1988) 14(1) *Feminist Studies* 33.

125 Audre Lorde, "The Master's Tools Will Never Dismantle the Master's House" (1979) in Audre Lorde (ed.), *Sister Outsider: Essays and Speeches* (Crossing Press, 2007) 110.

5 Deconstructing the lore

> The purportedly value-free aspects of standard philosophies of science and technology are complicitous with … a policy [that ensures some give so that others can take]. These make plausible to development designers Western imperial practices that actually increase the resources accessible to the "investing classes" in the North and their allies in the South, while decreasing them for the great majority of the world's citizens already the most economically and politically vulnerable.[1]

1 Introduction

Chapter 1 of this book outlined the ways in which patenting is gendered. Chapter 2 explained how this is in part due to the gender biases engrained in patent law itself. In particular, it showed how patentability reflects multiple gendered binaries that favour the masculine over the feminine. This was followed by an exposition into the knowledge governance system that patent law and patenting support and perpetuate. Chapter 3 showed how women are set up to fail. It highlighted how the "women in science, technology, engineering and mathematics (STEM)" rhetoric is dangerous, as it blames women when they do not succeed, despite the odds stacked against them, and absolves men and society from any responsibility. Chapter 4 analysed the negative consequences of gendered patent law and patenting on wealth distribution, reputational gain and the kinds of inventions that are created and commercialised, as well as who determines the future of knowledge development.

The instinctive reaction to Chapters 1–4 is to try to de-gender patent law. However, this might require the expansion of patentability. Such expansions are often met with counterarguments that we should be careful to not encroach too much upon the public domain. Courts have reasoned that discoveries, natural products and laws, and abstract methods are not patentable because they are "fundamental" or "upstream" technologies, which are necessary to create "downstream"

1 Sandra Harding, "A Socially Relevant Philosophy of Science" (2004) 19(1) *Hypatia* 25, 34.

DOI: 10.4324/9781003128502-6

technologies. A classic example would be $e = mc^2$. The law would deem this to be an unpatentable upstream natural law, which was merely "discovered" by mankind and which has multiple downstream applications. Those downstream applications would be patentable.

This chapter deconstructs the mythology around the "public domain" and its binary relationship with the propertised.[2] It argues that the public domain/privatised and upstream/downstream distinctions are further binaries that serve to reinforce extant hegemonic power. As suggested in the quote at the beginning of this chapter, the public domain is not "value free", but is used to ensure that those in power have access to resources they require. Thus, public domain arguments embedded within the patent law framework are not determinant of whether the knowledge governance system should protect the feminine and the non-Western. Put another way, if inventors and scientists under the existing knowledge governance system rely on feminine and non-Western knowledge as a free resources, they will of course argue against removing the feminine and non-Western from the public domain. They have a vested interest, making their arguments moot.

That said, the point is not that patents should protect every type of knowledge. Invention and innovation are cumulative, contingent and communal. This means that future invention and innovation would be hindered by 20 years of patent protection for all kinds of knowledge. However, this does not mean that the public domain/propertised dichotomy is justifiable. Instead, that patent protection can hinder follow-on invention highlights that patents and their exclusive rights create a poor knowledge governance system. This is a system that does not deal well with cumulative, contingent and communal creation.

Finally, patent law is by no means otherwise a perfect knowledge governance system. The final part of this chapter outlines how patents are otherwise problematic. For example, that they can inhibit access to inventions, have negative wealth distribution effects and might not fulfil their theorised functions.

2 Patent law's binary partner

2.1 A not so egalitarian concept

The public domain has multiple possible meanings, but generally includes knowledge no longer protected by intellectual property or that cannot constitute intellectual property.[3] It is often framed as the negative of the

2 This chapter updates and expands upon content from Jessica C Lai, "Patents, Knowledge Governance and Gender" (2020) 42(1) *European Intellectual Property Review* 623.

3 Though what exactly this entails is by no means agreed upon. There are two other focal points, being the freedom to use the knowledge and the accessibility thereof; see Pamela Samuelson, "Enriching Discourse on Public Domains" (2006) 55 *Duke Law Journal* 783, 816.

propertised.[4] The need for a "healthy" public domain is commonly raised to argue against the expansion of intellectual property rights.[5] Because invention is cumulative, innovation can be hindered by too much propertisation. The argument is that there must be sufficient resources in the public domain for it to be "viable" for invention to take place. However, as discussed in the following, these arguments regarding a "healthy" public domain appear to stand only against the disempowered. Consequently, it is the disempowered who give to the public domain, whereupon the empowered are in the position to take from it.

Proponents of the public domain often frame their arguments around the presumption that the public domain has hard and fast boundaries. These boundaries act to block the trend of propertisation. However, this cannot be correct because the public domain is the negative of property. It is what property leaves behind. It is not legally defined and protected. It has no positive constitution. As the negative of property, the public domain is prone to change. As the bounds of intellectual property alter, typically in expansive fashion, the public domain also alters in a reflectively contractive manner.

Another way to view this is that the boundaries of the public domain are just as much a matter of politics and policy as the scope of patentability. This is clear when we compare the way that legislators have reacted to the interests of the pharmaceutical, biotech and agritech industries compared to the interests of Indigenous peoples. Patent protection of the inventions from the pharmaceutical, biotech and agritech industries has generally expanded since the inception of patent law. For example, while patents for chemical products were once not patentable, they now are. Similarly, while most jurisdictions have historically not allowed patents for plant varieties,[6] this has shifted with advances in biotechnology.[7] In contradistinction, Indigenous peoples have been arguing for protection of their knowledge for decades with very few gains. The reasons given are either that protecting Indigenous knowledge would deprive the

4 The public domain is more correctly public domains, in part because there is no agreed upon meaning; James Boyle, "The Second Enclosure Movement and the Construction of the Public Domain" (2003) 66 *Law and Contemporary Problems* 33; Samuelson, "Enriching Discourse on Public Domains" (n 4) 786–813, who identifies 13 different public domains; and Pamela Samuelson, "Challenges in Mapping the Public Domain" in Lucie Guibault and P Bernt Hugenholtz (eds), *The Future of the Public Domain: Identifying the Commons in Information Law* (Kluwer Law International, 2006) 7.

5 See e.g. Boyle's "call to arms"; (n 4) 69–74.

6 Many jurisdictions protect plant varieties through *sui generis* rights. The United States has plant patents, but this is because they do not have plant variety or breeder rights.

7 E.g. *Pepper (follow-up to Tomatoes II and Broccoli II)* (2020) G 0003/19 EPO Boards of Appeal; *Method for Breeding Tomatoes Having Reduced Water Content and Product of the Method* (2015) G 0002/12 EPO Boards of Appeal; and *Method for Selective Increase of the Anticarcinogenic Glucosinolates in Brassica Species* (2015) G 0002/13 EPO Boards of Appeal.

public domain of fundamental (non-technical) knowledge,[8] or, in any case, it is too late as Indigenous knowledge is already in the public domain.[9]

Analogously, as discussed in Chapter 2, feminine knowledge is habitually relegated to the public domain. This is by defining it as constituting mere information, natural laws and natural products, or casting it as non-industrial. Feminine knowledge is then free to be filtered through masculine modes of invention, embodied in masculine technologies and patented. The public domain is gendered because it is the negative of gendered patent law. This can equally be said of Indigenous knowledge.

That the knowledge of the marginalised and disempowered is categorised as public domain, allowing it to be taken and propertised by the empowered, is exemplified in the imagery of the upstream/downstream binary. It is striking that feminine and Indigenous knowledge conveniently falls into the "upstream", while the masculine is predominantly categorised as "downstream". The latter is defined as having more utility and industrial application.[10] While the stream analogy might be apt for describing the flow of knowledge, it

8 See, e.g. Michael F Brown, "Culture, Property, and Peoplehood: A Comment on Carpenter, Katyal, and Riley's 'In Defense of Property'" (2010) 17 *International Journal of Cultural Property* 569. See also Moana Jackson, "The Property of the Māori Intellect: A Review of *The Politics of Māori Image and Design*" (2003) 7(1) *He Pukenga Kōrero* 32, 32; and Alexandra Xanthaki, *Indigenous Rights and United Nations Standards: Self-Determination, Culture and Land* (Cambridge University Press, 2007) 217–19. Indeed, there appears to be an automatic assumption that Indigenous knowledge is inherently in the public domain, as noted by Brigitte Vézina, "Are They In or Are They Out? Traditional Cultural Expressions and the Public Domain – Implications for Trade" in Christoph B Graber, Karolina Kuprecht and Jessica C Lai (eds), *International Trade in Indigenous Cultural Heritage: Legal and Policy Issues* (Edward Elgar, 2012) 196, 198–9; WIPO, Intergovernmental Committee on Intellectual Property and Genetic Resources, Traditional Knowledge and Folklore, Secretariat "Note on the Meanings of the Term 'Public Domain' in the Intellectual Property System with Special Reference to the Protection of Traditional Knowledge and Traditional Cultural Expressions/Expressions of Folklore" (2010) WIPO Doc. WIPO/GRTKF/IC/17/INF/8, [5]; Susy Frankel, *Intellectual Property in New Zealand* (2nd edn, LexisNexis Butterworths, 2011) 116; and Mariaan de Beer, "Protecting Echoes of the Past: Intellectual Property and Expressions of Culture" (20016) 12 *Canterbury Law Review* 94, 107.

9 Kristen A Carpenter, Sonia Katyal and Angela Riley, "Clarifying Cultural Property" (2010) 17 *International Journal of Cultural Property* 581, 590; and Graham Dutfield, "The Public and Private Domains" (2000) 21(3) *Science Communication* 274, 284. Charlotte Hess and Elinor Ostrom note that this is due to the confusion of common-property regimes as open-access regimes; "Ideas, Artifacts, and Facilities: Information as a Common-Pool Resource" (2003) *Law and Contemporary Problems* 111, 122–3.

10 Historically in the US, inventions had to be for the end-use (consumer) market rather than directed at researchers in order to have "utility"; *Brenner v Manson* (1966) 383 US 519; and Graeme B Dinwoodie and Rochelle Cooper Dreyfuss, "Patenting Science: Protecting the Domain of Accessible Knowledge" in Lucie Guibault and P Bernt Hugenholtz (eds), *The Future of the Public Domain: Identifying the Commons in Information Law* (Kluwer Law, 2006) 192, 200–1.

does not take into account the gendered nature of knowledge creation. It does nothing to help us understand why women are defined as creating upstream and men downstream. Moreover, the upstream/downstream binary reflects power and resource distribution. It usually takes more resources to create downstream. For example, it takes fewer resources to identify traits in plants and to crossbreed plants for those traits, than it does to genetically modify those plants to have those traits. Having fewer resources, including less education, women potentially get stuck upstream. This leads to women continuously giving to the stream and only the Western and masculine being able to take downstream. Furthermore, the binary is silent on women's negative experiences when they operate downstream.

Public domain arguments have rather patronisingly been used to deny Indigenous people protection of their intellectual knowledge on the basis that they, too, need a "healthy" public domain.[11] This disregards the fact that Indigenous people have been creating and continue to create, regardless of Western notions of the public domain. Moreover, it ignores the fact that not everyone has equal access to the public domain.

As the negative of the propertised, framed as that which must stay free so that innovation is not hindered, the public domain is part of the mythology of intellectual property.[12] This means that the public domain is romanticised much like the genius inventor (see Chapter 3). The public domain is mapped as an egalitarian space – one that everyone can enter, take from, build upon and perhaps propertise. This romance leads to the public domain discourse often being universalistic, presuming that the call to protect the public domain is on behalf of everyone. However, this universalism reflects libertarian idealism, making it naïve and disconnected from lived reality.[13] As discussed in Chapter 2 and this chapter, the feminine and non-Western is disproportionately sacrificed into the public domain. It is subsequently Western men who predominantly access the public domain and propertise what they find. After all, "materials and resources in the public sphere are not open to women in the same way as men",[14] nor to the colonised in the same way as the colonisers.[15]

11 Brad Sherman and Leanne Wiseman, "Towards an Indigenous Public Domain?" in Lucie Guibault and P Bernt Hugenholtz (eds), *The Future of the Public Domain: Identifying the Commons in Information Law* (Kluwer Law International, 2006) 260, 265–7.

12 Jessica Litman, "The Public Domain" (1990) 39(4) *Emory Law Journal* 965, who, with respect to copyright, discusses the pretence of "originality" and how it only works with the legal fiction of the public domain.

13 Kathy Bowrey and Jane Anderson, "The Politics of Global Information Sharing: Whose Cultural Agendas are Being Advanced?" (2009) 18(4) *Social & Legal Studies* 479.

14 Laura A Foster, "Situating Feminism, Patent Law, and the Public Domain" (2011) 20 *Columbia Journal of Gender & Law* 262, 318.

15 Bowrey and Anderson (n 13) 480, stated, "The whole notion of 'the public' in intellectual property presumes a notion of inclusion and representativeness that is at odds with Indigenous experiences within colonial contexts. Indigenous people and 'the public' should not be assumed to share a common interest."

And not everyone has the prerequisites necessary to take the knowledge and turn it into a patentable invention (namely, masculine technology).

Beyond gender, one's ability to exploit the public domain hinges on one's knowledge of and competence in how to do so. It is also contingent upon one's wealth, power and access to necessary infrastructure. In other words, existing privilege matters.[16] This is dependent on race, ethnicity, education and class, as well as gender. In this vein, Anupan Chander and Madhavi Sunder have argued that the public domain is employed as a further means to disadvantage and subordinate disempowered groups. Romantic notions of the public domain cause one to "[turn] a blind eye to the fact that for centuries the public domain has been a source for exploiting the labor and bodies of the disempowered – namely people of color, the poor, women, and people from the global South".[17] Categorised as not being novel, inventive or technical, and thus in the public domain, certain knowledge (the feminine and Indigenous knowledge) is devalued. In the public domain, this knowledge is free for use and propertisation through Western masculine science, which turns it into something that the law places value upon.[18] Therefore, the public domain has wealth distributional effects, just as property does, and the system functions to the systemic advantage of those with the resources and knowledge to exploit it.[19] In Chander and Sunder's words, the "commons … is not always kind to commoners".[20]

Yet, because the public domain is romanticised, its socio-political underpinnings and consequential distributive effects, benefitting those in power, remain opaque.[21] Paralleling the importance of showing that patent law is not neutral and objective, but is gendered and racialised, we need to tear down the veil that frames the public domain and shine a light on the constructs that underlie the romance. In the words of Carys Craig, "[a]s with any legal concept – and just like 'intellectual property' – the 'public domain' can work to

16 Jessica Silbey, "Intellectual Property Harms: A Paradigm for the Twenty-First Century" (2019) 99 *Boston University Law Review* 2447, 2462–3.

17 Anupan Chander and Madhavi Sunder, "The Romance of the Public Domain" (2004) 92 *California Law Review* 1331, 1335. See also Madhavi Sunder, "The Invention of Traditional Knowledge" (2007) 70 *Law and Contemporary Problems* 97.

18 Boatema Boetang, "Walking the Traditional-Modernity Tightrope: Gender Contradictions in Textile Production and Intellectual Property Law in Ghana" (2007) 15 *American University Journal of Gender, Society and Law* 341, 349, notes that categorising Indigenous knowledge as "traditional" feminises it "in its encounter with masculinized modernity". See also Sherman and Wiseman (n 11).

19 Chander and Sunder (n 17) 1337.

20 Ibid., 1338.

21 Eli M Salzberger, "Economic Analysis of the Public Domain" in Lucie Guibault and P Bernt Hugenholtz (eds), *The Future of the Public Domain: Identifying the Commons in Information Law* (Kluwer Law International, 2006) 27, 52–4, who notes that, if we are concerned about large corporations homogenising our cultural offerings, then we should equally be concerned that the public domain will be captured by the same forces.

suppress and to oppress, rationalizing as legal necessities outcomes that in fact reflect and perpetuate established inequalities on a global scale".[22] Thus, Kathy Bowrey and Jane Anderson stated that we need to ask "who benefits from greater access and whose cultural agendas are being advanced through this politics?"[23]

In essence, the public domain is a capital asset for those who are endowed with the resources to access and exploit it. This is chiefly the Western male of a certain class, often embodied by their institutions – STEM companies and research institutes. Viewed in this light, the public domain is not so much a *public* domain as a *private* domain shared by those with sufficient resources. This tends to be those who already have intellectual property. This is unsurprising, as it is Western males who have defined what constitutes a patentable invention. This includes delimiting what constitutes the public domain, which becomes their resource to use, develop and propertise. Wealth and power beget wealth and power.[24] The disempowered stay disempowered.

Overall, public domain arguments only stand against the disempowered. It is women and non-Western communities who have had to disproportionately give their knowledge to the public domain. This knowledge is then free to be taken and propertised, when filtered through Western masculine modes of invention, by men, who have the position and resources to exploit the public domain. Hence, while it is undoubtedly correct that our knowledge governance system must allow for cumulative invention, it is also undoubtedly true that the public domain is not a neutral, egalitarian and a-political space. This means that it should not be possible to simply quash claims for protection in an ungendered and unracialised manner based on the need for a healthy public domain. Instead, we need to look at the knowledge governance system as a whole and address how it is that we can best regulate knowledge and its production, whilst recognising the multiplicity of kinds of knowledge and ways of knowing.

2.2 Collapsing more binaries

The foregoing discussed two related binaries, the public domain/propertised and the upstream/downstream. The following explains how these binaries, like most binaries, are social constructs.

The stream analogy for invention and innovation has value in visual simplicity. However, in practice, knowledge and inventions are often both up- and

22 Carys J Craig, "Critical Copyright law and the Politics of 'IP'" in Emilio Chritodoulidis, Ruth Dukes, Marco Goldini (eds), *Research Handbook on Critical Legal Theory* (Edward Elgar, 2019) 301, 315.

23 Bowrey and Anderson (n 13) 481.

24 Dan L Burk, "Feminism and Dualism in Intellectual Property" (2007) 15(2) *American University Journal of Gender, Social Policy & the Law* 195, 202. See also Ruth Okediji, "Traditional Knowledge and the Public Domain" (2018) CIGI Papers No. 176, 15, who notes that "asserting the public domain appears to be principally about protecting *existing* beneficiaries of the IP system".

downstream.[25] For instance, an algorithm might have an immediate application in a piece of software. That same algorithm might be necessary to develop other programs. Yet another example, a genetic sequence can have an immediate commercial use in a diagnostic method but might also be necessary for future biotechnology research or in a medical treatment. The same is true for research tools, which are sold as end-products (albeit to researchers rather than the general consumer), but which are then used for further creation. Perhaps a simpler example would be the invention of a hand tool, such as a new kind of wrench used by everyday consumers. What if such a consumer were to use that wrench and invent a new kind of machine? Is that wrench then an upstream technology? Where do we, and indeed can we, draw the line between the upstream and downstream? We cannot. The public domain/propertised binary is also not clear cut. This is reflected in the tension between arguments that too much property is bad for invention, on the one side, and that public domain arguments cannot be universalistic, on the other side. In a sense, both sets of arguments are correct, dependent on the context and perspective. Furthermore, that there are so many different understandings of the public domain points to the artificial nature of the public domain/propertised binary. Pamela Samuelson reviewed literature on the public domain in an attempt to identify and categorise its various definitions. Samuelson concluded that the multiple understandings do not reflect that information resources are either intellectual property protected or in the public domain, as "these concepts are not binary opposites, but rather as points along a continuum".[26] The point along the continuum that any law draws a line to demarcate the public and the private is a matter of policy.[27] Moreover, as discussed above, it is a reflection of power.

Addressing the interwoven relationship between the public domain and the propertised, Carol Rose discussed *res publicae*, which she defined as "things belonging to the public and open to the public by operation of law".[28] She noted that *res publicae* is "by no means antagonistic to private property", rather the two function together.[29] Access to certain public goods would not make sense without private property – for example, access to trade routes only matters if there is something to trade.[30] Similarly, one can only speak of a move to

25 Rochelle Dreyfuss, "Protecting the Public Domain of Science: Has the Time for an Experimental Use Defense Arrived?" (2004) 46 *Arizona Law Review* 457, 463; and Robert P Merges, "Property Rights Theory and the Commons: The Case of Scientific Research" (1996) 13(2) *Social Philosophy & Policy* 145, 156.

26 Samuelson, "Enriching Discourse on Public Domains" (n 3) 785 and 820–1.

27 Julie E Cohen, "Copyright, Commodification, and Culture: Locating the Public Domain" in Lucie Guibault and P Bernt Hugenholtz (eds), *The Future of the Public Domain: Identifying the Commons in Information Law* (Kluwer Law International, 2006) 121, 123.

28 Carol M Rose, "Romans, Roads, and Romantic Creators: Traditions of Public Property in the Information Age" (2003) 66: *Law and Contemporary Problems* 89, 96.

29 Ibid., 99–100.

30 Ibid., 100.

privately enclose property if there is something has been created or discovered that is worth enclosing.[31] An example is the development of technologies to characterise and manipulate genetic sequences, which has led to attempts to propertise genetic sequences with patents. Thus, Rose stated that "it is a mistake to suppose that the public domain and private property are independent realms. Instead, the two are intimately intertwined, both historically and economically".[32] The exact manner in which the public domain and private property are intertwined differs depending on the exact situation at hand.

In this vein, Julie Cohen has critiqued the visual metaphor of the public domain as a physical space, geographically disconnected from the propertised.[33] She stated that "common resources [are] not simply … the distant backdrop for productive activity that is largely private, but … the infrastructure that supports private productive activity and enables its success".[34] There is a "continual interplay between private and public resources".[35] Thus, in practice, creation does not take place in "bounded space" and we should view the metaphor as "distributed spatiality – environment, landscape, network, milieu", as this "is more appropriate to convey the lived experience of the common in artistic culture".[36] Viewing creation as taking place within distributed spatiality reflects the interconnected character of the public and private.[37]

The constructed nature of the public domain/propertised binary can be illustrated with multiple examples from both the physical and intellectual worlds of resources or knowledge being regulated by mechanisms other than property.[38] Norms and customary practices commonly regulate sharing and use within a community, while typically being hostile to outside use. Rose categorised this as "limited common property", which is held in common among the members of a group, but exclusive vis-à-vis non-members.[39] Many Indigenous knowledge governance regimes have such systems.[40] Arun Agrawal has argued that these systems underscore that it does not make sense to speak of binaries, but rather "to talk about multiple domains and types of knowledges, with differing logics and epistemologies".[41] The Western world also has many

31 Ibid., 101.
32 Ibid., 101–103.
33 Cohen (n 27) 123.
34 Ibid., 139.
35 Ibid., 139.
36 Ibid., 154.
37 Ibid., 157.
38 See e.g. Elinor Ostrom, *Governing the Commons: The Evolution of Institutions for Collective Action* (Cambridge University Press, 1990); Hess and Ostrom (n 9); and Brett M Frischmann, Michael J Madison and Katherine J Strandburg (eds), *Governing Knowledge Commons* (Oxford University Press, 2014).
39 Carol M Rose, "The Several Futures of Property: Of Cyberspace and Folk Tales, Emission Trades and Ecosystems" (1998) 83(1) Minnesota Law Review 129, 132.
40 See e.g. Dutfield (n 9), who refers to these as "private domains".
41 Arun Agrawal, "Dismantling the Divide between Indigenous and Scientific Knowledge" (1995) 26 *Development and Change* 413, 433.

examples of non-property-related means of governing knowledge, from the way that copyright owners might allow for certain use of their works even if technically infringement, to the way that comedians may or may not steal each other's jokes.[42]

Rose described "limited common property" as "a property type that is neither entirely individualistic nor entirely public", and "ubiquitous, if unremarked".[43] Unremarked because, firstly, it is harder to draw legal boundaries around such diffuse systems and, secondly, because the hegemony shows a certain degree of cultural conceit towards systems that are "other".[44] Rose referred to both Indigenous communities and women as groups of "unrecognized social status", whose knowledge governance regimes are shown this conceit.[45] Yet, these systems favour group interaction towards creativity, while restricting behaviour that is disruptive of that creativity.[46] As discussed further below, creation in practice is not an individualistic endeavour and, indeed, studies show that there is a positive correlation between gender diversity and radical invention/innovation.[47] In 1998, Rose wrote that "adaptation to accommodate limited common property regimes may be one of the most important challenges facing our property law".[48]

Even if there is relevant property, scientists do not necessarily behave in a way that reflects the propertised/non-propertised dichotomy.[49] For instance, patentees do not sue all infringers. They are selective in how and against whom they enforce their patents. They might perhaps distinguish between commercial and non-commercial use, or fundamental research as opposed to product creation. In this selective enforcement, patentees leave some of their property to the public domain. At the same time, when there is no relevant intellectual property, norms and customs dictate how data, knowledge and tools are or are not shared. Often the distinctions drawn by researchers (and the norms these embody) are the same regardless of whether or not there is legally recognised property in play.[50] For example, third-party non-commercial use might be accepted regardless of whether there is a patent.

42 Dotan Oliar and Christopher Sprigman, "There's No Free Laugh (Anymore): The Emergence of Intellectual Property Norms and the Transformation of Stand-Up Comedy" (2008) 94 *Virginia Law Review* 1787.
43 Rose, "The Several Futures of Property" (n 39) 132.
44 Ibid., 140 and 152.
45 Ibid., 141 and 160. See also Linda Tuhiwai Smith, *Decolonizing Methodologies: Research and Indigenous Peoples* (2nd edn, Zed Books, 2012).
46 Rose, "Romans, Roads, and Romantic Creators" (n 28) 108.
47 Cristina Díaz-García et al., "Gender Diversity within R&D Teams: Its Impact on Radicalness of Innovation" (2013) 15(2) *Innovation: Management, Policy & Practice* 149; and Christian R Østergaard, Bram Timmermans and Kari Kristinsson, "Does a Different View Create Something New? The Effect of Employee Diversity on Innovation" (2011) 40 *Research Policy* 500; Martina Schraudner and Helga Lukoschat (eds), *Gender als Innovationspotenzial in Forschung und Entwicklung* (Fraunhofer Verlag, 2006).
48 Rose, "The Several Futures of Property" (n 39) 144.
49 Merges, "Property Rights Theory and the Commons" (n 25).
50 Ibid., 147.

Finally, property generates positive externalities, which feed into the public domain.[51] Eli Salzberger used the example of an architectural masterpiece. The public can enjoy the building visually. It also increases the value of neighbouring houses and may influence architectural designs. A patent law example would be that the disclosure of an invention in the patent specification will also disclose information and knowledge related to the invention that is not patentable. In light of these positive spill overs, Salzberger stated that "between private property and the public domain, there is a dichotomous line rather than a dichotomy".[52]

Therefore, it is distracting to construct the core tension of a knowledge governance system in terms of the public domain against the propertised, and thereby the upstream as opposed to the downstream. Such a construction leads to debates about where to draw the line, which invariably results in people declaring the sacredness of the public domain. It then becomes all too easy to deny the marginalised and disempowered protection for their knowledge. The discourse should instead focus on how to design a knowledge governance system that reflects how creation occurs – which, though heterogeneous, is cumulative, contingent and communal.

3 Cumulative, contingent and communal invention

The patent system is centred around the idea of the lone inventor having a "flash-of-genius" moment. This means that patent law is theorised around individual inventors – specifically, how to incentivise and reward them through property rights. Focusing on the incentive and reward functions of patents conceals and undervalues the importance of the cumulative, contingent and the communal. If the inventor creates *ex nihilo*, in a flash of genius, these things have little value. Focusing on the inventor rather than the inventive process allows the system to ignore everything and everyone that came before and, indeed, might have contributed towards the invention.[53] The enlightenment construction of the lone genius inventor has to be dismantled for the law to reflect how invention takes place in practice.

As discussed in Chapter 3, patent law's construction of inventors as highly individual beings contradicts feminine and Indigenous modes of invention, which often happen communally. The construction of inventors reflects the construction of men. Yet, this is a social construction and the "lone genius" is just as unrealistic for Western males as it is for women and the non-Western. Every inventor relies and builds upon what came before. Invention is incremental,[54] and happens cumulatively off the back of existing knowledge.[55] In

51 Salzberger (n 21) 55–6.
52 Ibid., 56.
53 Litman (n 12) 969. With respect to copyright authors and authorship, Litman stated that copyright is supposed to incentivise creativity, but this is lost when copyright uses property rights theorised around authors.
54 Merges, "Property Rights Theory and the Commons" (n 25) 162.
55 Mark A Lemley, "The Myth of the Sole Inventor" (2012) 110 *Michigan Law Review* 709; and David Lange "Reimagining the Public Domain" (2003) 66 *Law and*

the copyright context, Craig stated that the shared understanding that absolutely independent creation is possible "manifests some sort of shared human neurosis".[56] Furthermore, people invent depending on their communities, what resources they have and what they might require or desire. Reflecting this, when analysing her interviews with creators and inventors, Jessica Silbey stated: "In their critique of [intellectual property] law and hopes for a sustainable future, everyday creators and innovators champion a system in which trust and interdependence predominate and practices of sharing, collaboration, transparency, and reciprocity advance science and art."[57]

Patent law theory does recognise that invention is cumulative, because it recognises that the exclusive rights of patents can result in the under-use of patented inventions. Patents are nevertheless granted because this deadweight loss is considered to be a price paid in the short run to ensure technological progress in the long run and overall increased welfare.[58] Furthermore, Graeme Dinwoodie and Rochelle Cooper Dreyfuss have noted that concerns about a "healthy" public domain reflect an understanding that invention is cumulative.[59] Patent law reflects this understanding through its requirement that the patentee sufficiently discloses the invention (so that others may learn from it).[60] Furthermore, by comparing an invention to the prior art, the novelty and inventive step (non-obviousness) standards acknowledge that invention is cumulative.[61]

As noted in the foregoing, this acknowledgement that invention is cumulative leads to a line-drawing exercise,[62] where moves to expand patentability inevitably result in a discussion about the public domain. However, the public domain/propertised line-drawing exercise and patent law economic theory do not account for the inventive process being contingent and communal.

Focused on the inventor rather than the inventive process, patent law ignores that invention is a social (as well as individual) phenomenon, determined to a large degree by context.[63] In Donna Haraway's words, "[s]ocial reality is lived

Contemporary Problems 463, 472, "Creativity and appropriation are inseparable, as inseparable as creativity and memory".

56 Carys J Craig, *Copyright, Communication and Culture: Towards a Relational Theory of Copyright Law* (Edward Elgar, 2011) 106.

57 Silbey, "Intellectual Property Harms" (n 16) 2458.

58 Julien Pénin and Jean-Pierre Wack, "Research Tool Patents and Free-Libre Biotechnology: A Suggested Unified Framework" (2008) *Research Policy*, 37, pp. 1909–21, at p. 1917.

59 Dinwoodie and Cooper Dreyfuss, "Patenting Science" (n 10) 195.

60 Ibid.

61 Ibid., 196.

62 Ibid.

63 On the socially determined nature of invention, see e.g. William F Ogburn and Dorothy Thomas, "Are Inventions Inevitable? A Note on Social Evolution" (1922) 37(1) *Political Science Quarterly* 83.

social relations".[64] Invention does not come from nowhere. To a certain degree, it is path-dependent, as it relies on constituent cultural elements. This includes pre-existing technologies that are interpreted, re-interpreted, applied, built upon or to put together. Creation is, thus, "opportunistic" because it depends on the "borrowing and reworking of encountered objects and techniques".[65] Furthermore, creation depends on cultural preparation, such as the level and manner of education of the work force, methods and practices, and also the human qualities that a society imprints on individuals. Because invention is culturally and socially determined, it is recursive and rhetorical, reflecting its cultural and social context,[66] where inventors, their ideas, writings and works can only be understood in relation to one another.[67] Hence, invention involves a relational network of actors, resources and creative practices.[68]

In addition, invention occurs around socially identified needs and desires. Inventors invent for society (according to its preferences and needs) and there is a certain amount of creative inertia.[69] Put another way, once a field or technology goes in one direction, most people in that field tend to follow, leaving (possibly becoming blind to) alternative technologies and pathways, and resulting in a degree of standardisation.

Framing invention as relational and based on networks of people, resources, knowledge and culture and society, shifts our understanding of what is required in order to invent. This, in turn, affects how we should design our knowledge governance system. Yet, patent law reifies the genius of individuals, separate from the contingent and in contrast to the community. As stated by Malla Pollack, "society [is] demoted to something formed by human will (as opposed to humans as beings birthed into cultures and formed by nurturing)".[70] While it is undoubtedly true that invention requires individual efforts and much of this comes from the intrinsic motivations of individuals,[71] inventing is not individualistic. It involves those who patent law rewards because they contributed to the "conception" and realisation of the invention, as well as those

64 Donna Haraway, "A Cyborg Manifesto: Science, Technology, and Socialist-Feminism in the Late 20th Century" in Joel Weiss et al. (eds), *The International Handbook of Virtual Learning Environments* (Springer 2016) 117, 117; originally published in (1985) 80 *Socialist Review* 65.

65 Cohen (n 27) 123.

66 Ibid., 149.

67 Rose (n 28) 102.

68 Cohen (n 27) 138; and Silbey, "Intellectual Property Harms" (n 16) 2476.

69 Sociologists disagree about the exact relationship between technology and society. That is, to the extent that technology is self-perpetuating in an autonomous manner, and how much technological change affects social change in a scripted manner. For a summary of this, see Ronald R Kline, "Technological Determinism", James Wright (ed.), *International Encyclopedia of the Social & Behavioral Sciences* (2nd edn, Elsevier, 2015, vol. 24) 109.

70 Malla Pollack, "Towards a Feminist Theory of the Public Domain, or Rejecting the Gendered Scope of United States Copyrightable and Patentable Subject Matter" (2006) 12 *William and Mary Journal of Women and the Law* 603, 615.

71 Silbey, "Intellectual Property Harms" (n 16) 2455–6.

who assist these people in some way – whether a lab technician, secretary, janitor or family and friends – through support, exchange, discussion or collaboration.

The creation of the invention requires multiple and varying kinds of contributions.[72] Patent law places the contributions along a constructed spectrum of value. At the top of the spectrum are the heroic and romanticised genius inventors, who contribute mental labour through masculine modes of invention. For example, those who isolate and characterise a genetic sequence. It is these people whom patent law rewards. Down the spectrum are those who perform mental labour that results in feminine knowledge. This might be those who develop knowledge to identify which plants have medicinal properties. Patent law does not value these contributors.

On the other end of the spectrum are those who are removed from the conception of the invention (contributing mere labour of the body), who are ignored and devalued by patent law. Valuing the creative genius, patent law ignores that people other than those who conceive of the conceptual invention might contribute in other necessary ways. For example, perhaps without the moral and homemaking support of a partner, the conceiver of an invention would not have had the mental capacity to think of the invention. Yet, all but the romanticised genius are invisible to the patent system.

Property law overlooks communal creation because it is difficult to "recognize, monitor, transfer, and enforce" entitlements related to communal property regimes.[73] It is easier to identify the single (or discrete number of) creator(s) than the community of contributors, and to demarcate the "product of sudden innovation" or "sharply unusual intellectual product", than the incremental build-up of an idea or ideas.[74] However, creators are individual and communal beings. The construct of the lone individual is an enlightenment ideal that casts the individual in binary to the communal.

A knowledge governance system that fails to acknowledge the communal nature of the inventive process and the relational nature of the inventor cannot foster invention and innovation in an equitable manner. Instead, it may serve to disenfranchise some creators, who might view the patent system as inappropriate for their needs, at best, and/or harmful to their community (including via inequitable wealth distribution), at worst. In a similar vein, Silbey has noted that intellectual property's focus on extrinsically motivating creators ignores their intrinsic motivations, which "degrades people and the work they love [because] it refuses to recognize this alternative narrative of creativity and innovation that celebrates processes, collaborative systems, and the communities that produce them".[75] She continued:

72 Burk, "Feminism and Dualism in Intellectual Property" (n 24) 193–4.
73 Rose, "The Several Futures of Property" (n 39) 140.
74 Ibid., 152.
75 Silbey, "Intellectual Property Harms" (n 16).

> Everyday creators and innovators describe an inevitable dynamism in their relationships with others working as they do. They see structure and relationality where IP law and its dominant explanation for incentives and productivity see isolated individuals and profit maximization. When the law and legal solutions see only individuals and not the structures on which we rely, communities fall apart.
>
> Creators and innovators critique the system's misalignment with personal values and morals. They also complain of its failure to explain how each person or institutional partner may be integral to the health of creativity and innovation at large and thus should be individually sustained for the good of the whole, even if at the cost of a net sacrifice to one part to feed another. The system's deficiencies become personal because of its failure to attend to that which is the profoundly personal: one's sense of belonging, intrinsic value, and opportunity in increasingly congested and capricious socioeconomic times.[76]

Patent law does not just ignore individuals who do not contribute to the conception of the invention, or the communal nature of invention. It also ignores the agency of materials that go into inventions, whether they be biological cells, chemicals or machines, for example. This is part of the objectifying process of masculine science. There is a human scientist (the subject or agent) who objectifies a material. As noted in Chapter 2, science is often characterised as mastery, control or domination of nature. This represents another binary – human/object or culture/nature (see Chapter 2). Yet, non-human components are necessary for invention, both in terms of conception and also the materiality of the invention. Indeed, the vast number of serendipitous inventions, created through "error", or inventions that we cannot fully explain due to their complexity (particularly with biotechnology), speak to the agency of materials.[77] Moreover, in the words of Evelyn Fox Keller, modernity's constructions of human/object and culture/nature

> have never been universally embraced by the community of working scientists. … [gender ideology exerts pressure] that transforms a complex and pluralistic tradition into a monolithic rhetoric, overlaying, obscuring, and often distorting a wider diversity of practice.[78]

At the heart of this is the construction of what it is to "know". This is typically connected to the ability of (human) language. However, while the law on occasion dabbles with the potential subjectivity or agency of non-humans over which we can throw an anthropomorphic lens, such as monkeys or artificial

76 Ibid., 2474–5.
77 Dan L Burk, "Do Patents Have Gender?" (2011) 19 *American University Journal of Gender, Social Policy & the Law* 881, 912–916.
78 Evelyn Fox Keller, *Reflections on Gender and Science* (Yale University Press) 64–5.

intelligence,[79] the law does not entertain the importance of non-sentient materials. Yet,

> plants "know" how to convert water and carbon dioxide to glucose, and carbon "knows" to form a diamond, not graphite, under intense pressure. To make sense of these examples, therefore, the very definition of "knowledge" must be stretched beyond acquired understanding to include patternization, organization, repetition, and more. This is not to say that Nature is a sentient being, or that stones and dirt can now think for themselves, but it does lead one to wonder how far the bounds of knowledge may be pushed if objects can be, if only in a limited sense, "knowers."[80]

As Bruno Latour noted:

> there might exist many metaphysical shades between full causality and sheer non-existence [in terms of agency]: Things might authorise, allow, afford, encourage, permit, suggest, influence, block, render possible, forbid and so on.[81]

Giving agency to materials might be viewed as a feminist endeavour. This is because it runs counter to modernity and the subject/object and culture/nature binaries. That is, it is contrary to the construction of masculine science objectifying feminine nature. Giving materials agency might also shift power relations. Haraway stated that the pacification of a material "can seem to be either appropriations of a fixed and determined world reduced to resource for instrumentalist projects of destructive Western societies, or they can be seen as masks for interests, usually dominating interests".[82] This objectification of materials "guarantees and refreshes" the power of the user and knower. Thus, giving agency to materials might disrupt this power and domination.

So far, we have that invention is cumulative and requires access to, and is shaped by, what came before. The immediate reaction to this is typically to restrict what is protected by intellectual property and to broaden permissible uses and exceptions from infringement – that is, to argue for the public domain.

79 E.g. *Naruto, et al. v Slater, et al.* (2016) no 15-CV-04324 (ND Cal); and *Thaler v The Comptroller-General of Patents, Designs And Trade Marks* [2020] EWHC 2412 (Pat); and EP 18275163 and EP 18275174.

80 Landon Schnabel and Lindsey Breitwieser, "Recent Advances in Feminist Science and Technology Studies: Reconceptualizing Subjectivity and Knowledge" (2015) 20(1) *Advances in Gender Research* 43, 56.

81 Bruno Latour, "Non-humans" in Stephan Harrison, Steve Pile, Nigel J Thrift (eds), *Patterned Ground: Entanglements of Nature and Culture* (Reaktion Books, 2004) 224, 226.

82 Donna Haraway "Situated Knowledges: The Science Question in Feminism and the Privilege of Partial Perspective" (1988) 14(3) *Feminist Studies* 575, 591.

However, when we acknowledge that invention is contingent and communal, we necessarily question what value exactly the "inventor" has added and whether the notion of "inventorship" needs to be broadened. These appear to lead us to contradicting conclusions for the future direction of patent law. However, another way to view this is that the contradiction is a consequence of the patent system and its privatised/public domain, culture/nature, subject/object and individual/communal binaries creating a faulty knowledge governance system.

4 A faulty knowledge governance system

Once we acknowledge that the genius inventor and public domain are social constructs, cast in false binaries against the communal and the privatised, we can address the fact that property is weighed down by ideology that masks gendered constructs. Property is partly theorised on the basis that it prevents a tragedy of the commons, where people overuse common resources, or do not invest in goods or resources that are public, as they would not be guaranteed the fruits of their labour (see Chapter 4).[83] Hence, property supposedly maximises the exploitation of land and things, by allowing people to capture the return of their investment plus profit.[84] Patent law, more specifically, is a knowledge governance system that uses property to organise and structure the creation, exploitation and transfer of intellectual assets (see Chapter 4).

Where the property of some is protected, but not that of others – "partial propertisation" – this can result in distortion, unfair distribution, conflict and inefficiency.[85] Rose stated that "one cannot simply organize a single aspect of the whole, because that aspect will get attention at the expense of others; instead, one has to propertize all aspects – or failing that, fall back on some safety net of command and control".[86] For example, there is a valorisation of masculine inventions at the expense of feminine knowledge, and there is growing unrest about the lack of protection for Indigenous knowledge. She noted that "the first-best solution would be *more complete* property".[87] However, too many property rights can result in a tragedy of the anti-commons. A patent thicket of fragmented and overlapping patent rights can lead to information or knowledge not being further developed, because there are too many different owners who can block each other and other potential users.[88]

83 James Bessen and Michael J Meurer, *Patent Failure: How Judges, Bureaucrats, and Lawyers Put Innovators at Risk* (Princeton Univeristy Press, 2008) 6 and 34–5.
84 Harold Demsetz, "Toward a Theory of Property Rights" (1967) 57(2) *American Economic Review* 347; and Edmund W Kitch, "The Nature and Function of the Patent System" (1977) 20(2) *Journal of Law and Economics* 265.
85 Rose, "The Several Futures of Property" (n 39) 170–1 and 180.
86 Ibid., 171.
87 Carol M Rose, "The Several Futures of Property: Of Cyberspace and Folk Tales, Emission Trades and Ecosystems" (1998) 83(1) *Minnesota Law Review* 129, 172 (emphasis added).
88 Michael A Heller and Rebecca S Eisenberg, "Can Patents Deter Innovation? The Anticommons in Biomedical Research" (1998) 280 *Science* 698–701; Yann Joly,

In addition, patents can constrain access to inventions, as owners can use the exclusive rights to either refuse to licence the inventions or possibly to charge anti-competitive prices. This is exemplified in much of the debate around the "BRCA patents", which were patents covering two genes and related mutations associated with breast and cervical cancer. Much of the commentary centred on the fact that the patents were negative for women's health because the patents affected access to breast cancer testing.[89] Opponents of the BRCA patents argued that, by commoditising women and the female body, the patents represented masculine science colonising female bodies. In addition, the lack of competition meant that diagnostic testing of the BRCA genes placed an unaffordable cost on female healthcare, and essentially annihilated the development of competing products/services differentiated by quality, price and variety.[90] It was also not possible to get a second opinion because there was only one provider of a diagnostic test.[91]

It is also worth noting that not everyone wants property or patents. After all, they are masculine Western constructs. As Māori lawyer Moana Jackson stated regarding the appropriation of Māori knowledge:

> Now the response to that threat from some of our corporate warriors is well Māori people have to take out their own PVRs [plant variety rights], or their own patents over these plants but that seems to miss the point because if we buy into that regime that is contrary to our history that we can own the trees that they are no longer things with which we are meant to coexist but we like all good christians have dominion over them and that again just dismisses what I understand to be one of the cultural underpinnings of who we are. The second danger in taking out patents or copyrights is those copyrights or patents under Pākehā [non-Māori] law vest individual rights and if we are to learn anything when we talk about the collective nature of Māori society but we might decide that that tree

"Open Source Approaches in Biotechnology: Utopia Revisited" (2007) 59(2) *Maine Law Review* 385–405, 389–90 and 395; Hanns Ullrich, "Patent Pools – Policy and Problems" in Josef Drexl (ed.), *Research Handbook on Intellectual Property and Competition Law* (Edward Elgar, 2008) 139–61, at 143. See also Carl Shapiro, "Navigating the Patent Thicket: Cross Licenses, Patent Pools and Standard Setting" in Adam B Jaffe, Josh Lerner and Scott Stern (eds), *Innovation Policy and the Economy* (MIT Press, 2001, vol. I) 119, 119–26 and 149–50; Robert P Merges, "Institutions for Intellectual Property Transactions: The Case of Patent Pools" (1998), 4–12, www.law.berkeley.edu/files/pools%281%29.pdf; Silbey, "Intellectual Property Harms" (n 16) 2465–8.

89 E Richard Gold and Julia Carbone, "Myriad Genetics: In the Eye of the Policy Storm" (2010) 12(4) *Genetics in Medicine* S39.

90 Rochelle C Dreyfuss and James P Evans, "From Bilski back to Benson: Preemption, Inventing Around, and the Case of Genetic Diagnostics" (2011) 63(4) *Stanford Law Review* 1349, 1366.

91 Ibid., 1366; and ABC, "Body Corporate" (6 September 2010) *Four Corners*, www.abc.net.au/4corners/body-corporate/8952778.

> over there is a property that one individual can own to the exclusion of others so then we are debasing the things that we claim are the pillar of our society.[92]

Similarly, a leading expert on the protection of Māori knowledge, Aroha Mead, has stated that the commoditisation of nature and knowledge is "too bizarre to even comment on".[93] The emphasis is, thus, not necessarily on having Western property rights, but on how Indigenous peoples can maintain their knowledge governance systems. Agrawal has argued that the only way to empower the disadvantaged, particularly Indigenous peoples, is by breaking down dichotomies:

> It is only when we move away from the sterile dichotomy between indigenous and western, when we begin to recognize intra-group differentiation; and when we seek out bridges across the constructed chasm between the traditional and the scientific, that we will initiate a productive dialogue to safeguard the interests of those who are disadvantaged.[94]

In other words, rather than only having the propertised or the public domain, forcing everything to be in one or the other, we should break down the binary and recognise alternative means of knowledge governance.

In addition, to demand more propertisation to address the hegemony the patent system embodies is to valorise the very system that supports that hegemony. It reinforces the propertised vs public dichotomy, and perpetuates a system that falsely deifies the individual creator in contrast to the social, cultural and communal. In this vein, Silbey has noted that inequities in intellectual production and legal protection has resulted in a rights grab, where one is incentivised to be selfish in fear of losing out.[95] This feeds the hegemony, which amplifies the inequities. She stated that this will continue unless we address the social causes at the core.[96]

92 Moana Jackson, "Intellectual Property Rights and Implications for Māori" in Leonie Pihama and Cherryl Waerea-i-te-rangi Smith (eds), *Cultural and Intellectual Property Rights. Economics, Politics & Colonisation* (International Research Institute for Māori and Indigenous Education, University of Auckland, 1997, vol. 2) 30.

93 Aroha Mead, "Indigenous Rights to Land and Biological Resources. The Convention on Biological Diversity", *Biodiversity: Impacts on Government Business and the Economy*, International Institute for Research (NZ) Ltd and Department of Conservation (Auckland, New Zealand, 4–5 August 1994), in Aroha Mead, *Nga Tikanga, Nga Taonga. Cultural and Intellectual Property: The Rights of Indigenous Peoples* (Auckland, New Zealand: International Research Institute for Māori and Indigenous Education) 4, 6.

94 Agrawal (n 41) 433.

95 Silbey, "Intellectual Property Harms" (n 16) 2456.

96 Ibid., 2456.

Similarly, in the context of protecting Indigenous knowledge, Agrawal has stated that using Western tools to promote Indigenous interests has the effect of solidifying dichotomies and the power asymmetries that underlie them:

> The neo-indigenistus undermine their own arguments, almost unconsciously, because of their desire to hold on to the dichotomy between indigenous/scientific, and traditional/western; and because they are unwilling to recognize the intimate links between knowledge and power. Their attempt to classify, therefore, fails to rise above the structures of knowledge that it initially condemns, and ultimately seeks to transcend. … Non-recognition of the relationship between knowledge and power blinkers them to the fact that their own strategy [of using Western systems of knowledge protection] would only reproduce the control which elites exercise over scientific knowledge.[97]

Agrawal further noted that, while simply extending Western concepts might be the easier route, this is no excuse for trying to find the correct solution by recognising "the multiplicity of logics and practices that underlie the creation and maintenance of different knowledges".[98]

More still, property has wealth distribution effects. While relatively little has been written on this with respect to patents,[99] existing studies show that patents result in economic inequality, and increasing patent protection increases income inequality.[100] This is consistent with a qualitative study undertaken by Silbey, where she identified that the:

> overwhelming sense from the interview accounts is that there are "insiders" and "outsiders" in the IP system – those who have and quickly accumulate leverage and those who do not and are unlikely to do so. The description of "haves" and "have nots," or exclusion and inclusion in a system of opportunity, is also a picture of polarization – of giants and nobodies. There appear to be few companies or individuals who form a

97 Agrawal (n 41) 430–1.

98 Ibid., 432.

99 There is literature on distributive justice vis-à-vis pharmaceutical patents; Peter Lee, "Toward a Distributive Commons in Patent Law" (2009) 40 *Wisconsin Law Review* 917; Peter Lee, "Toward a Distributive Agenda for U.S. Patent Law" (2017) 55 *Houston Law Review* 321; Keith Aoki, "Distributive and Syncretic Motives in Intellectual Property Law (with Special Reference to Coercion, Agency, and Development)" (2007) 40 *UC Davis Law Review* 717.

100 Angus C Chu, "Effects of Patent Policy on Income and Consumption Inequality in a R&D Growth Model" (2010) 77(2) *Southern Economic Journal* 336; Angus C Chu and Guido Cozzi, "Effects of Patents versus R&D Subsidies on Income Inequality" (2018) 29 *Review of Economic Dynamics* 68; and Wenkai Tzeng "Poverty and Patents: Intellectual Property Policy and Economic Inequality" (2017) 5 *Indiana Journal of Law & Social Equality* 313.

"middle class" of the creative or innovative enterprises, creating a specter of scarcity and fear.[101]

This is to be expected, in light of patents being capital assets, which are generally owned by those with resources and which generate wealth at a greater rate than income gained through labour. It is, however, concerning when we consider the gendered nature of patenting, taken together with the fact that females generally earn less than males and own less of the world's capital wealth.[102] In addition, the ability to become an inventor is socially determined, dependent on gender, race, socio-economic background, environment, exposure to innovation growing up, and role models, amongst other things.[103] Those born into more affluent families, surrounded by invention and innovation, are more likely to patent later in life. The endowed become further endowed.

Finally, there is much empirical evidence that patents do not fulfil their theorised functions of incentivising invention (with perhaps the exception of the pharmaceutical industry).[104] This intuitively makes sense, as modern patents have only existed since around the mid-nineteenth century,[105] yet invention clearly took place before their development. There is also scant evidence that patents promote economic growth.[106] Indeed, Sanford Grossman and Joseph Stiglitz have shown that information-based markets cannot find equilibrium in

101 Silbey, "Intellectual Property Harms" (n 16) 2464.

102 HM Revenue and Customs, "UK Personal Wealth Statistics 2014 to 2016" (31 January 2019), www.gov.uk/government/statistics/uk-personal-wealth-statistics-2014-to-2016; Nicole Torres, "Closing the Gender Wealth Gap" (3 October 2019) *Harvard Business Review*, https://hbr.org/2019/10/closing-the-gender-wealth-gap; and Margaret Denton M and Linda Boos. "The Gender Wealth Gap: Structural and Material Constraints and Implications for Later Life" (2007) 19(3–4) *Journal of Women and Aging* 105; and Anne Fausto-Sterling, "Women and Science" (1981) 4(1) *Women's Studies International Quarterly* 41, 44–5.

103 Alexander M Bell et al., "Who Becomes an Inventor in America? The Importance of Exposure to Innovation" (2019) *The Quarterly Journal of Economics* 647.

104 Jessica Silbey, "Patent Variation: Discerning Diversity Among Patent Functions" (2013) 45 *Loyola University Chicago Law Journal* 441, 476; Bessen and Meurer (n 83) 14–16. Indeed, Bessen and Meurer conclude that – outside of the chemical and pharmaceutical industries – the aggregate costs of patents exceeded the aggregate private benefits of patents in the 1990s in the US (at 141). See also See also Frederic M Scherer, "A Half Century of Research on Patent Economics" (2010) 2(1) *The WIPO Journal* 20; and Silbey, "Intellectual Property Harms" (n 16) 2455–6.

105 The Venetian Patent Statute 1474 is usually attributed as the first patent legislation. In the common law system, this was the Statute of Monopolies 1623 (UK). However, the modern patent system has only existed since around 1850; Brad Sherman and Lionel Bently, *The Making of Modern Intellectual Property Law: The British Experience, 1760–1911* (Cambridge University Press, 1999).

106 As discussed in Bessen and Meurer (n 83) 81–4; Sigrid Sterckx "The Ethics of Patenting – Uneasy Justifications" in P Drahos (ed), *Death of Patents* (Lawtext Publishing and Queen Mary Intellectual Property Research Institute, 2005) 195, 200–2.

a competitive economy.[107] In addition, patents are seldom an effective means of disseminating knowledge. Most inventions can be reverse engineered (i.e. the patent disclosure is not required), patent documents are written in inaccessible language and empirical studies show that most scientist do not refer to patents in their literature searches.[108] Patents do appear to fulfil their theorised post-grant functions of signalling information about the invention and inventor, and structuring and facilitating commercialisation.

The patent system is also justified on the basis that the patent registry creates certainty, as to what exactly the property covers and what can be transacted/contracted around.[109] However, despite examination by a patent office, a patent can always be revoked or be narrowed.[110] There is no absolute certainty. In addition, patents are expensive to obtain, sometimes impossible to police, and enforcement is costly and sporadic. That patents are expensive to obtain, maintain and enforce perpetuates the hegemonic nature of the system. It will be those with resources who can benefit from the system. Enforcement of a patent also only occurs when it makes financial and/or strategic sense, and it is in accordance with the customary norms of an industry. For example, it might be common industry practice to allow non-commercial use. These are the same considerations made when enforcing copyright, which is unregistered.

Typically, when a patent is enforced in court, the defendant will challenge the validity of the patent and the court must then assess whether the patent should be revoked. It can, thus, be risky for a patentee to enforce a patent and often patentees prefer to use cease and desist letters and/or to seek licences. This is, again, also true for copyright enforcement. Hence, regardless that one intellectual property regime is registered and the other is not, the same

107 Sanford J Grossman and Joseph E Stiglitz, "On the Impossibility of Informationally Efficient Markets" (1980) 70(3) *The American Economic Review* 393.

108 Stuart JH Graham et al., "High Technology Entrepreneurs and the Patent System: Results of the 2008 Berkeley Patent Survey" (2009) 24(4) *Berkeley Tech LJ* 1255, 1320–3; Bronwyn H Hall and Dietmar Harhoff, "Recent Research on the Economics of Patents" (2012) 4 *Annual Review of Economics* 541, 542 and 550 and Appendix 2, 5–6; Nicolas van Zeebroeck et al., "Patents and Academic Research: A State of the Art" (2008) 9(2) *Journal of Intellectual Capital* 246, 252–7; Wesley M Cohen et al., "R&D Spillovers, Patents and the Incentives to Innovate in Japan and the United States" (2002) 31 *Research Policy* 1349, 1362–4; Sean B Seymour, "The Teaching Function of Patents" (2010) 85(2) *Notre Dame Law Review* 621, 625–6, 628–41; Alan Devlin, "The Misunderstood Function of Disclosure in Patent Law" (2010) 23(2) *Harvard Journal of Law & Technology* 401; and Dan L Burk, "Patent Silences" (2016) 69 *Vanderbilt Law Review* 1603.

109 There has been a suggestion that one way to address gendered patenting is by protecting unregistered patents, the way that unregistered trademarks are protected and copyright is unregistered; Miriam Marcowitz-Bitton, Yotam Kaplan and Emily Michikiko Morris, "Unregistered Patents and Gender Equality" (2020 43 *Harvard Journal of Law & Gender* 47. However, this only addresses the access issues that women face in getting patents. It does not address the gendered nature of patentability itself or any of the other issues identified in this book (particularly in Chapter 5).

110 Bessen and Meurer (n 83) 9–10 and 65–7.

considerations are made when deciding whether to enforce the intellectual property and there is always the risk that a court determines that there is no valid intellectual property.

5 Where to from here?

A common argument against protecting kinds of knowledge that have hitherto not been protected by patents is that it would make poor the public domain. This chapter has shown that: (1) this argument is weak because it masks the political nature of the public domain/propertised dichotomy, which protects the empowered while keeping the marginalised disempowered; and, in any case, (2) the public domain/propertised dichotomy is the wrong focus, as discussing where to draw lines is a distraction from challenging the hegemony that create the dichotomy. Furthermore, this chapter has shown how the knowledge governance system created by patents cannot account for the fact that invention and innovation are contingent and communal. At the same time, propertisation is not always desirable and does not always achieve its theorised aims.

Therefore, it is important to remember that patent law represents one way that knowledge can be fostered and governed. In the context of human history, patents are relatively new and very much embody a Western paradigm.[111] Invention, innovation and the transfer of knowledge clearly took place in its absence.

This is exemplified by the significant body of literature on the alternative ways that Indigenous peoples' laws govern knowledge. To illustrate, Peter Drahos has noted that "[i]n essence, intellectual property systems and indigenous governance systems solve access problems to resources in different ways".[112] However, while the Western system is backed by law and power, Indigenous governance mechanisms go unrecognised and disrespected.[113] A parallel can be made with feminine knowledge. This has undoubtedly been created, fostered and disseminated throughout human history. Yet, Western lawmakers have dismissed this knowledge as unscientific and non-technical.

111 Above n 105.

112 Peter Drahos, "When Cosmology Meets Property: Indigenous People's Innovation and Intellectual Property" (2011) 29(3) *Prometheus* 233, 239–40.

113 "Statement by the Tulalip Tribes of Washington on Folklore, Indigenous Knowledge, and the Public Domain" (9 July 2003) WIPO Intergovernmental Committee on Intellectual Property and Genetic Resources, Traditional Knowledge and Folklore, Fifth Session, 4, www.wipo.int/tk/en/igc/ngo/tulaliptribes.pdf; UN, Department of Economic and Social Affairs, Secretariat of the Permanent Forum on Indigenous Issues, *State of the World's Indigenous Peoples* (United Nations, 2009) 74. See also Mark C Suchman, "Invention and Ritual: Notes on the Interrelation of Magic and Intellectual Property in Preliterate Societies" (1989) 89 *Columbia Law Review* 1264, who concludes that even oral-based societies without governmental IP structures will seek to protect their knowledge and innovations, usually via mechanisms similar to trade secrecy.

Instead, feminine knowledge and the systems around its creation have been deemed to be unworthy of protection.

Failing to change this will result in the gendered and racialised nature of patent law and patenting continuing to disproportionately distribute wealth in favour of Western males. The question, thus, becomes whether we can imagine a knowledge governance system that ensures creation and commercialisation of inventions in a more egalitarian manner. The system must also distribute wealth more equally, whilst allowing for access. This necessitates stepping back from the presumption that the patent system is the primary driver of invention and innovation and thinking about how knowledge is created. This is addressed in Chapters 6 and 7.

6 Of monsters and men

1 Introduction

Chapters 1–5 outlined how patent law reflects gendered binaries to create a knowledge governance ecosystem that is negatively biased against women. This includes mind/body, culture/nature, subject/object, individual/communal and public/private. The patent system is a narrow knowledge governance system, which – while purporting to be objective – predominantly promotes the interests of the Western, masculine and already endowed. Chapters 4 and 5 analysed in depth the negative effects of the current patent system in this regard.

This chapter examines how we might conceive knowledge freer from the binaries embedded in patent law and its mythology.[1] This allows us to consider potential alternative knowledge governance systems, which are examined in Chapter 7. As outlined in the foregoing chapters, we must rethink knowledge governance because we have to stop telling individuals that they have to play masculine roles in order to partake in the knowledge economy. Furthermore, we need to stop reifying the masculine and, as a result, perpetually casting the feminine into the public domain, where it is free for the privileged to appropriate and turn into the patentable, which, in turn, solidifies the dichotomy between the masculine and feminine.

Instead, we need to design a knowledge governance system that values the multiple contributions and contributors along chains of production and that is not so deeply entrenched in constructed binaries that do not reflect creative processes. After all, as discussed in Chapters 3 and 4, a diversity of perspectives and knowledge types (often dependent on demographic background) can result in better innovation. Right now, most of the observable diversity in the Western world does not extend beyond the masculine domination of the feminine. Evelyn Fox Keller has noted this with respect to physics' colonisation of biology (the rational and abstract colonisation of the natural and local).[2] This

1 I am indebted to Dorothea Endres for her invaluable comments on an earlier draft of this chapter. She pushed me to find my voice and to dare to share my own thoughts. Thus, any errors or misunderstandings remain unashamedly my own.

2 Evelyn Fox Keller, "A Clash of Two Cultures" (2007) 445 *Nature* 603.

DOI: 10.4324/9781003128502-7

colonisation has resulted in biology being viewed as more objective and, thus, more technical and industrial. This begs the question of what knowledge might look like if the feminine were given similar epistemic value and were capable of colonising the masculine. Put another way, what might knowledge and innovation look like if our knowledge governance system were less gendered and less hierarchical in a gendered way?

Valuing different kinds of contributors and contributions can only be achieved when we break down binaries. This is different from switching between binary partners, which is the common reaction to observing binaries and the inequities they can result in. For example, a reaction to the Enlightened "individual" has often been to push forward the opposite – the communal. Similarly, the immediate reaction to learning that patent law protects the masculine is to suggest that we should reify the feminine public domain (see Chapter 5). However, binaries form a dialectic pair, where one is constituted by the other, or one is defined in negative relation to the other.[3] As a dialectic pair, it does not make sense to choose one or the other. They exist in interdependence. One is not an alternative to the other as one does not have any meaning without the other.[4]

Moreover, switching between binaries does not make sense as both halves can share the common logic of denying difference and multiplicity. To illustrate, Iris Young noted this in relation to the individual and the community dyad.[5] The Enlightened individual is a "solid, self-sufficient unity" and all individuals are judged by universalistic means, marginalising the different. A community is defined by social subjects who are in a relation of unity, homogenising those within the community, but rejecting difference embodied in those outside. The community creates an "us" and "them", even within political movements (e.g. feminism).[6] Young stated:

> The projection of the ideal of community as the radical other of existing society denies difference in the sense of the contradictions and ambiguities of social life. Instead of dichotomizing the pure and the impure into two stages of history or two kinds of social relations, a liberating politics should conceive the social process in which we move as a multiplicity of actions and structures which cohere and contradict, some of them exploitative and some of them liberating.[7]

3 Carol Gould, *Marx's Social Ontology* (MIT Press, 1978) 9: "The subjects are therefore mutually interdependent and the relations between them are internal because each subject is what it is – a subject – through its relation to the other, namely, through being recognized as a subject by the other. These individuals therefore form a communal but differentiated subject that expresses itself in and through each individual. The whole or unity that is recons[t]ituted in these internal relations among the individuals is thus mediated or differentiated by their individuality, but unified by their commonality."

4 Iris M Young, "The Ideal of Community and the Politics of Difference" (1986) 12 (1) *Social Theory and Practice* 1, 6–7.

5 Ibid., 7.

6 Ibid., 13.

Young, therefore, argued that "radical politics must begin from historical givens, and conceive radical change not as the negation of the given, but rather as making something good from many elements of the given".[8] In other words, the issues caused by one half of a binary cannot be resolved by simply pushing for the other half.[9] Indeed, this serves to underscore the binary. Instead, we need to collapse binaries and decide what we can take from the whole to create the society we want.

The purpose of collapsing binaries is not to homogenise. Individuals are different, some of which is biologically based. The purpose is instead the opposite of homogenisation – recognising that people behave beyond their socially constructed binary roles in very individual ways and that equality involves giving analogous rights and opportunities despite difference. One could argue that there is a contradiction here – how can the law reflecting gendered binaries be detrimental to women, if people do not indeed conform with constructed binary roles or such conformity is not essential? This can be addressed by recognising that a binary system is simply a poor fit for a world of multiplicity. Furthermore, as noted in the Introduction of this book, people can be punished for not conforming to societal expectations. Indeed, we observe this in the way that women are often treated in science, technology, engineering and mathematics (STEM) (see Chapter 3).

This chapter explores selected ontological and epistemological theories of knowledge that might help us to understand "knowledge". The binaries of modernity are deeply ingrained in society to the extent that they have the appearance of being essential. A goal of this chapter is to emphasise that this is only a façade and it is possible to view knowledge, its creators and creation, differently. It does so, first, by taking a metaphor created by Donna Haraway and developed by Susan Leigh Star, the cyborg or monster, which facilitates a disintegration of the modern binary construction of the world. This helps us to imagine a less binary world and "sets the scene" for an examination of three theories on knowledge: standpoint theory; new materialism; and actor-network theory (ANT). While somewhat older, standpoint theory is an important starting point because it helps us to understand that knowledge is not universally or absolutely objective. It is always affected by the social, historical and political location of the knower. This strips away the veneer that masculine knowledge is objective and universal, whereas feminine knowledge is subjective and local. While standpoint theory is valuable for shifting subjectivity, it does not deal with the fact that modernity casts humans as outside of nature – the former is the subject and the latter the object. The second theory examined, new materialism, does so. New materialism breaks down the subject/

8 Ibid., 19.

9 Joan W Scott, "Deconstructing Equality-versus-Difference: Or, the Uses of Post-structuralist Theory for Feminism" (1988) 14(1) *Feminist Studies* 33, 33, stated, "We need theory that will enable us to articulate ways of thinking about (and thus acting upon) gender without either simply reversing the old hierarchies or confirming them. And we need theory that will be useful and relevant for political practice."

object binary through theorising that humans and matter co-constitute one another. Matter matters. How exactly matter matters can be gleaned from ANT, which explains how knowledge becomes stabilised (or accepted) within the context of networks of interdependent humans and non-humans.

The various theories discussed are brought together in Part 4 of this chapter to guide the development of a new knowledge governance system freer from binaries and the biases they reflect, which is examined in Chapter 7.

2 A metaphor of cyborgs and monsters

Modernity's binaries are so ingrained in society that they have the appearance of being essential. We need tools to look at these binaries from an external perspective to open an exploration into a non-binary approach to experience and perception. Seeing the world from a non-binary perspective also allows us to question the social relations that give rise to what it means to conform to certain societal standards, or to exist heterogenous to them. This allows us to then confront the "standardised" (including knowledge and ways of knowing) and the invisible work that must be undertaken to maintain this.

In 1985, Haraway asked whether a born hybrid – a cyborg,[10] born into a world where it must live, but does not and cannot conform – could allow us to imagine a world free of gender and of the binaries used for universalisation and domination.[11] The experience of the cyborg is a metaphor for that of women. The gendered body is a cyborg – a "monster" that represents constant otherness. Like women, cyborgs question what "self" means and how this has been constructed by society. Haraway stated that there was no place for women in networks of people and spaces, "only geometries of difference and contradiction".[12]

Because the cyborg is born a hybrid – both culture and nature, and both organism and machine – it automatically breaks down these binaries. The cyborg does not start as nature and have its nature-culture quality shift with contestation. Instead, the cyborg is born contested. The cyborg thus exemplifies that binaries are social constructs. After all, the cyborg is also not clearly either public or private, individual or communal, or subject or object, and does not have a mind and body as conceived by modernity. It also need not be a

10 A cyborg is a being with both organic and biomechatronic body parts.

11 Donna Haraway, "A Cyborg Manifesto: Science, Technology, and Socialist-Feminism in the Late 20th Century" in Joel Weiss et al. (eds), *The International Handbook of Virtual Learning Environments* (Springer 2016) 117, 140; originally published in (1985) 80 *Socialist Review* 65. She identifies the following binaries as "troubling" with respect to being "systemic to the logics and practices of domination of women, people of colour, nature, workers, animals" (at 143): "self/other, mind/body, culture/nature, male/female, civilized/primitive, reality/appearance, whole/part, agent/resource, maker/made, active/passive, right/wrong, truth/illusion, total/partial, God/man".

12 Ibid., 136.

specific gender.[13] Thus, "[c]yborg imagery can suggest a way out of the maze of dualisms in which we have explained our bodies and our tools to ourselves"[14] and "[crack] the matrices of domination and [open] geometric possibilities."[15]

Haraway viewed her cyborg as local (or situated by its cultural, political, historical and social location) rather than universal, as "[t]here is no drive in cyborgs to produce total theory, but there is an intimate experience of boundaries, their construction, and deconstruction".[16] Of course, a twenty-first century cyborg might in fact be searching for something universal, as it will reflect its master coder, who might programme this into the cyborg.[17] However, Haraway was referring to a Frankenstein-like monster – a cyborg born into the world trying to fit in through local experience in 1985, not programmed to the extent it would be if it were a twenty-first century cyborg.[18]

Cyborgs (like all people) do not live in a single social location, or single network, where they have one kind of conforming/non-conforming experience. Haraway stated that we are all:

> necessarily living in more worlds than one, always living in multiple worlds. There is no way that the world is totally colonized by a single system of spatiotemporalities. Everybody lives in more than one world all the time, and learns how to do so, even inside oneself as well as in any social collectivity. Out of that, it seems to me, the question of agency becomes, in principle, easy. In practice, it's a question of use it or lose it. Agency is not something that pre-exists a situation of political action, in which you sort of lift up a veil of discoveries and then go do something.

13 Haraway, "A Cyborg Manifesto" (n 11) 118. Haraway was more resolute in her statement that "The cyborg is a creature in a post-gender world". I am less so, as in the twenty-first century, it is clear that technology embodies the biases of society and much technology is made feminine; see e.g. Monica Nickelsburg, "Why is AI Female? How our Ideas About Sex and Service Influence the Personalities We Give Machines" (4 April 2016) *Geekwire*, www.geekwire.com/2016/why-is-ai-female-how-our-ideas-about-sex-and-service-influence-the-personalities-we-give-machines; Chandra Steele, "The Real Reason Voice Assistants Are Female (and Why it Matters)" *PC Mag* (5 January 2018), https://au.pcmag.com/smart-home/51146/the-real-reason-voice-assistants-are-female-and-why-it-matters.

14 Haraway, "A Cyborg Manifesto" (n 11) 147.

15 Ibid, 140; and Donna Haraway, "Nature, Politics, and Possibilities: A Debate and Discussion with David Harvey and Donna Haraway" (1995) 13 *Environmental and Planning D: Society and Space* 507, 514.

16 Haraway, "A Cyborg Manifesto" (n 11), 146.

17 Twenty-first century information technology is largely based on "big data" and trying to find knowledge out of this. On how technology embodies the biases of society, see (n 13); and Joy Buolamwini, "Artificial Intelligence Has a Problem With Gender and Racial Bias. Here's How to Solve It" (7 February 2019) *Time*, https://time.com/5520558/artificial-intelligence-racial-gender-bias.

18 Haraway differentiated her cyborg from Frankenstein's monster; Haraway, "A Cyborg Manifesto" (n 11) 119.

> Agency is, rather, the practice of actualizing the consequences of multiple lived worlds.[19]

Each social actor is a part of multiple networks – some to which that individual conforms, others to which that same individual does not conform, and others to which the individual is a cyborg or monster self, neither conforming nor non-conforming.[20] Developing Haraway's cyborg metaphor, Star discussed monsters regarding:

> the multiplicity of participating in many social worlds – the experience of being marginal. By experience and by affinity, some of us begin not with Pasteur [the "genius scientist" examined by Latour through ANT], but with the monster, the outcast. Our multiplicity has not been the multiple personality of the· executive, but that of the half breed. We are the ones who have done the invisible work of creating a unity of action in the face of a multiplicity of selves, as well as, and at the same time, the invisible work of lending unity to the face of the torturer or of the executive. We have usually been the delegated to, the disciplined. Our selves are thus in two senses monstrous selves, cyborgs, impure, first in the sense of uniting split selves and secondly in the sense of being that which goes unrepresented in encounters with technology. This experience is about multivocality or heterogeneity, but not only that. We are at once heterogeneous, split apart, multiple – and through living in multiple worlds without delegation, we have experience of a self unified only through action, work and the patchwork of collective biography ...[21]

Cyborgs and monsters are ever-present, but ever-invisible. They are "permanently escaping, subverting, but nevertheless in relationship with the standardized technologies. It is not nonconformity, but heterogeneity".[22] Star was saying that the world is designed to be a certain "standardised" way, which cyborgs and monsters have no choice but to be in relation with, even if they do not (or cannot) conform. This might be through avoidance/escape or subversion, reflecting heterogeneity.

Star continued: "In a sense, a cyborg *is* the relationship between standardized and local experience; that which is between the categories, yet in relationship to them."[23] Cyborgs and monsters must do constant invisible work to maintain

19 Haraway, "Nature, Politics, and Possibilities" (n 15) 515.

20 Susan Leigh Star, "Power, Technology and the Phenomenology of Conventions: On Being Allergic to Onions" (1990) 38(S1) *The Sociological Review* 26. See also David Harvey, "Nature, Politics, and Possibilities: A Debate and Discussion with David Harvey and Donna Haraway" (1995) 13 *Environmental and Planning D: Society and Space* 507, 513, "bodies are being made not in the free sense of any autonomous kind of process, but are being made in relationships with certain sets of processes which may be contradictory".

21 Star (n 20) 29.

22 Ibid., 39.

23 Ibid. (emphasis in original).

the standardised for some, but not all.[24] Like women, the cyborg or the monster is always there, living with the standardised, heterogenous to it, yet forced to be in relation to the standardised, indeed even do invisible work to maintain it. "It's not so much that women have been left out, but that we were both in and out at the same time."[25]

We can take this metaphor, as developed by Haraway and Star, and apply it to knowledge and innovation, or more specifically women in STEM fields. Women are born into a world where STEM is designed to reflect masculine modes of production. The "standard" of what is knowledge and how this is generated is the masculine. Yet, women cannot refuse to conform if they wish to be in STEM, patent and commercialise their inventions. So, women enter STEM and often exist heterogeneously within it, accepting discrimination and misogynistic behaviour. They often even "play masculine" to fit in and maintain the culture, or end up in administrative or managerial roles to support STEM as it exists.

While the born-hybrid cyborg or monster is a metaphor for women and is helpful for visualising the non-binary within an oppressive world, hybridity does not only apply to women. Males are also born into a world that tells them what it is to be a "real man". They also are in relation to the standardised and may, within certain contexts, in fact not conform. There may be social locations within which males might seek to permanently escape or subvert certain standards, thereby behaving heterogeneously. We are all cyborgs.

In a discussion with Haraway, Harvey asked, "If we are all cyborgs, then what are the possibilities that exist from that position for a radical politics?"[26] In the next part we discuss three different theories that help us to answer this question.

3 Selected theories of knowledge

Patent law has been developed around universalistic ideals of truth and knowledge, as embodied in the binary constructs of modernity. The following discusses selected literature from epistemology and ontology in an effort to find a new way to frame knowledge governance that is egalitarian and experiential. Broadly speaking, ontology is the study of being (what is) and epistemology the study of knowledge (how we know things). Because both deal with the concepts of nature, truth and universals, these two branches of philosophy are intimately connected. As areas of philosophy that address how knowledge is generated and what is, they should implicitly affect the theorisation of patent law (or knowledge governance) and the regulation of knowledge. However, patent law is mostly justified on law and economics based on a modern understanding of inventors and invention, or who generates knowledge and what knowledge is (see Chapter 4).

24 Ibid., 44.
25 Ibid., 50.
26 Harvey, "Nature, Politics, and Possibilities" (n 20) 514.

One should note that there is not a singular uncontested theory of epistemology or ontology. Discussions on epistemology and ontology are multifaceted and diverse to the extent that it is impossible to do justice to their rich contributions within the limited space of this chapter. The purpose of the discussion is neither to offer a full explication of each theory, nor to create a new strand of theory. Instead, the aim of this exploration is to learn from my interpretations of the theories to show that there are different ways of viewing knowledge and truth or nature, which differ from universalistic truths about nature derived from individual human subjects' actions on objects. This is with the intention of finding an alternative way to regulate knowledge that better reflects how knowledge is generated and that is freer of gendered binaries, which is developed in Chapter 7.

3.1 Standpoint theory

As discussed throughout this book, gendered binaries affect what constitutes "knowledge". Michel Foucault famously theorised that knowledge and power are dyadic and co-constituting.[27] This framing of knowledge and power was made within his broader "discourse theory", according to which power is distributed throughout a "discourse", which was a historically contingent social system made up of discursive practices that (re)produces knowledge and meaning. What is accepted as knowledge is determined by power formations. Put another way, knowledge is only generated at social locations where there is power. "Truth", then, is dictated by power, or "regimes of truth" are created within discursive systems of knowledge (through social meaning-making or signification via the sensory representations). What is accepted as knowledge and accepted as truth is contingent upon the historical and political. The production and reproduction of knowledge sustain the power that created it. Note that this is not saying that there is no such thing as absolute truth, but is instead a commentary on what is accepted as truth.[28] According to Foucault, because power and knowledge are co-constituting, it is not possible to remove power from knowledge. However, power is also wielded by those who resist it, as they are also within the discourse. Consequently, it should be possible to shift the loci of power/knowledge convergences within a system.[29] Resistance is, in

27 Michel Foucault, *Discipline and Punish: 1970–1975* (2nd edn, Vintage Books, 1995) 27; Michel Foucault, *The History of Sexuality* (Pantheon Books: 1978, vol. I) 93–5. For a commentary on power/knowledge, see Joseph Rouse, "Power/Knowledge" in Gary Gutting (ed), *The Cambridge Companion to Foucault* (2nd edn, Cambridge University Press, 2005) 95.

28 Interview with Michel Foucault by Alessandro Fontana and Pasquale Pasquino, in Paul Rabinow (ed), *The Foucault Reader* (Pantheon Books, 1984) 74; and Linda Martín Alcoff, "Foucault's Normative Epistemology" in Christopher Falzon, Timothy O'Leary and Jana Sawicki (eds), *A Companion to Foucault* (Blackwell Publishing, 2013) 207, 219–20.

29 Interview with Michel Foucault by Alessandro Fontana and Pasquale Pasquino (n 28) 75.

essence, an attempt to change the loci of knowledge/power convergences.[30] Though Foucault's work was descriptive and critical, and was never intended to be normative, standpoint theory develops on Foucault's theory through an attempt to shift knowledge/power convergences.[31]

Per modernity (see Chapter 2), the subject of knowledge is impliedly a generic and therefore disembodied human being, but is in fact usually a Western man. Women and non-Western peoples often lack subjectivity – they are objects. Modern "objectivity" requires that the viewer is everywhere (universal) but nowhere (not tied to a cultural, political, historical and social location), and there is a singular viewpoint of reality and truth, which is attained and discerned from a particular methodology. In contrast, standpoint theory (or standpoint epistemology) is a postmodern theory that attempts to overcome the universalistic nature of the modern construction of knowledge. While there are many versions and interpretations of this theory, standpoint theory generally holds that knowledge is created by and for a class of socially situated knowers.[32] Knowledge is embodied and situated within (or from the perspective of) its cultural, political, historical and social location.[33] It is local. Standpoint theory broadens subjectivity to everyone – everyone's knowledge is only local. It is limited by their location, or partial, "which is not to be rejected, but which is not to be over-extended either".[34] This general form of standpoint theory is about individuals' viewpoints, set within their social locations. As discussed further in the following, this makes it relativistic.

The most obvious way that standpoint theory affects modern binaries is by expanding subjectivity beyond only Western men, changing the subject/object binary. Standpoint theory also breaks down the mind/body duality, which – as discussed in Chapter 2 – is woven throughout patent law to favour the masculine mind over the feminine body. In her ground-breaking article on situated knowledge from 1988, Haraway formulated an embodied nature of all vision.[35]

30 See Rouse (n 27) 112–15.
31 For a comparison and contrasting of Foucault and certain perspectives of standpoint theory, see Susan Hekman, "Truth and Method: Feminist Standpoint Theory Revisited" (1997) 22(2) *Signs: Journal of Women in Culture and Society* 341.
32 See e.g. Donna Haraway, "Animal Sociology and a Natural Economy of the Body Politic, Part II: The Past is the Contested Zone" (1978) 4(1) *Signs: Journal of Women in Culture and Society* 37; and Helen E Longino and Ruth Doell, "Body, Bias, and Behaviour: A Comparative Analysis of Reasoning in Two Areas of Biological Science" (1983) 9(2) *Signs: Journal of Women in Culture and Society* 206; Emily Martin, "The Egg and the Sperm: How Science has Constructed a Romance Based on Stereotypical Male-Female Roles" (1991) 16(3) *Signs: Journal of Women in Culture and Society* 485.
33 Dorothy E Smith, *The Conceptual Practices of Power: A Feminist Sociology of Knowledge* (Northeastern University Press, 1990) 11–28; and Dorothy E Smith, "Women's Perspective as a Radical Critique of Sociology" in Evelyn Fox Keller and Helen E Longino (eds), *Feminism and Science* (Oxford University Press, 1996) 17.
34 Mary Tiles, "A Science of Mars or of Venus" (1987) 62 *Philosophy* 293, 299–300.
35 Donna Haraway, "Situated Knowledges: The Science Question in Feminism and the Privilege of Partial Perspective" (1988) 14(3) *Feminist Studies* 575.

Haraway framed feminist objectivity through situating knowledge in its viewer, both in terms of the subject and location. Embodied, there is no mind/body binary. Knowledge of the object becomes embodied in the cultural, social and political context of the subject. Subject and object are not split,[36] and the viewer becomes responsible for the knowledge.[37] This is consistent with her cyborg, which is also both embodied and local.

Understanding that knowledge is situated helps us to overcome the ideal of universal truth and universal objectivity, upon which patent law depends. All knowledge, regardless of its locality, is discursively constituted. As noted in Chapter 3, there is no such thing as absolutely objective knowledge, which is free from the social, cultural, historical and political lenses that create and interpret it. All social groups "produce different patterns of knowledge and, equally importantly, of ignorance".[38] This is not to say that there is no absolute truth, but rather that perception, interpretation and expression are dependent on one's social, cultural, historical and political location, which generate social truths.

Not acknowledging that all knowledge is situated creates blind spots to institutionalised biases. Within the patent law context, it makes one blind to how the law is interpreted to primarily benefit the Western and the masculine (see Chapter 2). This has the effect of making knowledge less objective. Thus, one could argue that the problem is not that Western masculine knowledge is too objectifying, but that it is not objectifying enough.[39] Put another way, as Western masculine knowledge is blind to the gendered binaries it embodies because they are ubiquitous and taken as essential, it cannot root them out. Knowledge needs to be objectified more in order to identify and excise bias. A purpose of standpoint theorists is, therefore, to try to create knowledge that is "more objective" than current Western masculine standards. That is, by localising knowledge, it attempts to maximise objectivity, while recognising that all knowledge is situated. Similarly, through offering diverse viewpoints, standpoint theory aims to create knowledge that is less partial and distorted.[40]

According to some commentators, the starting point is looking at the situated knowledge of the marginalised.[41] Dominant groups are epistemically

36 See also Evelyn Fox Keller, *Reflections on Gender and Science* (Yale University Press, 1985) 95–126, on the relationship between the subject and object, and interdependence of objects.

37 Haraway, "Situated Knowledges" (n 35) 583–4; Sandra Harding, "Rethinking Standpoint Epistemology: What is 'Strong Objectivity?'" (1992) 36(3) *The Centennial Review* 437, 453.

38 Sandra Harding, "A Socially Relevant Philosophy of Science" (2004) 19(1) *Hypatia* 25, 35.

39 Harding, "Rethinking Standpoint Epistemology" (n 37) 438.

40 Harding referred to this as "strong objectivity"; ibid. David Harvey has called it "real hard 'objective' knowledge, deep objective knowledge"; Harvey, "Nature, Politics, and Possibilities" (n 20) 508.

41 Harding, "Rethinking Standpoint Epistemology" (n 37). See also Nancy Hartsock, "Postmodernism and Political Change: Issues for Feminist Theory" (1990) *Cultural Critique* 15.

disadvantaged in terms of generating more objective knowledge,[42] because they are less likely to critically examine themselves. They do not have "strong reflexivity" and are less able to see the blind spots from their social locations.[43] This can result in dominant accounts "legitimating exploitative 'practical politics' even when those who produce them have good intentions".[44] In contrast, the oppressed are more likely to be self-critical and not see themselves as representing something universal.[45] It is only through embedding the knowledges of socially dominant groups within the knowledges of marginalised groups that it becomes possible to systematically identify and eliminate cultural, political and social lenses, thus maximising objectivity.[46] In other words, a diversity of perspectives can allow the construction of more and better (more objective) scientific methods.

Building on this, Star argued that we should use multiplicity "as the point of departure for *all* analysis, instead of adding perspectives to an essentially monolithic model".[47] That is, we must gather the viewpoints of cyborgs and monsters – their heterogenous (neither conforming nor unconforming) experiences across different social locations – as there is "power in collective multiplicity".[48] Jane Flax stated that focusing on multiplicity would mean that "reality" would be unstable:

> there is no force or reality "outside" our social relations and activity (e.g., history, reason, progress, science, some transcendental essence) that will rescue us from partiality and differences. Our lives and alliances belong with those who seek to further decenter the world – although we should reserve the right to be suspicious of their motives and visions as well. Feminist theories, like other forms of post-modernism, should encourage us to tolerate and interpret ambivalence, ambiguity, and multiplicity as well as to expose the roots of our needs for imposing order and structure no matter how arbitrary and oppressive these needs may be.
>
> If we do our work well, "reality" will appear even more unstable, complex, and disorderly than it does now.[49]

This instability of knowledge is not a bad thing. Having multiple perspectives allows for understanding difference and continually challenging the status quo. This is not to say that there cannot be periods when a piece of knowledge is stable (or standardised). How knowledge becomes stabilised is discussed below

42 Harding, "Rethinking Standpoint Epistemology" (n 37) 442.
43 Ibid., 443.
44 Ibid., 442.
45 Nancy Hartsock, "Rethinking Modernism: Minority vs. Majority Theories" (1987) *Cultural Critique* 187, 205.
46 Harding, "Rethinking Standpoint Epistemology" (n 37) 440.
47 Star (n 20) 34 (emphasis in original).
48 Ibid., 50.
49 Jane Flax, "Postmodernism and Gender Relations in Feminist Theory" (1987) 12(4) *Signs: Journal of Women in Culture and Society* 621, 642–3.

vis-à-vis ANT. However, that knowledge should always be open to contestation.

3.1.1 Critiques

There are three core critiques of standpoint theory that potentially limit its ability to inform the foundations of a knowledge governance system. The first is that there are dangers involved with prioritising certain viewpoints, as all viewpoints are relevant, not just those of the dominant and/or the marginalised.[50] Another way to see this is that this is the creation of a further binary – dominant/marginalised, which may have unintended consequences. In the context of knowledge governance and innovation, it might mean that only the knowledge of the dominant and marginalised is given value in the eyes of the law and subsequently commercialised.

Second (and related), standpoint theory can homogenise experiences, for example, of "women" or of a certain class or a certain race,[51] or of the dominant and the marginalised. If postmodernism rejects essentialism (that there is an inherent reason for the constitution of gender) and any pretence to absolute objectivity, but instead recognises that our realities are discursively constructed, constituted within multiple sets of social contexts and social relations, there is no "woman" or "women". This means that there is no women's standpoint. Any standpoint is necessarily partial, defined and limited by its exact location. Flax argued:

> Thinking about women may illuminate some aspects of a society that have been previously suppressed within the dominant view. But none of us can speak for "woman" because no such person exists except within a specific set of (already gendered) relations – to "man" and to many concrete and different women. Indeed, the notion of a feminist standpoint that is truer than previous (male) ones seems to rest upon many problematic and unexamined assumptions. These include an optimistic belief that people act rationally in their own interests and that reality has a structure that perfect reason (perfected) can discover. Both of these assumptions in turn depend upon uncritical appropriation of the Enlightenment ideas discussed earlier [that there is reason divorced from the contingent].[52]

Here Flax is alluding to a deeper problem with standpoint theory. Namely, that it plays into certain binaries of modernity by trying to find the pure from the impure. In addition, simply turning to women's standpoints reinforces gendered binaries by playing into the "otherness" that women are to men. Flax continued her critique:

50 Katharine T Bartlett, "Feminist Legal Methods" (1990) 103 *Harvard Law Review* 829, 873; and Hekman (n 31).
51 Hekman (n 31); and Helen E Longino, "Subjects, Power, and Knowledge: Description and Prescription in Feminist Philosophies of Science" in Linda Alcoff and Elizabeth Potter (eds), *Feminist Epistemologies* (Taylor & Francis, 1992) 101, 107.
52 Flax (n 49) 642.

> Furthermore, the notion of such a standpoint also assumes that the oppressed are not in fundamental ways damaged by their social experience. On the contrary, this position assumes that the oppressed have a privileged (and not just different) relation and ability to comprehend a reality that "out there" waiting for our representation. It also presupposes gendered social relations in which there is a category of beings who are fundamentally like each other by virtue of their sex – that is, it assumes the otherness men assign to women. Such a standpoint also assumes that women, unlike men, can be free of determination from their own participation in relations of domination such as those rooted in the social relations of race, class, homophobia.[53]

In essence, Flax is saying that playing into the "otherness" presumes that the other has a privileged position from which they can be subject to what is "out there" to be objectified. In other words, while standpoint theory changes the subject/object binary, it continues to rely on it. Flax also alludes to the fact that being marginalised in one sense does not mean that one is not socially dominant in another. To illustrate, one might be a woman marginalised next to men, but Caucasian and dominant over women of colour.[54]

Finally, standpoint theory creates knowledge that it is relativistic. By situating knowledge within its context, the theory denies that humans can discover, generate or express any universal or natural truths. Nature and matter are purely the objects of human subjectivity. That is, the social disproportionately takes precedent over the natural. How does knowledge develop and how is there epistemic truth or ontological being if knowledge is always local? In other words, how can we have truth (something universalistic) if knowledge is always relative? At the same time, standpoint theory alone does not tell us either how to deal with competing viewpoints, particularly not those that are meant to ground science and technology, or whether there is a means to transform or integrate multiple perspectives into one.[55]

53 Ibid.

54 See e.g. Sandra Harding, "Postcolonial and Feminist Philosophies of Science and Technology: Convergence and Dissonances" (2009) 12(4) *Postcolonial Studies* 401, 414. In defence of standpoint theory in postcolonial contexts, Harding stated: "Yet standpoint methodology/epistemology may be too Western to be fully useful elsewhere quite apart from this particular gender issue. After all, it is positioned against what are perceived as 'positivist' regulatory ideals and practices in Western-origin natural and social sciences. It was formulated initially within the Marxian and Enlightenment philosophic and methodological legacies, even as it protests significant aspects of them. Positivism is not one of the most problematic aspects of many Third World societies, as philosopher Uma Narayan pointed out about India several decades ago. Moreover, she noted that standpoint theory's appeal to the value of women's experience can lose its critical edge in societies that conceptualize sex/gender differences as fundamentally complementary rather than hierarchical (and regardless of whether such differences are in fact treated as hierarchical)" (at 414).

55 Longino (n 51) 109; and see Hekman (n 31).

It is a general criticism of poststructural and postmodern theories that they are good at deconstructing, but do not provide us with a means to reconstruct, as they do not tell us what is "good" as opposed to what is "bad". There needs to be a way of judging different knowledges to find more objective knowledge, as otherwise science cannot develop. Science needs reference points, common understandings and repeatability. The difficulty is how to judge different knowledges without replicating modernity's universalistic, homogenising and biased approach, because – in Haraway's words – "relativism and totalization are both 'god tricks' promising vision from everywhere and nowhere equally and fully".[56]

3.1.2 "More objective" knowledge

Haraway, David Harvey and Helen Longino have theorised means by which one could evaluate different situated knowledges to try to overcome arguments of relativism (that situated knowledge is relative) and hyper-social constructivism (that knowledge becomes too local to be useful, in our context, for innovation), and obtain more objective knowledge. These lie in situating situated knowledges.

We cannot avoid attempts at finding universality – to do so would mean that one cannot say anything or develop science and innovation, as one would have to accept all heterogeneous viewpoints.[57] However, we should accept universality that is non-oppressive,[58] and that is framed in a "dialectical relation to particularity, positionality and group difference".[59] That is, situating universality such that is interdependent with its location. This has the effect of situating the situated knowledge in dialectic relation to the different:

> "Situatedness" is then taken out of its wooden attachment to identifiable individuals and their biographies and is itself situated as a play of difference. ... Individuals are heterogeneously constructed subjects, internalizing "otherness" by virtue of their relations to the world.[60]

In terms of creating more objective knowledge, Haraway noted the importance of addressing the irrationality of science:

56 Haraway, "Situated Knowledges" (n 35) 584; Evelyn Fox Keller, *Secrets of Life, Secrets of Death: Essays on Language, Gender and Science* (New York: Routledge, 1992) 33–6.

57 David Harvey, "Class Relations, Social Justice and the Politics of Difference" in Michal Keith and Steve Pile (eds), *Place and the Politics of Identity* (Tayler & Francis, 1993) 41, 62; Harvey referred to political speech rather the scientific knowledge. See also Hekman (n 31) 361–3, who argues that we should be able to adapt existing (even if masculine) logic and values for feminist purposes.

58 Young (n 4).

59 Harvey, "Class Relations, Social Justice and the Politics of Difference" (n 57) 57.

60 Ibid., 58.

> one of the things we have to do, and this is where some of the inroads are beginning to tell, is by looking at some of the profoundly irrational ways in which science works and the profoundly irrational forms of its organization. You can actually reclaim the notion of rationality in a way that is profoundly oppositional to some of the practices that are going on throughout much of science, without necessarily saying it's all a load of rubbish, or becoming a sort of mystic and sitting under a banyan tree.[61]

Another way to view this is that counter accounts reveal the opaque cultural, political and social locations of the accounts of socially dominant groups. This then allows socially dominant groups to critically analyse their locations, methods of knowledge production and the way that these can subjugate the marginalised. However, this does not necessarily mean that a critical analysis of the dominant position will result in the adoption of the opposite position.

Objectivity is achieved through critical positioning, which grounds knowledge, giving it a point of projection.[62] This is positioned rationality. Haraway explains:

> contingency and relationality are not equal to relativism; that radical historical contingency is about understanding the modes of materiality in the world; that understanding issues of possibility or understanding issues of apparatuses of production is materiality; and that it's semiotic all the way down. There is no gap between materiality and semiosis; the meaning-making processes and the materiality of the world are dynamic, historical, contingent, specific; that bodies and institutions and machines are made, not made up.[63]

As a dialectic, a situated knowledge and the different "defines the other in such a way as to make the universality criterion always open to negotiation through the particularities of difference".[64] After all,

> individuals developing such situated knowledge are not themselves homogeneous entities but bundles of heterogeneous impulses, many of which derive from an internalization of "the other" within the self. Such a conception of the subject renders situatedness itself heterogeneous and differentiated. In the last instance, it is the social construction of situatedness which matters.[65]

61 Haraway, "Nature, Politics, and Possibilities" (n 15) 527.
62 Haraway, "Situated Knowledges" (n 35) 586–7. Cf. Pierre Bourdieu, "Participant Objectivation" (2003) 9 *Journal of the Royal Anthropological Institute* 281.
63 Haraway, "Nature, Politics, and Possibilities" (n 15) 509.
64 Harvey, "Class Relations, Social Justice and the Politics of Difference" (n 57) 62.
65 Ibid., 63.

Haraway's theory of situated knowledge acknowledges the "complex, contradictory, structuring and structured body" that gives a viewpoint.[66] This keeps it open to discourse and criticism, rather than closed and final, and thereby vulnerable.[67] This "privileges contestation, deconstruction, passionate construction, webbed connections, and hope for transformation of knowledge and ways of seeing".[68] Adding to the openness of knowledge, one's situatedness is fluid. In Harvey's words:

> we have to understand the fluidity and flexibility with which situatedness is constituted by the processes of working the world, the transformative work that individuals do; so that the situation is not something that is fixed. It is itself in flux and therefore situated knowledges are knowledges which are not built from some fixed standpoint but are integrated into the processes which are structuring and restructuring the world.[69]

Knowledge is never final. It is constantly challenged and corrected. Through this understanding of knowledge,

> science becomes the paradigmatic model, not of closure, but of that which is contestable and contested. Science becomes the myth, not of what escapes human agency and responsibility in a realm about the fray, but, rather, of accountability and responsibility for translations and solidarities linking the cacophonous visions and visionary voices that characterize the knowledges of the subjugated.[70]

Note that Haraway is changing the "myth" of what science is. That is, away from the rational, absolutely universal and objective, towards that which is more local, open and contestable, and that over which knowledge holders are responsible.

This is similar to Longino's proposal for generating scientific knowledge from contradicting standpoints, which is communal and competitive.[71] Longino theorised that humans are all in relations of interdependence and "that scientific knowledge is constructed not by individuals applying a method to the material to be known but by individuals in interaction with one another in ways that modify their observations, theories and hypotheses, and patterns of reasoning".[72] A community needs multiple alternative points of view to identify background presumptions and determined shared values that shape observation and reasoning.[73]

66 Haraway, "Situated Knowledges" (n 35) 589.
67 Ibid., 589–90.
68 Haraway, "Situated Knowledges" (n 35) 585.
69 Haraway, "Nature, Politics, and Possibilities" (n 15) 508.
70 Haraway, "Situated Knowledges" (n 35) 590.
71 Longino (n 51).
72 Ibid., 111.
73 Ibid., 112. On finding commonalities as a means to overcome relativism, see Hartsock, "Rethinking Modernism" (n 45); and Hartsock, "Postmodernism and Political Change" (n 41).

Scientific knowledge is created through contestation and consensus within a community made up of diverse viewpoints. Longino stated:

> Scientific knowledge, on this view, is an outcome of the critical dialogue in which individuals and groups holding different points of view engage with each other. It is constructed not by individuals but by an interactive dialogic community. A community's practice of inquiry is productive of knowledge to the extent that it facilitates transformative criticism.[74]

Haraway and Longino's theories of objectivity through contestation make them non-relativistic and more relational. This is because knowledge is not from the perspective of individuals (which would be relativistic) but is found between people who are interdependent within a system of relations. Relational theories differ from modern and Enlightenment ideals of the individual as the unit for analysis, as relational theories have the starting point that humans are born into and shaped by relationships. Theorising knowledge as something relational breaks down the individual/communal dichotomy. Knowledge becomes something both individual (from the perspective of individuals) and communal (dependent on social relations and contestation). As discussed further below, looking at knowledge in a relational way also allows us to address how knowledge becomes something "standard" (or stable) and how this is affected by social relations (including power and gender).

Longino additionally stated that there are "legitimate constraints on what counts as reasonable to believe apart from the individual's own beliefs".[75] She continued:

> Equality of intellectual authority does not mean that anything goes but that everyone is regarded as equally capable of providing arguments germane to the construction of scientific knowledge. The position outlined here holds that both nature and logic impose constraints. …
>
> this notion of knowledge through interactive intersubjectivity idealizes the view from everywhere (perhaps better thought of as views from *many wheres*).[76]

Note that, as well as logic, Longino alluded to the importance of nature. Nature must set boundaries on what is knowledge as opposed to what is a belief. It cannot be that the culture half of the culture/nature binary defines and dominates nature, as this reinforces that binary. The importance of nature (or of matter) is discussed in the following from the perspective of theory of new materialism.

74 Longino (n 51) 112.
75 Ibid., 113.
76 Ibid. (emphasis in original).

3.2 New materialism

A core issue in epistemology lies in the dichotomy between nature and culture (modernity), or between the material and the socially constructed.[77] Put another way, are there natural truths (realism)? If there are natural truths, to what extent are they observable, measurable and capable of reflection by humans (relativism), or is all knowledge socially constructed (extreme postmodernism)? Nature cannot speak for itself, resulting in knowledge being framed and expressed through structures that are socially, politically and historically constituted. Does this mean that the agency of nature is subsumed within anthropocentrism? The role of nature or matter is discussed in the following.

In her seminal 2003 article on "Posthumanist Performativity", Karen Barad questioned how it is that "language came to be more trustworthy than matter".[78] A "return to matter" or new materialism is an attempt to try to overcome hyper-social constructivism and relativism. New materialists generally step away from subjectivity being centred on human beings, human exceptionalism, and things and truth being only a matter of social construction. New materialism opposes the ideas that all human activity (including perception and thought) and its products are socially constructed rather than natural, and that meaning is a matter of language and semiotics. Barad, thus, argued that we need to take a performative understanding of ontology, shifting from linguistic representations to discursive practices. "Agential realism" accepts the human role in "the intertwined practices of knowing and becoming".[79]

The culture/nature and mind/body dualities have long been used to keep women out of certain public and political spheres (see Chapter 2). According to these binaries, it is men who have reason and who are objective and intellectual (culture and the mind), whereas women are without reason, subjective and do only devalued physical work (nature and the body). By placing value in matter, new materialist approaches have the potential to be deployed to break down the perception that culture acts upon nature and that matter is not of relevance.[80] In other words, new materialism potentially gives the feminine as much salience as the masculine.

77 On the turn away from hyper-social constructivism, see Iris van der Tuin, "New Feminist Materialisms" (2011) 34 *Women's Studies International Forum* 271.

78 Karen Barad, "Posthumanist Performativity: Toward an Understanding of How Matter Comes to Matter" (2003) 28(3) *Signs: Journal of Woman in Culture and Society* 801.

79 Ibid., 812.

80 This is similarly true with affective theories, which use the science of emotions, as women have been socially constructed as emotional. See e.g. Carolyn Pedwell and Anne Whiteshead, "Affecting Feminism: Questions of Feeling in Feminist Theory" (2012) 13(2) *Feminist Theory* 115; Clare Hemmings, "Invoking Affect: Cultural Theory and the Ontological Turn" (2005) 19(5) *Cultural Studies* 548; Clare Hemmings, "Affective Solidarity: Feminist Reflexivity and Political Transformation" (2012) 13(2) *Feminist Theory* 147; and Linda Åhäll, "Affect as Methodology: Feminism and the Politics of Emotion" (2018) 12 *International Political Sociology* 36.

New materialism views matter, or material configurations of the world, as discursive practices that affect reality, experience and meaning-making. Discursive practices are not only a human phenomenon. This means that matter embodies specific exclusionary practices, or dictating constraints, conditions and practices.[81] As Longino argued in the context of standpoint theory (noted above), nature imposes constraints. In turn, discourse ("what constrains and enables what can be said")[82] is affected by matter. Put another way, matter cannot be divorced from culture or discourse.

Matter and humans intra-act to co-constitute one another and create meaning – they are not static.[83] Within intra-actions, matter is not an inert product of discursive practices, "passively awaiting signification".[84] In other words, matter is not simply out there waiting for humans to discover, identify, define and describe. It "is always already an ongoing historicity".[85] That is, matter is there with or without human interaction or observation – it has its own ongoing historical authenticity. Within intra-actions with humans, matter is an active agent in the creation of meaning because it too has discursive practices. Matter, humans and meaning are continually going through boundary-making (discursive) processes through intra-actions.

Because of the continual boundary-making process, intra-actions do not presume any prior existence of independent entities.[86] Barad stated:

> matter does not refer to a fixed substance; rather, matter is substance in its intra-active becoming – not a thing, but a doing, a congealing of agency. Matter is a stabilizing and destabilizing process of iterative intra-activity. Phenomena – the smallest material units (relational "atoms") – come to matter through this process of ongoing intra-activity. That is, matter refers to the materiality/materialization of phenomena, not to an inherent fixed property of abstract independently existing objects of Newtonian physics …[87]

It is intra-action that creates the distinction between the agents, or between subject and object:

> Indeed, it is through such practices that the differential boundaries between "humans" and "nonhumans," "culture" and "nature," the "social" and the "scientific" are constituted. Phenomena are constitutive of reality. Reality is not composed of things-in-themselves or things-behind-phenomena but "things"-in-phenomena. The world is intraactivity in its differential mattering.[88]

81 Ibid., 819.
82 Ibid.
83 Ibid., 820–21 (emphasis removed from original).
84 Ibid., 821.
85 Ibid.
86 Ibid., 815.
87 Ibid., 822 (emphasis removed from original).
88 Ibid., 817.

New materialism also theorises a co-constitution of mind and body, resulting in an embodied human being and also embodied subjectivity.[89] Subjectivity lies not only in the disembodied mind (masculine), but also in the material body (to include the feminine). This embodied being engages in networks of interdependent physical and metaphysical (natural and cultural) forces to co-constitute subjectivity. This subjectivity arises out of human-matter entanglements:

> the universe is agential intra-activity in its becoming. The primary ontological units are not "things" but phenomena – dynamic topological reconfigurings/entanglements/relationalities/(re)articulations. And the primary semantic units are not "words" but material-discursive practices through which boundaries are constituted. This dynamism is agency. Agency is not an attribute but the ongoing reconfigurings of the world.[90]

That is, intra-action means that subjectivity is continually becoming. Both human beings and matter have agency (or subjectivity) through intra-acting, doing and being. As discussed further below, viewing matter as having agency affects the way that we think about the inventor and the invention.

Furthermore, intra-action results in relations that are "material phenomena".[91] Material phenomena are defined by the inseparability of the human and the matter. In Barad's words:

> This account refuses the representationalist fixation on "words" and "things" and the problematic of their relationality, advocating instead *a causal relationship between specific exclusionary practices embodied as specific material configurations of the world* (i.e., discursive practices/(con)figurations rather than "words") *and specific material phenomena* (i.e., relations rather than "things"). This causal relationship between the apparatuses of bodily production and the phenomena produced is one of "agential intra-action."[92]

New materialist subjects are not hybrids like Haraway's cyborg (or per ANT discussed below), but rather human-matter entanglements that results in inseparability of entangled material phenomena. This essentially distributes subjectivity beyond human beings and the inanimate, and beyond individual actors. This is quite different from standpoint theory, as there is no subject and object, or observer of the external world. Unlike standpoint theory, new materialism does not simply change the subject/object binary, but breaks it down. Similarly, new materialism collapses the culture/nature binary, as humans are not "simply located at particular places *in* the world; rather, we are part *of* the world in its ongoing

89 Elizabeth Grosz, "Feminism, Materialism, and Freedom" in Diana Coole et al. (eds), *New Materialisms: Ontology, Agency, and Politics* (Duke University Press, 2010) 139.
90 Barad (n 78) 818.
91 Ibid., 814 (emphasis in original).
92 Ibid. (emphasis in original).

intra-activity".[93] As a result, agential realism dissolves the distinction between ontology and epistemology:

> Practices of knowing and being are not isolatable, but rather they are mutually implicated. We do not obtain knowledge by standing outside of the world; we know because "we" are of the world. We are part of the world in its differential becoming. The separation of epistemology from ontology is a reverberation of a metaphysics that assumes an inherent difference between human and nonhuman, subject and object, mind and body, matter and discourse. *Onto-epistem-ology* – the study of practices of knowing in being – is probably a better way to think about the kind of understandings that are needed to come to terms with how specific intra-actions matter.[94]

New materialism is a relational theory, as the "onto-epistemological" is found in relations. Different from Haraway's development of standpoint theory outlined above, which is also relational, in new materialism relations can be with matter.

New materialism and specifically Barad's interpretation thereof are not without their critics. For example, Sara Ahmed and Nikki Sullivan have separately contradicted the stereotypical framing of feminist poststructuralist critique as ignoring the corporeal, being "matter-phobic", and instead focused on rhetoric and semiotics.[95] Sara Irni and Angela Wiley have raised concerns that the "return to matter" might lead to a loss of all the gains made by postcolonial critiques, as race will be excluded from the discussion.[96] Irni argued that this results from a very natural-sciences understanding of "matter", which leaves out other "matter", such as women's material living conditions, labour, health and intimacy, which are structured by race amongst other things.[97] Wiley expanded on this, stating that the return to matter would result in a return to Eurocentric science, as "this genealogy of materialism imagines a debate about the matter of matter that excludes diverse and longstanding counterhegemonic knowledges about our worlds."[98] After all, "[i]n new materialism, as in other areas of feminist theory, the unmarked and presumably race-neutral body is implicitly white".[99]

93 Ibid., 828 (emphasis in original).
94 Ibid., 829 (emphasis added).
95 Sara Ahmed, "Open Forum. Imaginary Prohibitions. Some Preliminary Remarks on the Founding Gesture of the 'New Materialism'" (2008) 15(1) *European Journal of Women's Studies* 23; and Nikki Sullivan, "The Somatechnics of Perception and the Matter of the Non/human: A Critical Response to New Materialism" (2012) 19(3) *European Journal of Women's Studies* 299.
96 Sari Irni, "The Politics of Materiality: Affective Encounters in a Transdisciplinary Debate" (2013) 20(4) *European Journal of Women's Studies* 347; Angela Wiley, "A World of Materialisms: Postcolonial Feminist Science Studies and the New Natural" (2016) 41(6) *Science, Technology, & Human Values* 991.
97 Irni (n 96) 349–53.
98 Wiley (n 96) 999.
99 Ibid., 1002.

Barad's new materialism is descriptive – it describes what is rather than showing what could or should be. Landon Schnabel has questioned the political deployability of new materialism. When humans are the centre of subjectivity, it is easier to set political and moral judgements.[100] The same argument can be made regarding the usefulness of new materialism for developing a new knowledge governance system. For example, the theory does not tell us how to address competing onto-epistemes, or assist with critiquing a knowledge governance system that gives more legal protection to certain kinds of knowledge over others. In this regard, Wiley argued that weaving in feminist postcolonial critique could give new materialism the ability to effect change. In her words, "[p]ostcolonial feminist science studies can operate as occasion and resource for knowing, imagining, and making our worlds anew".[101] Wiley stated that taking feminist postcolonial critique into account would "yield a world of materialisms. A postcolonial feminist materialism would proliferate knowledges and thus narrative and empirical resources for transforming our worlds."[102] She argued that new materialism should be framed as "ways of reconceiving/conceiving the imagined proper objects of Western science", as this "would not only position these projects as destabilizing challenges to the epistemological hegemony of Science but also make them accountable to a postcolonial insistence on the importance of power".[103]

Wiley's critique weaves in standpoint theory by calling for multiple materialisms, which is akin to the call for a need for multiple viewpoints. In addition, she draws on a Foucauldian understanding of the relationship between knowledge and power, by arguing for the importance of challenging colonial (re)productions of co-constituting knowledge and power, through ensuring that non-Western and non-masculine materialisms are also given salience. By interweaving existing feminist standpoint theory into new materialism, Wiley opens the door to linking developments such as Haraway's situated knowledges (discussed above), which could be used to theorise how to generate "more objective" onto-epistemes.

For our purposes, what is valuable from new materialism is the idea that matter matters. It is not a passive thing awaiting human discovery or action. Instead, humans and matter intra-act to co-constitute. There is no hard and fast delineation of the human, on the one side, and "discovered" natural laws or natural products on the other side. This affects our understanding of the invention and the inventor, which, in turn, breaks down the divide between discoveries and inventions.

Though new materialism is a relational theory, it does not actually tell us about relations. New materialism is focused on how relations result in humans and matter being interdependent and co-constituting. We turn to ANT to look more directly at relations between humans and matter (and other things), and how knowledge is stabilised (or standardised) within those relations.

100 Landon Schnabel, "The Question of Subjectivity in Three Emerging Feminist Science Studies Frameworks" (2014) 44 *Women's Studies International Forum* 10, 14.
101 Wiley (n 96) 1009.
102 Ibid., 1008–9.
103 Ibid., 1005.

3.3 Actor-network theory

ANT is used in the social sciences to describe relationships between people and all other "things" as networks.[104] These networks include all things (human or otherwise) that in some way affect the production of scientific statements and theories. The descriptive nature of ANT makes it comparable with Foucauldian discourse analysis – both use saturated descriptions to explain the social world. However, ANT "networks" differ from Foucauldian "discourses", as they are not historically (or contextually) contingent but constitute what is. Nothing exists outside of the networks. In other words, a description of all the relations in a network tells you everything that is within and that affects that network.

Per ANT, human actors are not objective observers, making ANT post-modern. ANT frames human actors (particularly researchers) as entangled participants amongst other humans, animals, objects, methods and instruments, amongst other things, all of which act upon each other. All these things in the network are "actants" and have agency or subjectivity. There is no culture/nature binary. Because networks include anything – inanimate and animate – that can affect the production of scientific statements and theories, ANT is both materialist and posthumanist. According to ANT, agencies of actions need not be conscious or have intention.[105] Bruno Latour wrote:

> It is because humans, nonhumans, and even angels are never sufficient in themselves and because there is no one direction going from one type of delegation to the other, that it is so useless to impose a priori divisions between which skills are human and which ones are not human, which characters are personified and which remain abstract, which delegation is forbidden and which is permissible, which type of delegation is stronger or more durable than the other.[106]

While ANT shares similarities with Barad's new materialism, it differs in its focus on networks of actants and the way knowledge is stabilised (or made durable) within those networks. According to ANT, agents act upon each other through relational practices, with scientists translating facts and artefacts

104 See e.g. Bruno Latour, *Science in Action* (Open University Press, 1987); and Bruno Latour, *Reassembling the Social: An Introduction to Actor-Network-Theory* (Oxford University Press, 2007); Michel Callon, "Actor-Network Theory – The Market Test" (1999) 47(1) *The Sociological Review* 181; John Law, *A Sociology of Monsters: Essays on Power, Technology, and Domination* (Routledge, 1991). On ANT generally, see Fabian Muniesa, "Actor Network Theory" in James D Wright (ed.), *International Encyclopedia of the Social & Behavioral Sciences* (2nd edn, Elsevier, 2015, vol.1) 80.

105 Indeed, Callon and Law urge caution in considering intention, as intention is often tied to language, which removes agency from that unable to use words to account for intention. See Michel Callon and John Law, "Agency and the Hybrid Collectif" (1995) 94 *South Atlantic Quarterly* 481.

106 Bruno Latour, "Mixing Humans and Nonhumans Together: The Sociology of a Door-Closer" (1988) 35(3) *Social Problems* 298, 305.

throughout the network. If these facts and artefacts are successfully translated (subscribed to) throughout the network, the network and the knowledge are stabilised.[107] Successful translation and stabilisation of knowledge require that the knowledge becomes unquestioned throughout the network, or "black-boxed", which is

> the way scientific and technical work is made invisible by its own success. When a machine runs efficiently, when a matter of fact is settled, one need focus only on its inputs and outputs and not on its internal complexity. Thus, paradoxically, the more science and technology succeed, the more opaque and obscure they become.[108]

The more that is black-boxed, the more the knowledge is stable and predictable. It is not only knowledge and technology that become stabilised, but also the performances of actors and power relations within the network; the scientist becomes the actor, seen as the cause of network effects, and other roles are ascribed.[109] Note that there are similarities between ANT's "stabilised" and Star's "standardised" – both are things that are accepted and unquestioned.

In difference to general standpoint theory, ANT is not relative but relational. That is, it is not that knowledge, experience and being are "true" only in reference to other variables, but that what "is" is the found in the relational. While Haraway's approach to standpoint theory is relational in the sense that it situates situated knowledges, making them interdependent, with ANT, relations are the unit of analysis. There is no subject and object, but relations. There are no human viewpoints (subject) of nature (object), but rather actants (human, animate and inanimate) are mutually constituted, or structured and structuring. More in line with Barad's new materialism, per ANT the individual and the community are materially intertwined – "constructed in and through one another within specific contexts and relations of power … each is implicated with and dependent on the other for meaning".[110]

As a relational theory, ANT does not distinguish between the nodes of the network and the network as actors. Entities within a network participate in collective and distributed actions. All actions are a result of the actor-network. For example, if a scientific statement or theory comes out of a network, it is an

107 Bruno Latour, "Technology is Society Made Durable" (1991) 38(S1) *The Sociological Review* 103, 129.

108 Bruno Latour, *Pandora's Hope: Essays on the Reality of Science Studies* (Harvard University Press, 1999) 304. Cf. Pierre Bourdieu, *Outline of a Theory of Practice* (Cambridge University Press, 1977) 164, on beliefs that appear self-evident and are undisputed, which Bourdieu refers to as "doxa", "so as to distinguish it from an orthodox or heterodox belief implying awareness and recognition of the possibility of different or antagonistic beliefs".

109 Latour, "Technology is Society Made Durable" (n 107) 118.

110 Carolyn Pedwell, "Weaving Relational Webs: Theorizing Cultural Difference and Embodied Practice" (2008) 9(1) *Feminist Theory* 87, 93.

action of the entire network. However, power and agency are not necessarily distributed equally within a network. Not all actions are equal.[111] Recognising everything that can affect scientific statements and theories as actors flattens the hierarchy of different kinds of actors. For our purposes, agency is spread beyond just the human inventor who came up with the conceptual aspects of an invention. Viewing humans as actors within a network also overcomes the individual/communal dichotomy, as it frames the individual as inherently communal – affected by other humans in an interdependent relationship. However, as power and agency are not necessarily distributed equally and not all actions are equal, it is possible that different individuals contributed differently towards scientific statements and theories. It is also possible that different actors within the network have more or less of an effect on what becomes stabilised.

The stabilisation of networks (through black-boxing) and power relations is what allows for the construction of dualities, such as culture/nature and human/non-human. That is, the binaries omnipresent in Western societies exist because certain knowledge has been successfully translated and stabilised throughout networks. Relational ordering (how nodes of the network relate to and are co-constituted by the network) means that the knowledge and the binaries it embodies are continually practiced, enacted and re-enacted, thus maintaining them. Note that this is similar to Foucault's understanding of the (re)production of knowledge and power, discussed above.

While ANT explains why there are binaries, it simultaneously makes it clear that they are not essential. Like Barad's new materialism, which breaks the divide between epistemology and ontology, ANT bridges social constructivism and realism (or culture and nature) by theorising that the social and nature are coproduced as a performative function of science. In other words, by doing science (using instruments, graphs, figures and linguistic tools), scientists both describe and produce nature. Natural entities are materialised in the laboratory. The translation of facts and artefacts throughout the network both represents and constructs nature. Latour stated:

> when studying science and technology, we are not to follow a given statement through *context*. We are to follow the simultaneous production of a "text" and a "context". In other words, any division we make between society on the one hand and scientific or technical content on the other is necessarily arbitrary.[112]

That is, culture does not contextualise nature or have a semiotic relationship to it. Knowledge does not represent nature from an external or outside perspective. It does not explain nature or exist apart from it. By producing cultural products, we assemble what is nature. Science is performative. Thus, there is no duality between nature and culture.[113] Instead, there are socio-material

111 Latour, "Technology is Society Made Durable" (n 107) 128.
112 Ibid., 106 (emphasis in original).
113 Bruno Latour, *We Have Never Been Modern* (Harvard University Press, 1993).

networks within which social phenomena are constituted, and what constitutes nature is accepted cultural ideas of what is "real" or "true".

Entities and their networks co-create one another and create new forms of social action. Established networks have stabilised forms of social action. Once a network has been solidified, an actor's particular locality (or network) affects his/her background assumptions, methodologies, measurements, interpretation, production and acceptance of knowledge.

ANT holds that there are natural truths; however, they cannot be known to humans without understanding the network within which knowledge is generated. It is not social constructivism, as it does not merely explain knowledge vis-à-vis the context of its production. Instead, methods and techniques have a performative role in constituting what they are used to create.[114] That is, in the production of knowledge, content and context are coproduced. It is non-dualistic, as both content and context are subject to analysis.

Similar to Barad's new materialism and Haraway's situated knowledge (discussed above), what is "nature" or "true" according to ANT is continuously contested and remade. Because of the heterogeneous and changing make up of networks, networks are easily destabilised, for example, with the entry or exit of individuals. Furthermore, the "actors involved … consist of a range of mutable identities, engaged in complex processes of negotiating their own and each other's identities".[115] Any network is one of "dynamic construction".[116] Mutable identities mean that any network stability can only be temporary. The same is true of "culture" and also power and domination, because networks and the technologies they encompass can evolve. "Domination is never a capital that can be stored in a bank. It has to be deployed, black-boxed, repaired, maintained."[117]

As noted in the foregoing, ANT understands technology as an actor and part of a network of actors in society. Latour argued that we need to look beyond "social relations", weaving these "into a fabric that includes non-human actants", as non-humans "offer the possibility of holding society together as a durable whole".[118] This is because the reality is that "[w]e are never faced with objects or social relations, we are faced with chains which are associations of humans (h) and non-humans (NH). No one has ever seen a social relation by itself … nor a technical relation".[119] Elsewhere, Latour stated that "[t]he bizarre idea that society might be made up of human relations is a mirror image of the

114 Note that this is similar to Foucault's discourses (historically contingent social systems), which Foucault describes as material in effect because of "practices that systematically form the objects of which they speak"; Michel Foucault, *Archaeology of Knowledge and the Discourse on Language* (1969) (trans. AM Sheridan Smith, Pantheon Books, 1972) 49.

115 Vicky Singleton, "Feminism, Sociology and Scientific Knowledge and Postmodernism: Politics, Theory and Me" (1996) 26 *Social Studies of Science* 445, 463.

116 Ibid.

117 Latour, "Technology is Society Made Durable" (n 107) 118.

118 Ibid., 103.

119 Ibid., 110.

other no less bizarre idea that techniques might be made up of nonhuman relations".[120]

Stability (or durability) of social relations is only achieved with non-humans.[121] This is because humans interact with so many non-human things on a daily basis, which embody social relations, that these are part of the social world. In Latour's words:

> If, in our societies, there are thousands of such lieutenants to which we have delegated competences [in technological characters, delegates or representatives], it means that what defines our social relations is, for the most part, prescribed back to us by nonhumans. Knowledge, morality, craft, force, sociability are not properties of humans but of humans *accompanied* by their retinue of delegated characters. Since each of those delegates ties together part of our social world, it means that studying social relations without the nonhumans is impossible ...[122]

This creates an environment of techno-social character.[123] Within this, innovation and technology are not separate from the social. There is no "innovation" or "technology" contextualised by the social. An innovation or technology is simply part of the network. As noted above, as a relational theory, there is no distinction between the nodes of the network and the network as actors.

Latour has also addressed the human/object (culture/nature) dichotomy and theorised around the "hybrid" character of humans and technologies.[124] Within certain networks, some interactions are so common that it becomes senseless to categorise entities and effects as either nature or culture. Instead, Latour explains that there are "nature-cultures" or "quasi-objects",[125] which are hybrid entities. Latour's hybrids are not necessarily a mix of culture and nature, or human and technology, but something that is neither one nor the other in the binary.

There are analogies between Latour's hybrids and Haraway's cyborg, as it is possible that a human is born into a relation with a technology that is nature-culture, making it cyborg like. Nevertheless, Haraway has criticised ANT on the basis that it is a descriptive theory rather than a critical theory.[126] Unlike standpoint theory, ANT

120 Latour, "Mixing Humans and Nonhumans Together" (n 106) 308.

121 Latour, "Technology is Society Made Durable" (n 107) 111.

122 Latour, "Mixing Humans and Nonhumans Together" (n 106) 310 (emphasis in original). See also 308.

123 See also Gunther Teubner, "Rights of Non-Humans? Electronic Agents and Animals as New Actors in Politics and Law" (2006) 33(4) *Journal of Law and Society* 497; and Vaios Karavas, "The Force of Code: Law's Transformation under Information Technological Conditions" (2009) 10(4) *German Law Journal* 463.

124 Latour, "Mixing Humans and Nonhumans Together" (n 106); and Latour, *We Have Never Been Modern* (n 113).

125 Latour, *We Have Never Been Modern* (n 113) 104.

126 Donna Haraway, *Modest_witness@second_Millenium. The FemaleMan_Meets_OncoMouse* (Routledge, 1997).

does not have the ability to take into account factors such as gender, race and class. ANT does not consider how these factors might affect translations, power relations and social actions. It is a-political and ethics free.[127] Because there is nothing external to a network, Latour has stated that power and power relations are an effect of networks, rather than a cause.[128] In other words, according to Latour, power and domination result from the stabilisation of networks and expected behaviour. Any moral obligations arise from the stabilised network and the interactions between actants – they are internal rather than external.

There is value in description (whether ANT or Foucauldian). It can allow one to know, understand and judge.[129] ANT focuses on relations, for example, the interpersonal, institutional and structural, which reveal power and oppression. Focusing on the relational can reveal how conditions, structures and institutions might marginalise and oppress, and entrench inequalities and injustices. Without description, social relations (including power and gender relations) might remain invisible, opaque to scrutiny. Only through identification can one engage, dismantle and repair. However, accounting for characteristics such as gender, race and class might require that our network descriptions are centred on actors other than the "hero" scientists.[130] Note that, in reply to the criticism that ANT is only descriptive and cannot be politically deployed, Latour stated that "saturated" descriptions are sufficient, as we then have all viewpoints and trajectories, and can vary the observer's point of view. The point is perhaps that we do indeed have to vary the point of view.[131] It is through saturated descriptions of the relations of the non-"heroes" and how their knowledge is translated and black-boxed (or not), and the power, gender and other relations at play, that we can politicise ANT.

Saturated descriptions of networks should be centred around heterogenous cyborgs or monsters – from the standpoint of those who "have no choice but to live inside the system of commensurability which is being established, but who don't and can't quite fit".[132] If we were to focus an ANT description on female inventors, we would gain understanding about their social relations within their networks and the work that they must do to maintain the network, and whether their knowledge and ways of knowing are stabilised (black-boxed or standardised) or how their power relations within the network affect stabilisation.

127 See e.g. Arianne Françoise Conty, "The Politics of Nature: New Materialist Response to the Anthropocene" (2018) 35(7) *Theory, Culture & Society* 73.
128 Bruno Latour, "The Powers of Association" (1984) 32(1S) *The Sociological Review* 264.
129 Latour, "Technology is Society Made Durable" (n 107) 130, noted that there is nothing about ANT that prevents judgement. But, before one can make a judgement, one must first describe the network.
130 Latour is well-known for his work on Louis Pasteur; Bruno Latour, *The Pasteurization of France* (trans. Alan Sheridan and John Law, Cambridge University Press, 1988).
131 Latour, "Technology is Society Made Durable" (n 107) 129–30.
132 Star (n 20); and Haraway, "Nature, Politics, and Possibilities" (n 15) 514.

Overall, what we can take from ANT is the value of relationality instead of relativity. That is, viewing actants, methods, artefacts and knowledge as co-constituting, because this overcomes dualities. We could focus on the relational to better effect change in what is co-constituted and also what knowledge is stabilised (or accepted) within networks. However, before we can effect such change, we need to politicise ANT by centring an actor-network analysis on those other than "hero" scientists.

4 A techno-social relational network of situated knowledges?

The foregoing discussion exemplifies that there are many ways to conceive of "knowledge" that differ significantly from modernism. The following takes certain aspects of the three theories examined above to frame "knowledge" in a way helpful for designing an alternative knowledge governance system, which is done in Chapter 7.

Situated knowledges can be viewed as networks – embodied within a viewer, who sits within an ANT-like network of all things that affect knowledge generation. Unlike ANT networks, these are embedded in social, political and historical locations, more like Foucauldian discourses, as this allows for politicisation and consequently change. However, the word "network" is used as the network imagery is valuable. The development of "more objective" knowledge would be constructed by situating these situated networked accounts within the milieu of other situated networked accounts, allowing for contestation of the layered webs. Furthermore, we can conceptualise networks with respect to Julie Cohen's "distributed spatiality – environment, landscape, network, milieu", where the privatised and public domain share interwoven space in a distributed network (discussed in Chapter 5).[133] In other words, the situated networked accounts would expand through the private and the public, with no definitive borders between the private and public and no distinct value given to one over the other.

If we factor in that humans and matter are co-constituting, giving the latter agency, we can place matter in the networks of knowledge generation. Knowledge is not only situated in the viewer and social location, in relation to other social actors, but also in relation to matter. This is in contradistinction to modernity, which only views humans as having agency through their thought, language and ability to act with intention. When knowledge is situated and materials have agency, we can break down a further binary inherent in masculine "objective" science – the divide between humans and technology. This binary sees man as the objectifier, technology as the object. Yet, technology embodies gender relations and, when this technology is used and interpreted, it affects those relations.[134] In Haraway's words, "every technology is a frozen moment of social practice and

133 Julie E Cohen, "Copyright, Commodification, and Culture: Locating the Public Domain" in Lucie Guibault and P Bernt Hugenholtz (eds), *The Future of the Public Domain: Identifying the Commons in Information Law* (Kluwer Law International, 2006) 121, 154 and 157.

134 Judy Wajcman, "Feminist Theories of Technology" (2010) 34 *Cambridge Journal of Economics* 143, 150–1. See also Ronald R Kline, "Technological Determinism" in

may be not so frozen. ... Machines are arrangements of practice, and that certainly includes the personal body".[135] All things are "barely stabilized historical processes".[136] When matter has agency, it is not a mere object to be observed and manipulated. Matter has a performative role in co-constituting knowledge and meaning. This affects our perception of inventorship and the hierarchy of contributions towards inventions.

This steps away from the focus on individual creators, acknowledging that invention is cumulative, contingent and communal, and that it is a discourse or dialogic. The understanding that knowledge is interdependent with its context is consistent with relational theories (discussed above). If our distributed networks are imbued with social, political and historical locations, knowledge generation necessarily occurs within a network of social relations.[137] Flax has argued that social relations must include gender relations:

> Unless we see gender as a social relation, rather than as an opposition of inherently different beings, we will not be able to identify the varieties and limitations of different women's (or men's) powers and oppressions within particular societies.[138]

I would add that it also includes techno-social relations. Knowledge generation is not just cumulative, contingent and communal vis-à-vis other social actors, but also the animate and inanimate. Social relations are co-created with, embodied within and reliant upon the animate and inanimate.

Craig, Joseph Turcotte and Rosemary Coombe have discussed how relational feminism allows us to recognise the duality of creators, as communally dependent social beings, having individual autonomy, identity or voice.[139] A "relational" creator is "situated within, and constituted by, the communities in which she exists, and the texts and discourses with which she is surrounded, which also shape her consciousness and expressive activities".[140] Relational theory, thus, understands autonomy in relational terms, as intrinsically social.[141] If the starting point is that humans are intrinsically social, then one cannot be genuinely autonomous without community – there is interdependence.[142] Put

James D Wright (ed.), *International Encyclopedia of the Social & Behavioral Sciences* (2nd edn, Elsevier, 2015, vol. 24) 109.

135 Haraway, "Nature, Politics, and Possibilities" (n 15) 520.

136 Ibid.

137 On the copyright context, see Carys J Craig, *Copyright, Communication and Culture: Towards a Relational Theory of Copyright Law* (Edward Elgar, 2011).

138 Flax (n 49) 641.

139 Carys J Craig, Joseph F Turcotte and Rosemary J Coombe, "What is Feminist About Open Access?: A Relational Approach to Copyright in the Academy" (2011) 1(1) *Feminists@law* 1, 10–11. See also Craig (n 137) 31–64.

140 Craig, Turcotte and Coombe (n 139) 13.

141 Ibid., 11.

142 Craig (n 137) 46–7.

another way, one cannot truly act individually without engagement with others, existing knowledge and materials.

A situated and relational approach, therefore, helps us to dismantle a binary inherent in the inventorship discussion: the isolated individual and the immersed communal being. Neither is reified. Neither is removed of its specificity. Instead, the individual and the community are seen as entangled and interdependent. Individual creation is socially and culturally determined, directed by the pre- and co-existing. Such an understanding is notably consistent with a common Indigenous worldview of knowledge, which focuses on the relationship with that knowledge per se and vis-à-vis the community, future generations and the environment.[143]

A relational approach also inherently places knowledge in others' networks, allowing for knowledge to be continually subject to dialogue and change.[144] Knowledge becomes based on the "social relation of 'conversation.' The world neither speaks itself nor disappears in favour of a master decoder. The codes of the world are not still, waiting only to be read. The world is not raw material for humanization".[145] Viewing knowledge as the social relation of conversation allows us to deconstruct the nature/culture binary. There is no human subject or culture that decodes nature. Instead, there is co-constitution of nature and culture, by and through the other, or in Haraway's words, "naturecultures", and the co-constitution of subjectivity.[146] Therefore, with respect to inventorship, a relational understanding recasts the "inventor", as both autonomous and communal, and the formation of subjectivity is not necessarily limited to human beings. Furthermore, in relation to patentability, there is neither a sharp distinction between natural laws and natural products (not patentable) and inventions (patentable), nor between the upstream and downstream.

Viewing knowledge and knowledge production as being situated and relational additionally allows us to consider the public domain and privatised dichotomy in a new light. The network imagery, together with the understanding that the public domain and privatised are co-constituting, might increase the focus on openness and egalitarianism, thereby breaking down the sharp divide between the public domain and the privatised.[147] Social relations, history and context can be factored in, including power relations, gender, class,

143 Peter Drahos and Susy Frankel, "Indigenous Peoples' Innovation and Intellectual Property: The Issues" in Peter Drahos and Susy Frankel (eds), *Indigenous Peoples' Innovation: Intellectual Property Pathways to Development* (ANU E-Press, 2012) 1, 9–10.

144 This understanding of the creator and creation is, thus, dialogic Craig (n 137) 40. See also Pedwell (n 110) 93.

145 Haraway, "Situated Knowledges" (n 35) 593.

146 Donna Haraway, *The Companion Species Manifesto: Dogs, People, and Significant Otherness* (Prickly Paradigm, 2003).

147 Laura A Foster, "Situating Feminism, Patent Law, and the Public Domain" (2011) 20 *Columbia Journal of Gender & Law* 262, 339.

race and colonisation. Knowledge and its production become heterogeneous and contingent, and less hierarchical.

In terms of creating some kind of universality, Harvey proposed that we need epistemology that can tell the difference between significant and insignificant differences or "othernesses". This is an epistemology that "can understand the social processes of construction of situatedness, otherness, difference, political identity and the like".[148] That is, epistemologies that can understand the specific process of co-constitution and differences between locations.[149] Therefore, similarity and solidarity are found between situated knowledges through understanding why there are differences (often related to power dynamics or social power), rather than just looking at differences per se. This gets rid of insignificant differences, allowing for some universality. In a similar vein, Mary Tiles has noted that a situated approach that gives more agency to materials does not mean abandoning standards of objectivity, such as being able to obtain reliably repeatable results.[150] It means that the success or failure of projects must be "set and judged against a background of conditions which determine and limit their significance".[151]

According to Harvey, "more objective" knowledge is created when it acquires durability through social relations of situated knowledges:

> While identity does not rest upon sameness or essence, it does acquire durability and permanence according to the stories we tell ourselves and others about our history. Although identity internalizes otherness, it nevertheless delimits and renders relatively durable both the field of "othernesses" brought into play and the relation of those others to a particular sense of selfhood.[152]

Here, ANT is useful, as it helps us to identify how networks and knowledge within them become stable. Viewpoints (or scientific statements or theories) will compete, insignificant differences will be discarded, and once a viewpoint is black-boxed throughout the network, accepted and unquestioned, it is stabilised (or standardised) and it becomes "more objective" knowledge. Knowledge is not just a matter of competing viewpoints. It is a matter of translation and dialogue, where social truths are derived through techno-social relations. What is translated and accepted as "true" is what makes the most sense within a context of techno-social relations.

5 "Take homes"

The purpose of this chapter was to identify different ways of theorising knowledge, which can be used to develop a new knowledge governance system free from binaries and the biases they embody. The theories discussed

148 Harvey (n 57) 63.
149 Ibid.
150 Tiles (n 34) 306.
151 Ibid.
152 Harvey, "Class Relations, Social Justice and the Politics of Difference" (n 57) 58.

attempt to overcome the binaries created by modernity, without falling into hyper-social constructivism and relativism. In other words, while knowledge and being depend on one's social, historical and political location, there must be some way to develop more objective or universal knowledge, and which acknowledges the role of matter or nature.

Here, I have found it useful to understand humans, matter and knowledge as situated within techno-social relational networks. Understanding that all knowledge is situated strips away the reification of certain sources and kinds of knowledge. When we account for Haraway and Star's heterogeneous cyborg or monster as the actors, who are forced to operate within stabilised networks to which they cannot conform, we start to question the techno-social relations at play. For example, the gender, historical or political relations that affect co-constitution. If we were to create a saturated description of a cyborg's actor-network, it would reflect very different power relations than the actor-networks of "heroes". Doing so is important for effecting political change. In addition, more objective knowledge is created through overlaying networks and finding similarity and solidarity.

Within such relational networks, there is interdependence and co-constitution of the individual and the communal, the subject and the object, and humans and knowledge. Matter has agency, as it acts upon humans just as humans act upon it, in an intra-action of co-constitution. This shifts our understanding of the inventor and the invention. The inventor is no longer the human who contributed the "concept" behind an invention. Inventorship is distributed throughout the network of humans and matter that allow for the invention. The sharp dichotomy between the "made" and the "natural" disappears, as meaning, matter or the natural are co-created through intra-actions with humans. In addition, the network imagery allows us to understand the interdependence of the public domain and the privatised, which also has the effect of flattening hierarchies of creators and knowledge.

Overall, we want the situated techno-social network descriptions of a diverse range of people, across their multiple social locations, so that we can develop more objective knowledge. Different theories of knowledge and being are also clear that hierarchies of, and distinctions between, creators and knowledge embodied in patent law are a result of modernism and not inherent. The following chapter carries these "take homes" forward to create a more egalitarian knowledge governance system.

7 Reconstructing the law

> [T]he principle which regulates the existing social relations between the two sexes – the legal subordination of one sex to the other – is wrong in itself, and now one of the chief hindrances to human improvement; and that it ought to be replaced by a principle of perfect equality, admitting no power or privilege on the one side, nor disability on the other.[1]

1 Introduction

This book has shown that patenting is gendered (Chapter 1) because patent law creates a biased knowledge governance system. This is reflected in the law itself (Chapter 2), which embodies multiple gendered binaries, as well as the innovation environment that the law supports (Chapter 3). This has negative consequences for women because of the role that patents play in incentivising inventors and invention, and in structuring the commercialisation of inventions – it is the masculine and males which and who predominantly benefit from the patent system (Chapter 4). In John Stuart Mill's words, quoted at the beginning of this chapter, "the legal subordination of one sex to the other – is wrong in itself" and should be ameliorated. Attempts at this typically try to promote the feminine and women. This might be through legally protecting the feminine and the public domain (the binary dialectic of the masculine and property, respectively), or pushing for more "women in science, technology, engineering and mathematics (STEM)". However, both of these are misguided. The solution to the biases engendered by binaries cannot come from flipping the binaries, or reinforcing them by telling women to work in STEM. Instead, binaries need to be broken down (Chapter 5). Moreover, as indicated throughout this book, the "women in STEM" rhetoric is a distraction from the underlying power relations that result in patent law being gendered and women having to be in STEM to patent.

These power relations are dictated by modernity. Yet, we need not theorise knowledge through the modern lens. Indeed, with the understanding that binaries are socially constructed rather than essential, philosophers have been trying to theorise their way out of modernity for the last century. As discussed in Chapter 6, one

1 John Stuart Mill, *The Subjection of Women* (Savill, Edwards & Co, 1869) 1.

DOI: 10.4324/9781003128502-8

can view knowledge as embodied and situated within social, political and historical contexts, embedded within techno-social relational networks. The different theories discussed exhibit that we need not maintain the existing patent law conceptualisations of the inventor and the invention, or of the public domain and the privatised.

More specifically, we can step away from an incentive-based property system that is balanced against a healthy and dynamic public domain to develop a system that allows for and fosters innovation. After all, framing knowledge as either propertised or in the public domain is yet another constructed binary, and it is one that "masks the ways in which the commons often functions more in the interests of traditional property owners than in the interests of commoners."[2] In addition, we may wish to develop a knowledge governance system that concentrates on incentivising the inventive process, distributed across a network of humans and matter, rather than being focused on individuals.

Ultimately, what is required is a system that best supports generation, dissemination, development and maintenance of knowledge, and the multiple modes in which this occurs in practice. This needs to be done in an egalitarian manner. Ideally, it would also be a system that promotes a fair distribution of wealth. All of these considerations are served by dismantling the view of the public domain as part of a binary system of propertised vs not propertised, and reimagining inventorship and the invention. This chapter examines what such a system might look like.

This chapter starts by discussing various alternative constructions of the public domain.[3] This is followed by an examination of the existing attempts to use the intellectual property system and the "grey" space between property and the public domain to address issues of distributive justice. Part 4 of this chapter then outlines a proposal for a possible knowledge governance system that reflects the learnings from this book. This is followed by some concluding thoughts.

2 A positive and structured public domain

As noted in the introduction of this chapter, one method of addressing the masculine nature of the propertised is to push for more recognition and protection of the feminine public domain. Malla Pollack has argued that the public domain is inherently feminine, because: (1) it is not commodified; (2) it recognises communal roots of creation; (3) it instantiates nurturing by being a space where one gives freely; and (4) it provides essential nourishment ("it is the birthing and lactating mother").[4] The core argument is that, rather than arguing for propertisation (e.g. patentability) of the feminine, we should shrink what

2 Anupan Chander and Madhavi Sunder, "The Romance of the Public Domain" (2004) 92 *California Law Review* 1331, 1343.

3 This chapter updates and expands upon content from Jessica C Lai, "Patents, Knowledge Governance and Gender" (2020) 42(1) *European Intellectual Property Review* 623.

4 Malla Pollack, "Towards a Feminist Theory of the Public Domain, or Rejecting the Gendered Scope of United States Copyrightable and Patentable Subject Matter" (2006) 12 *William and Mary Journal of Women and the Law* 603, 620–3.

is propertised and thereby broaden the feminine public domain. Terra Gearhart-Serna has similarly discussed how the openness of the public domain might actually make it a good knowledge framework for Indigenous women's knowledge.[5]

Pollack's and Gearhart-Serna's suggestions do not take us beyond the binary of the propertised and the public domain. Indeed, the suggestions rely on the binary. Yet, as the co-constituted dyadic partner of property, the existing public domain cannot function as a substitute knowledge governance system. It exists in interdependence with the propertised. In other words, it has no meaning without the propertised. Furthermore, as discussed in Chapter 5, the public domain is equally as gendered and racialised as the propertised, and it is constructed to ensure that the knowledge of women and the non-Western is available to be appropriated and propertised by the masculine and Western. The existing public domain is not an egalitarian space. Simply placing more in the public domain might serve to perpetuate the divide between the disempowered and the empowered. As stated by Chander and Sunder:

> the fashionable understanding of the public domain as "the opposite of property" is misleading. The binary framework suggests that, normatively, the public domain stands in opposition to intellectual property – that the public domain is a bulwark against propertization and an alternative to intellectual property. But in fact the public domain is essential to our private property system because it offers a sphere of free works upon which capitalists can draw without either seeking consent or drawing liability.[6]

In other words, the public domain "often functions in service of property, not in opposition to it".[7] It is "a device that permits the rest of the system to work by leaving the raw material of authorship [and inventorship] for authors [and inventors] to use".[8]

In order for the public domain to function as an alternative knowledge governance system, we would have to stop constructing it as the negative of property. In other words, we would have to break down the dichotomisation of the privatised and public domain. The first step towards this would be to legally recognise the public domain, thereby giving it positive constitution.[9] Because the public domain has no legally defined or protected boundaries, it is relatively easy for intellectual property to expand into the public domain. The

5 Terra L Gearhart-Serna, "Women's Work, Women's Knowing: Intellectual Property and the Recognition of Women's Traditional Knowledge" (2010) 21(2) *Yale Journal of Law and Feminism* 372, 395–8.

6 Chander and Sunder (n 2) 1343.

7 Ibid., 1346.

8 Jessica Litman, "The Public Domain" (1990) 39(4) *Emory Law Journal* 965, 968.

9 David Lange, "Recognizing the Public Domain" (1981) 44 *Law and Contemporary Problems* 147, 150 stated "no exclusive right should ever have affirmative recognition unless its conceptual opposite is also recognized. Each right ought to be marked off clearly against the public domain". Lange made multiple suggestions for how to protect the public domain from encroachment (at 175–8).

opposite is not true. Séverinne Dussolier has criticised the negative nature of the public domain, stating that it

> draws some empty space, empty of any exclusivity, but also empty of any protection of that very freedom to use. More than no-rights land, it is a wasteland, a fallow land. Calling it a domain seems preposterous and qualifying it as public only hints at its pretension to ensure public access and use to its resources, with no guarantee.[10]

Dussolier argued that the public domain should be positive, with "its own consistence or body" so that it has protection, rather than being a "spectre of the property right".[11] Similarly, David Lange has stated that the problems relating to the expanding scope of intellectual property "will not be resolved until courts have come to see the public domain not merely as an unexplored abstraction but as a field of individual rights fully as important as any of the new property rights".[12]

However, reifying the negative will not suffice.[13] As stated by Ruth Okediji, "[t]o carve out meaningful space for a rights-based international framework for traditional knowledge, the undifferentiated notion of the public domain requires discipline".[14] In this vein, Chander and Sunder stated that "leaving a resource in the public domain is not enough to satisfy societal ideals. It matters how that public domain is to be structured".[15] In other words, it is not enough to simply pick one binary half over the other, as this does not change the relationship between the two halves. Discipline and structure could be achieved through giving the public domain positive constitution via legal recognition and regulatory structure. This structure should reflect how creation takes place in practice, including issues relating to access to the public domain.[16]

10 Séverinne Dussolier, "Inclusivity in Intellectual Property" in Graeme B Dinwoodie, *Intellectual Property and General Legal Principles: Is IP* Lex Specialis*?* (Edward Elgar, 2015) 101, 106.

11 Ibid.

12 Lange, "Recognizing the Public Domain" (n 9) 178. See also Laura A Foster, "Situating Feminism, Patent Law, and the Public Domain" (2011) 20 *Columbia Journal of Gender & Law* 262, 282–96, on seeing patented objects as a hybrid of the propertised and the public domain and how this gives them equal value.

13 Cf. James Boyle "The Second Enclosure Movement and the Construction of the Public Domain" (2003) 66 *Law and Contemporary Problems* 33, who called for reification because there is a need to develop vocabulary about the public domains. This is because language matters and can be used to "counter the language of sacred property"; (70) "Naming encourages study" (at 72); "Having concrete language allows people to rally behind a common cause" (at 73).

14 Ruth Okediji, "Traditional Knowledge and the Public Domain" (2018) CIGI Papers No. 176, 10.

15 Chander and Sunder (n 2) 1337.

16 Julie E Cohen, "Copyright, Commodification, and Culture: Locating the Public Domain" in Lucie Guibault and P Bernt Hugenholtz (eds), *The Future of the Public Domain: Identifying the Commons in Information Law* (Kluwer Law International, 2006) 121, 158.

Graeme Dinwoodie and Rochelle Cooper Dreyfuss have similarly suggested that we might ensure access to the public domain through users' rights. They note the importance of doing so because the "the public domain is more than a place where old intellectual property goes to die".[17] Incursions of intellectual property can be better fought off if the public domain represents an affirmative source of entitlements.[18] The public domain and propertised dichotomy is broken down when the law is developed to recognise rights and privileges in relation to the public domain and obligations vis-à-vis property.[19] This is because the propertised would have some public character, and the public domain would have some private qualities.

There is disagreement as to whether the rights in relation to the public domain would be individualistic or collective. Lange has suggested that we could view the public domain as a "status" akin to citizenship, which "arises from the exercise of the creative imagination, thus to confer entitlements, privileges and immunities in the service of that exercise; a status independently and affirmatively recognized in law, sometimes collective in nature and sometimes individual, but omnipresent, portable and defining".[20] Lange clearly framed the positive entitlements of his public domain as being sometimes individual and sometimes collective. In contrast, Pollack defined the public domain as something collective, "which is shared by the community, the property held in common".[21] She stated that a "feminist-friendly public domain can be theorized as an owned public domain where the 'ownership' interest each community member holds is the right not to be excluded".[22] As discussed in Chapter 5, the individual/community is another binary, one that requires deconstructing.

Dussolier has argued that the public domain should not only be positive, but also *inclusive*. By this she means that the public domain should be regarded as the opposite of exclusivity, framed positively to mean "inclusivity". Whereas exclusivity is characterised by exclusion and individuality, inclusivity is "(1) the absence of a power to exclude others, which leads to inclusion of others in the use and (2) the collectiveness of use, as opposed to the individuality of exclusive rights".[23] Furthermore, while exclusivity engenders and functions via asymmetric power, inclusivity should be "equal and symmetric" entitlements in all users.[24]

It is worth noting that Indigenous peoples have similarly argued that the negative public domain is purely an intellectual property construct that does not take

17 Graeme B Dinwoodie and Rochelle Cooper Dreyfuss, "Patenting Science: Protecting the Domain of Accessible Knowledge" in Lucie Guibault and P Bernt Hugenholtz, *The Future of the Public Domain. Identifying the Commons in Information Law* (Kluwer Law International, 2006) 192, 200.

18 Ibid., 476.

19 Cohen (n 16) 165.

20 David Lange "Reimagining the Public Domain" (2003) 66 *Law and Contemporary Problems* 463, 474.

21 Pollack (n 4) 624.

22 Ibid., 625.

23 Dussolier (n 10) 104.

24 Ibid., 104–5.

into account the "private domains" created through their customary laws.[25] The Tulalip Tribes of Washington stated:

> There is no public domain in traditional knowledge. For the Māori, as lawyer Maui Solomon has emphasized, it makes no sense to talk about rights without also talking about obligations for the use of knowledge and resources, and this view is common, if not universal, among indigenous peoples. Although individuals might hold knowledge, their right is collectively determined, and it is rare that individuals have the right to use knowledge in a free and unconstrained manner. They are bound by the laws of their tribe and of the Creator.
>
> In this sense, the idea of "already disclosed" and "non-disclosed" knowledge also is a false distinction.[26]

Put another way, their knowledge might be presumed to be in the Western public domain, but this is not to say that it is unregulated. Instead, there is knowledge that falls outside of the Western and modern propertised/public domain binary, though politics and power result in that knowledge being subsumed within it.

A positive and inclusive public domain is more suitable to recognise and maintain various knowledge governance systems, able to substitute patents. As Dussolier noted,

> Inclusivity could also renew our thinking about what intellectual property is, particularly when we seek to apply it to traditional knowledge and folklore. An intellectual property right that could be able to grant inclusive rights would better pay tribute to the collective and shared use. In consequence, maybe traditional knowledge could enrich our notion of intellectual property, without being trapped by it?[27]

A positive and inclusive public domain would fit between our current conceptualisation of the exclusive-propertised and the negative public domain.

The presumption that feminine and Indigenous knowledge can be used without restraint fades away when the public domain is reframed as positive and inclusive. The reframing recognises that knowledge might be "shared" and "open" within a certain group or community, but this would not mean that it is free for the taking. This would mean that feminine knowledge could not

25 World Intellectual Property Organization (WIPO), "Culture as a Commodity? Intellectual Property and Expressions of Traditional Cultures" (2003) 4 *WIPO Magazine* 9–14, 12; and Graham Dutfield, "The Public and Private Domains" (2000) 21(3) *Science Communication* 274, 285.

26 "Statement by the Tulalip Tribes of Washington on Folklore, Indigenous Knowledge, and the Public Domain" (9 July 2003), WIPO Intergovernmental Committee on Intellectual Property and Genetic Resources, Traditional Knowledge and Folklore, Fifth Session, 2, www.wipo.int/tk/en/igc/ngo/tulaliptribes.pdf. See also Moana Jackson, "The Property of the Māori Intellect: A Review of *The Politics of Māori Image and Design*" (2003) 7(1) *He Pukenga Kōrero* 32, 32.

27 Dussolier (n 10) 117.

simply be taken, filtered through the masculine and patented. Furthermore, a positive and inclusive public domain could result in actors having positive obligations – that is, individuals are not disconnected from their knowledge of or their community. Thus, within a positive and inclusive public domain, relations between creators, communities and knowledge could be maintained, fostered and governed. This would be more consistent with a situated and relationally networked understanding of knowledge.

3 Attempts to blur the binary

3.1 Using intellectual property

There are active attempts to blur the line between property and the public domain. A well-known example is the open access or "copyleft" movement. This includes the Creative Commons project, which creates standardised licences, which copyright owners can use to licence their works in a manner contrary to the "all rights reserved" presumption of copyright.[28] Copyright owners can use Creative Commons licences to license out their works to the public for free, under certain conditions stipulating which rights they wish to retain and which they wish to waive. For example, they might stipulate that use must be non-commercial, or no derivatives may be made. The Creative Commons is a means to fight against the perceived modern-day tendency to overprotect works to the detriment of the public domain, future creativity and freedom of expression.[29] In other words, it is based on the understanding that creativity is cumulative and communal. There are analogous endeavours structured around patent law, such as open biotech projects and non-enforcement pledges.[30]

Arguments have been made for expanding the Creative Commons approach to address the concerns and needs of Indigenous peoples. This would be through "indigenous-knowledge-specific licences",[31] developed in a culturally appropriate manner, to directly address Indigenous peoples' perspectives and interests.[32]

28 I have called it a "pseudo" public domain, because there are still restrictions on use even for the rights waived, such as that the user: attribute the original author, likewise share his/her work, not make any derivatives, or only make non-commercial use.

29 Lawrence Lessig, *Free Culture* (The Penguin Press, 2004) 8–9.

30 See e.g. Yochai Benkler, "Commons-Based Strategies and the Problems of Patents" (2004) 305 *Science* 1110.

31 Jane E Anderson, "Indigenous/Traditional Knowledge & Intellectual Property" (2010) Centre for the Study of the Public Domain Issue Paper, [3.3.2.5], www.law.duke.edu/cspd/itkpaper.

32 Ibid., [3.3.2.4]. The same problem has been identified in the proposal to extend the Fairtrade Label to Indigenous goods and services and the development of standards required for obtaining the certification mark; see Christoph B Graber and Jessica C Lai, "Indigenous Cultural Heritage and Fair Trade – Voluntary Certification

Open access models can allow for distributed (decentralised) or communal production.[33] In this vein, Carys Craig, Joseph Turcotte and Rosemary Coombe have outlined how the open access movement is feminist. This is because both the open access movement and feminist critiques of intellectual property challenge the individual-creator paradigm and recognise that creation occurs in specific social and cultural contexts. Both also understand the value and power inherent in information/knowledge, and seek to disrupt hegemonic power structures that protect the status quo through sharing and dialogue.[34]

Open access models are not without their problems and critics. Their success relies on social acceptance and broad infiltration, which in turn depends on one-size-fits-all licences. Such licences cannot reflect the different needs and expectations of heterogeneous groups.[35] For example, presuming that standardised licences can be developed that are suitable for all Indigenous peoples is unrealistic. There are also concerns relating to who should decide on the terms of the licences.[36] For example, which Indigenous groups might end up drafting the licensing terms? It is worth noting that, even amongst the marginalised, there are power hierarchies. It is possible that one-size-fits-all licences either reflect the requirements of the powerful, or suit the needs of the slightly more powerful marginalised, but not the most marginalised.

From a more fundamental perspective, the open models are based on the existing intellectual property framework. They do not work in the absence of either copyright or patents. Thus, the binaries that affect patentability remain. In addition, open access models do not function when something is in the negative public domain. Instead, open access models are "contractually constructed commons" within the propertised realm.[37] To illustrate, Jessica Silbey has shown that the open access movement continues property's idealisation of individual autonomy and consent.[38] Furthermore, one can question who has access to these constructed commons. Who takes advantage of Creative Commons licences or patent pledges? Who knows they exist and can employ and enforce them? Like the romanticised public domain, it will be those with the means and resources, who understand the open access model and how to exploit it, who will benefit from it.

Standards in the Light of WIPO and WTO Law and Policymaking" (2011) 29(3) *Prometheus* 287, 300.

33 As noted by Boyle, "The importance of open-source software is not that it introduces us to a wholly new idea; it is that it makes us see clearly a very old idea", Boyle (n 13) 47.

34 Carys J Craig, Joseph F Turcotte and Rosemary J Coombe, "What is Feminist About Open Access?: A Relational Approach to Copyright in the Academy" (2011) 1(1) *Feminists@law* 1, 26–31.

35 Anderson (n 31) 3.3.2.2 and 3.4.3.1.

36 Molly Torsen and Jane Anderson, *Intellectual Property and the Safeguarding of Traditional Cultures* (WIPO, 2010) 49.

37 Pamela Samuelson, "Enriching Discourse on Public Domains" (2006) 55 *Duke Law Journal* 783, 832.

38 Jessica Silbey, "Comparative Tales of Origins and Access: Intellectual Property and the Rhetoric of Social Change" (2010) 616(1) *Case Western Reserve Law Review* 195.

3.2 Working in the grey

There are existing approaches that do not rely on there being intellectual property, including the *domaine public payant* (paying public domain) system, access and benefit sharing (ABS) agreements, and attribution rights. These three approaches give some positive constitution to things in that are legally property free.

The *domaine public payant* creates a liability rule that allows artistic or expressive works that are in the public domain to be used without restriction, subject to the payment of a fee.[39] Due to the requirement that payment be made for use of something in the public domain, it blurs the line between the propertised and the public domain. Suggestions have been made to extend this in the more technical-knowledge context. This would involve the use of compulsory licensing, which would require that users of knowledge in the public domain pay source communities for their use.[40] It would be licensing of something that is property free. It is compulsory licensing, as the relevant descendants or communities would not have any right to object to third-party use, but merely to be compensated for it.

The *domaine public payant* is only about remuneration. Relevant communities are not granted any control over their knowledge,[41] making it distinct from the classical property regime. No exclusive rights are created and nothing would be taken out of the public domain. However, paywall fences would be erected. Problematically, the system requires that knowledge is discretely recognisable (a "thing" to be licensed) and clearly stemming from a particular source. It does not work for more diffuse knowledge, or knowledge shared across multiple groups.

There is a growing movement to push for ABS agreements with Indigenous communities when their knowledge and/or genetic resources are used to derive something of commercial value.[42] Through an ABS agreement, a source community grants access to their knowledge or genetic resources in exchange

39 Tunis Model of Law on Copyright for Developing Countries (1976), s 17. See also Bangui Agreement (1977), art. 59; and WIPO, Intergovernmental Committee on Intellectual Property and Genetic Resources, Traditional Knowledge and Folklore, Secretariat, "Note on the Meanings of the Term 'Public Domain' in the Intellectual Property System with Special Reference to the Protection of Traditional Knowledge and Traditional Cultural Expressions/Expressions of Folklore" (2010) WIPO Doc. WIPO/GRTKF/IC/17/INF/8, [55]–[58].

40 Discussed by Jacques de Werra, "Fighting Against Biopiracy: Does the Obligation to Disclose in Patent Applications Truly Help" (2009) 42 *Vanderbilt Journal of Transnational Law* 143, 169–71.

41 Antony Taubman, "Saving the Village: Conserving Jurisprudential Diversity in the International Protection of Traditional Knowledge" in Keith E Maskus and Jerome H Reichman (eds), *International Public Goods and Transfer of Technology Under a Globalized Intellectual Property Regime* (Cambridge University Press, 2005) 521, 532.

42 See e.g. Rio Convention on Biological Diversity (CBD), 1760 UNTS 79; 31 ILM 818 (opened for signature 5 June 1992, entered into force 29 December 1993), art. 8(j); and Nagoya Protocol on Access to Genetic Resources and the Fair and Equitable Sharing of Benefits Arising from their Utilization to the Convention on

for some financial benefit (such as an upfront payment and/or royalties from any resultant commercialisation) and possibly some technology transfer to assist the source community to develop their technological capacity. ABS is often discussed together with the idea of obtaining prior-informed consent (PIC) to use Indigenous knowledge and genetic resources. In other words, the ideal is that one gets PIC to undertake research and signs an ABS agreement to ensure the source community is rewarded in some way.

Laura Foster has suggested that ABS could be a means of ensuring that women are financially rewarded for the use of their knowledge.[43] In other words, when feminine knowledge is presumed to be in the public domain, taken, filtered through the masculine, patented and commercialised, the women from whom the knowledge originates would partake in the financial benefits. This might be through royalty payments. By making access to something in the public domain contingent on obtaining some benefit, ABS agreements – like the *domaine public payant* – overcome the strict delineation between the propertised and the public domain.

Finally, Gearhart-Serna has suggested a "public domain plus" regime, where the use of women's traditional knowledge would require attribution or acknowledgement of the women and the source community.[44] The concept of attribution is familiar in the copyright realm.[45] Authors of copyrighted works have a moral right to be named as the authors of their works. Attribution is less familiar in the patent law context, where only those who contributed to the conception part of an invention must be named as inventors (see Chapters 3 and 5). Attribution would share some of the reputational gains from patenting with the creators of feminine knowledge. This could result in some indirect financial benefits, such as future collaborations or job opportunities. However, direct financial benefits would require ABS. The reputational gains and indirect benefits would arguably be limited. As noted throughout this book, Western culture has been socialised to valorise genius inventors, and not everyone who came before and around them. To a certain degree, attribution in the patent law environment would do little more over and above the fact that patent applications typically note prior art when describing the background for the invention. Furthermore, it is well known that "first authors" or "first inventors" on lists of authors and inventors obtain most of the reputational gain from publication and patenting (see Chapter 4).

Giving property-like characteristics to the public domain addresses the fact that creation is both cumulative and not discrete – all inventions embody

Biological Diversity (Nagoya Protocol), UN Doc. UNEP/CBD/COP/DEC/X/1 (adopted on 29 October 2010).

43 Laura A Foster, "Situating Feminism, Patent Law, and the Public Domain" (n 12) 296.

44 Gearhart-Serna (n 5) 395–8.

45 For a particular application of attribution in the Indigenous context, see the Haka Ka Mate Attribution Act 2014 (NZ).

knowledge that was already known. It also implicitly acknowledges that the processes and results of creation are not always separable from their context. However, the approaches discussed do not account for communal creation. Furthermore, they are all universalistic, allowing little space for the heterogeneity of how knowledge is generated, developed and maintained, and how various creators and communities govern their knowledge. The approaches also potentially transplant Western and masculine ideals of remuneration, consent and contract arrangements,[46] which may not be suitable or desirable. In fact, from a legal and transactional perspective, the approaches might make it easier for the Western and the masculine to continue to exploit the knowledge and resources of certain peoples and to do so "guilt free", without truly addressing the concerns of the communities from which the knowledge and resources come. Connected to this, these approaches do little to address the social relations that frame situated networks of knowledge. For example, they do not address that certain knowledge is in the public domain because of political, power and gender relations.

4 Stepping away from attempts at a unified theory

> The unoppressive city is thus defined as openness to unassimilated otherness. Of course, we do not have such openness to difference our current social relations. I am asserting an ideal, which consists in a politics of difference. Assuming that group differentiation is a given of social life for us, how can the relationships of group identities embody justice, respect and the absence of oppression? The relationship among group identities and cultures in our societies is blotted by racism, sexism, xenophobia, homophobia, suspicion mockery. A politics of difference lays down institutional ideological means for recognizing and affirming differently identifying groups in two basic senses: giving political representation to group interests and celebrating the distinctive cultures and characteristics of different groups. …
>
> … the concept of social relations that embody openness to unassimilated otherness with justice and appreciation needs to be developed. Radical politics, moreover, must develop discourse and institutions for bringing differently identified groups together without suppressing or subsuming the differences.[47]

Section 2 of this chapter discussed ways that the public domain and privatised dichotomy could be collapsed in an abstract sense. Section 3 outlined existing attempts to do so and how they have fallen short of addressing the presumptions of modernity and the social relations embedded in patent law and the public domain. It is not surprising that these attempts cannot address the in-

46 Laura A Foster, "Decolonizing Patent Law: Postcolonial Technoscience and Indigenous Knowledge in South Africa" (2017) 28(3) *Feminist Formations* 148, 161–2, who notes that patents and ABS agreements are tools of neoliberalism, which reinforce capitalism and allow for transnational flow of capital and knowledge.

47 Iris M Young, "The Ideal of Community and the Politics of Difference" (1986) 12 (1) *Social Theory and Practice* 1, 22–3.

built biases of patent law, as they are all based on universalistic Western and masculine concepts.

We need to stop constructing binaries and trying to solve them with universalistic ideals. That is, we need to step away from trying to find a single homogentisic way of regulating knowledge. After all, local and context-specific theories have proven sufficient for the advancement of knowledge generation.[48] Helen Longino has suggested that "we look at the aims of inquiry (at least some) as satisfied by embracing multiple and, in some cases, incompatible theories that satisfy local standards".[49] She argued that we can do this if we frame science as a practice or set of practices, and we view scientific theories as models.[50] In her words:

> If we understand science as practice, then we understand inquiry as ongoing, that is, we give up the idea that there is a terminus of inquiry that just is the set of truths about the world. ... Scientific knowledge from this perspective is not the static end point of inquiry but a cognitive or intellectual expression of an ongoing interaction with our natural and social environments. ... Scientific knowledge, then, is a body of diverse theories and their articulations onto the world that changes over time in response to the changing cognitive needs of those who develop and use the theories, in response to the new questions and anomalous empirical data revealed by applying theories, and in response to changes in associated theories. ... If we recognize the partiality of theories, as we can when we treat as models, we can recognize pluralism in the community as one of the conditions for the continued development of scientific knowledge in this sense.[51]

An example of the partiality of a plurality of models is classical Newtonian physics of motion and models of quantum mechanics. Newtonian physics works well for modelling the observable world. However, it breaks down at the quantum level, for which there are multiple competing models, some of which work better than others depending on the context. There is no unified theory.

There is something to be gained from multiple models. Longino stated:

> Some [models] will be more appropriate for some domains, others for others, and some for none. We can't know this unless models get sufficiently elaborated to be used as guides for interactions. Thus, this joint perspective implies the advocacy of subcommunities characterized by local standards. To the extent that they address a common domain and to the

48 Evelyn Fox Keller, *Secrets of Life, Secrets of Death: Essays on Language, Gender and Science* (Routledge, 1992) 180–181.

49 Helen E Longino, "Subjects, Power, and Knowledge: Description and Prescription in Feminist Philosophies of Science" in Linda Alcoff and Elizabeth Potter (eds), *Feminist Epistemologies* (Taylor & Francis, 1992) 101, 114.

50 Ibid.

51 Ibid., 116.

> extent that they share some standards in common, these subcommunities must be in critical dialogue with each other as well as with those subcommunities identified with more mainstream science. The point of dialogue from this point of view is not to produce a general and universal consensus but to make possible the refinement, correction, rejection, and sharing of models. Alliances, mergers, and revisions of standards as well as of models are all possible consequences of this dialogic interaction.[52]

Yet another illustration is a traditional medicine and the isolated active ingredient in pill form. The latter might never come to fruition without the knowledge of the former. It is through dialogue that the relationship between the two forms of knowledge is clarified. Potentially they can learn from one another. However, both forms are appropriate within their social locations.

Furthermore, as discussed in Chapter 5, we know that there are many different local means to successfully facilitate, maintain and regulate invention. Thus, we need to develop a system that accepts the multiplicity of ways that knowledge is generated and governed, beyond socially constructed dichotomies. We must do so to ensure that everyone can participate equally in the knowledge economy and, moreover, have an equal say in what that knowledge economy looks like and whom it benefits.

This section steps away from the existence of patents and the public domain that they create being a given. In doing so, it shifts the position of inventing, inventorship and knowledge from the individual and the universal to the situated and the relational. This allows us to think about the effects that rights and obligations can have on relationships between people and between people and things. In turn, we can think about the kinds of relationships and networks that we want and how to use the law to achieve these.[53] This is consistent with one of the core tenets of property law, that it regulates the relationship between people and objects, and between people with respect to objects.[54] This is typically ignored in the theorisation of patent law. Nevertheless, the rights that a society chooses to grant to achieve the relationships it wants need not be property based.

It is worth noting that giving patents (as well as copyright and trade marks) legal status as "property" is a relatively new phenomenon. As Peter Drahos has eruditely pointed out, these rights were historically used as public policy instruments.[55] Thus, we should not feel bound by the legal mechanism for knowledge governance being property. Parallel to this, we should not be enamoured by the romanticisation of the public domain.

52 Ibid., 117.

53 Craig, Turcotte and Coombe (n 34) 11. See also Carys J Craig, *Copyright, Communication and Culture: Towards a Relational Theory of Copyright Law* (Edward Elgar, 2011).

54 Wesley Newcomb Hohfeld, "Some Fundamental Legal Conceptions as Applied in Judicial Reasoning" (1913) 23(1) *Yale Law Journal* 16, 28–33 (on "jural relations"); and Felix S Cohen, "Dialogue on Private Property" (1954) 4(2) *Rutgers Law Review* 357, 361–3 ("on social relations").

55 Peter Drahos, *A Philosophy of Intellectual Property* (Dartmouth Publishing, 1996).

4.1 Protecting "limited common property" systems

We could replace the patent system with laws that protect the norms of what Carol Rose termed "limited common property" systems (see Chapter 5),[56] or Indigenous peoples have referred to as their "private domains". History shows that humans create, and communities develop norms to regulate access and use of creations, regardless of whether there is a patent system. The norms might include obligations, as well as rights. Legal protection of those norms would not be as unusual as it appears on first blush. As discussed in Chapter 5, the common law and law of equity are replete with examples of obligations and rights arising from common usage, and there being no trespass or infringement due to the failure of a rightsholder to enforce their rights, creating legally recognised expectations.[57] In other words, the law protects reasonable expectations.

Such a suggestion will undoubtedly have opponents for being "backward" or "primitive". However, the theories discussed in Chapter 6 underscore that modernity and its binaries are not essential, but socially constructed and used to maintain hegemonic power. Philosophers have been trying to theorise alternative and more representative conceptualisations of knowledge and being. At the same time, Indigenous peoples' knowledge governance systems are largely pre-modern. Perhaps, then, we should stop thinking of Indigenous knowledge as "primitive" and "non-scientific", and viewing its governance as inferior, and we could, instead, learn something from pre-modern societies.

Those wishing to enforce the norms of their community would have to present evidence that the creation came from them or their community. They would also have to prove the defendants have breached the customary norms of that community. This would be a "situated" approach – local to the community. There is no mythical all-seeing person having ordinary skill in the art (PHOSITA). This would allow for independent creation.

The proposed legal framework would not base protection on the field, discipline or subject matter. This is important, firstly, because disciplines can be complicit with social power.[58] The thread throughout this book arguing that "women in STEM" rhetoric is a distraction, at best, or dangerous, at worst, is a reflection of this. STEM embodies social power. Proponents of the need for more "women in STEM", without deconstructing and reconstructing what "STEM" constitutes, are complicit in imbuing it with power. In Sandra Harding's words:

56 Carol M Rose, "The Several Futures of Property: Of Cyberspace and Folk Tales, Emission Trades and Ecosystems" (1998) 83(1) *Minnesota Law Review* 129, 162, stated that "many kinds of intellectual production may be best fostered in a 'limited commons,' where members encourage one another internally but still preserve a domain of their own, separate from the rest of the world".

57 See e.g. Carol M Rose, "The Comedy of the Commons: Commerce, Custom, and Inherently Public Property" (1986) 53(3) *University of Chicago Law Review* 711.

58 Sandra Harding, "Standpoint Theories: Productively Controversial" (2009) 24(4) *Hypatia* 192, 197.

> Disciplines are powerful epistemologically and politically. Oppressed groups cannot afford to simply ignore them just because they have become aligned with regressive scientific and political practices any more than they can afford to ignore regressive legal or economic practices. Disciplinary assumptions and practices must be reappropriated and directed to emancipatory ends.[59]

Applied to the context of this book, Harding is saying that the disempowered cannot ignore "STEM" and the wealth and power it represents. However, if they enter it without reflecting on "STEM" (e.g. what is it to do "science" or what is "technology"), they reinforce and perpetuate power relations. As Harding noted:

> How research disciplines conceptualize the world they study changes those worlds – in the natural as well as the social sciences, we now know. The activities of sociologists and political philosophers are complicit with different activities of the dominant institutions; thus changing conceptual frameworks in those disciplines can affect how women are served by, say, a welfare system and a legal system.[60]

The proposed approach does more than change conceptual frameworks, instead stepping back and away from Western and masculine notions of "science", "technology" and "invention".

Secondly, not being restricted to discipline or field leaves open the door to a more holistic approach to knowledge governance. The proposed approach does not attempt to distinguish between the artistic (what would be protected by copyright or design law) and the technical (the realm of patent law). It does not attempt to categorise different kinds of abstract or intellectual "things". This is more consistent with a non-modernistic and common Indigenous worldview.[61] Indeed, it is consistent with the fact that the intellectual does not fall neatly within the confines of different kinds of intellectual property.[62] For example, software has always awkwardly straddled both copyright and patent protection.

The lack of a specific scope of protection will not represent chaos in comparison to patent law. Under the existing system, to defend validity challenges, patentees must bring evidence and expert witnesses to support that their inventions are new and inventive vis-à-vis PHOSITA. In other words, even

59 Ibid., 197–8.

60 Ibid., 198.

61 This might affect the term of the exclusive marketing rights. On the ideal term of protection for the artistic as opposed to the technical, see Rebecca Giblin, "Reimagining Copyright's Duration" in Rebecca Giblin and Kimberlee Weatherall (eds), *What if We could Reimagine Copyright?* (ANU Press, 2017) 177.

62 Neil Wilkof and Shmnad Basheer (eds), *Overlapping Intellectual Property Rights* (Oxford University Press, 2012).

granted patents must be defended and proven to be valid. Moreover, most people are not precisely aware of the law on the books. People do not abstain from murder because it is a crime, or from taking someone else's car because it is a tort. People mostly behave in accordance with social expectations and norms, which usually keeps them in line with the law. If there is deviation, enforcement will only occur if the community deems it worth the cost. This is equally true with the patent system – patentees typically only enforce their patents if it is in accordance with their industry norms, and it makes strategic and/or financial sense.

The approach is non-universalistic. There is not one understanding of science or knowledge, or a scientist and inventor. That said, there would have to be some limitations, which would add a layer of universalism. For example, the customary norms could not be otherwise illegal. Related to this, the law could not enforce norms that are contrary to certain ideals. For example, norms that are discriminatory based on sex, gender, race, religion and so on. "Community" would likely have to be legally definition, but within that definition of community, rights would have to be inclusive.

4.1 Marketing rights

Short-term rights to market exclusivity for the first person to market a good or service could accompany the protection of limited common property systems. This could be, for example, for five years. Like any law, the exact details of how such a system would work would require careful drafting.[63] However, at the core is the idea that, if one discovers or creates something that another person is willing to exchange value for, one would get those marketing rights. The applicant would have to disclose the details of their creation (e.g. how it is made or how it works). The disclosure would allow for others to understand and build upon the product or service. The customary norms of the community from which the individual created would determine whether that individual would have the right (or "entitlement") to apply for the marketing rights. This would reflect a situated and relational understanding of creators, which takes into account the context of the creation and whether that context comes with any obligations.

Because there would be limited definition of what could get marketing rights, exclusive marketing rights of this nature would be non-directive. That is, they would not incentivise creativity towards certain subject matter. This is contrast to patent rights, which direct creation and commercialisation towards that which is patentable. For example, it would include a method of counselling treatment, method of education, or knowledge that a particular plant can be used to treat a certain ailment. Furthermore, terms such as "science", "technology" or

63 On the use of exclusive marketing rights to overcome first-mover disadvantages, see Michael Abramowicz and John F Duffy, "Intellectual Property for Market Experimentation" (2008) 83 *New York University Law Review* 337.

"invention" would not be required, making the approach comparatively de-gendered and de-racialised.

What is "new" could be defined relative to what is currently on the market. This is in contradistinction to patent law, where novelty is measured against all pre-existing information or knowledge.[64] This would have the effect of situating knowledge more.[65] It also steps away from a value-laden assessment of novelty (see Chapter 2) and assists in de-gendering "newness". Under such an understanding of "new", it would be possible to get exclusive marketing rights for undertaking the risk of bringing something to market, even if it pertains to pre-existing information or knowledge. This is as long as it is not presently being marketed.

The term of exclusive marketing rights would be relatively short (compared to the potential 20-year patent term). This being the case, there would be no need to assess the level of inventiveness. Indeed, there would be no need to assess any other measure of quality. Thus, the services of the mythical and masculine PHOSITA would no longer be required. Maintaining such a system should be relatively low-cost, due to there being no subject matter eligibility, or assessments of non-obviousness, utility or universal novelty. In other words, assessing the applications should be relatively straightforward, which means it should be relatively low-cost to apply for such rights. This is important as it makes the system more accessible for the disadvantaged or marginalised. In comparison, patents are expensive to obtain and maintain.

Short-term, exclusive marketing rights better reflect that creation is communal and cumulative. While patent rights are predominantly exclusive rights to make and use, marketing rights would not prevent non-market-related uses of the creation or others from building on it. This is so long as the uses are not contrary to customary norms, as discussed above. For example, others who had been using the creation privately could continue to do so. Others could also use it in research, improve it, even create follow-on inventions (again, so long as this is consistent with the community's norms). Recognising that others might be using the knowledge or might wish to use or develop it, breaks down the individual/communal binary. It reflects a relational understanding of knowledge generation and has the effect of flattening the hierarchy of contributors. It also acknowledges that knowledge is never final, but continually contested and developed within different networks.

64 To a certain extent, this is how the patent system in England started out, where novelty was defined locally rather than universally, and one could invent via importing. See Jessica C Lai, "A Tale of Two Histories: The 'Invention' and its Incentive Theory" in Jessica C Lai and Antoinette Maget Dominicé (eds), *Intellectual Property and Access to Im/material Goods* (Edward Elgar, 2016) 94, 96–100.

65 Donna Haraway, "Situated Knowledges: The Science Question in Feminism and the Privilege of Partial Perspective" (1988) 14(3) *Feminist Studies* 575. See also Dan L Burk, "Do Patents Have Gender?" (2011) 19 *American University Journal of Gender, Social Policy & the Law* 881, 907–9, on the possibility of situating PHOSITA.

The approach allows for the agency of matter, which form part of the network of conversation (see Chapter 6).[66] Matter embodies discursive practices, and humans and matter intra-act to co-create boundaries and meaning.[67] Recognising the contingent and communal nature of invention, as well as the agency of matter, creates a flatter hierarchy of invention.[68] Unlike patent law, primacy would not be given to the "manmade", in contrast to the "natural". The proposed marketing rights are not centred around the ideal of individuals who objectify their surroundings, as there is no assessment of the "intellectual" creation vis-à-vis "nature". This means that there are no culture/nature or mind/body binaries. When matter has agency and the human/matter interaction is viewed as interdependent, calls for sharing materials (such as source code or biological specimens) are stronger. This is because the human-matter relationship is not one of culture mastering nature. Matter matters. Thus, the person with the exclusive marketing rights should be required to share any materials relating to the creation for a reasonable fee. Allowing for non-market use and requiring that any materials are shared breaks down the public domain/privatised binary, as that over which the exclusive marketing rights exist is still open to others.

Arguments that these marketing rights might not be capable incentivising invention are moot, as empirical evidence shows that patents do not fulfil this function in practice.[69] Nevertheless, a structure that facilitates commercialisation is required. Hence, the legislation should be clear that the rights should be capable of assignment or being licensed. That said, the exclusive marketing rights should not be property rights, as property law comes with certain ideology related to natural rights theory, for example. Though not property, but capable of being assigned and licensed, the exclusive marketing rights would be something that could be transacted around, which is necessary for commercialisation.

It might make sense to vary the exact term and scope of the marketing rights depending on whether one brings a new product/service to market or whether the marketed creation is a new feature or improvement of an existing product/service. There should also be the possibility to postpone the starting point of the term of market exclusivity under certain circumstances, such as having to go through clinical trials and/or regulatory approval. For example, pharmaceuticals and agricultural chemicals have to go through regulatory review, which includes submitting data on safety and efficacy. Allowing a delay in the

66 Haraway (n 65) 592.

67 Karen Barad, "Posthumanist Performativity: Toward and Understanding of How Matter Comes to Matter" (2003) 28(3) *Signs: Journal of Woman in Culture and Society* 801.

68 Burk, "Do Patents Have Gender?" (n 65) 916; and Dan L Burk, "Feminism and Dualism in Intellectual Property" (2007) 15(2) *American University Journal of Gender, Social Policy & the Law* 195.

69 See e.g. Adam D Moore, "Intellectual Property, Innovation, and Social Progress: The Case Against Incentive Based Arguments" (2003) 26(3) *Hamline Law Review* 602; and Browyn H Hall and Dietmar Harhoff, "Recent Research on the Economics of Patents" (2012) 4 *Annual Review of Economics* 541.

starting point of the market exclusivity would also address the fact that the chemical and pharmaceutical industries are the only industries where there is some empirical evidence indicating the need for an incentive to invent.[70]

Overall, the proposed approach would protect, and thereby give legal credence to, a multiplicity of ways of knowing, kinds of knowledge and means of regulating the knowledge. This is in stark contrast to the patent system, which is a one-size-fits-all Western and exclusivity-based system, that is essentially set up such that women and Indigenous peoples are always giving upstream to Western-masculine science to take downstream, patent and commercialise. As discussed in Chapter 3, creation occurs in an intricate ecosystem,[71] not a singular uni-directional stream. However, the patent system is only interested in the end-products of the creative process.[72] Rose analogised the way we should view the knowledge ecosystem with the physical environment, stating:

> Radical environmentalists have long stressed that the environment must be understood as an entire interactive system, and, in particular, that human beings should practice a non-instrumentalist ethic that places human activities in the context of interconnected ecosystems. On this account, the environmental whole is greater than the sum of the parts; the isolation of one element for pragmatic "resource development" may unravel the larger networks of biota that mutually support one other. This view has implications for property: it suggests that while property may indeed focus our attention, it misguidedly focuses our attention on the parts rather than the whole. An attempt to divide an ecosystem entirely into bit and pieces of property would thus detract from what is needed, that is, a holistic view of an ecosystem or indeed the earth in its entirety.[73]

The whole ecosystem is recognised in the proposed approach. This is because it acknowledges that both the upstream and downstream, as well as everything in between, are relevant and require regulation. Moreover, it recognises that the ecosystem is in fact comprised of a relational network of streams that intertwine with one another and together with a variety of other factors, such as the social, cultural and material. Instead of the downstream getting strong rights and the upstream getting few rights, the proposed regulation decreases the level of

70 Jessica Silbey, "Patent Variation: Discerning Diversity Among Patent Functions" (2013) 45 *Loyola University Chicago Law Journal* 441, 476; James Bessen and Michael J Meurer, *Patent Failure: How Judges, Bureaucrats, and Lawyers Put Innovators at Risk* (Princeton University Press, 2008) 14–6 and 141; and FM Scherer, "A Half Century of Research on Patent Economics" (2010) 2(1) *WIPO Journal* 20.

71 Jessica C Lai, "Patents and Gender: A Contextual Analysis" (2020) 10(3) *Queen Mary Journal of Intellectual Property* 283.

72 Rose, "The Several Futures of Property" (n 56) 161, who states that "it may be the 'spaces,' rather than the products from those spaces, that most require a rethinking of intellectual property protection-the LCP [limited common property] as a set of *activities* rather than, or in addition to, a set of products".

73 Rose, "The Several Futures of Property" (n 56) 174–5.

rights, but distributes them more equally throughout the ecosystem. In doing so, it blurs the upstream/downstream dichotomy and implicitly also the public domain/privatised binary.

Being non-universalistic, the suggested approach would potentially be consistent with Indigenous peoples' knowledge governance systems. In particular, it does not use the logic of Western property and its in-built binaries.[74] Instead, it allows for an understanding that there is no hard distinction between nature and culture, or the tangible and intangible, for example.[75]

5 Concluding thoughts

The law is a reflection of hegemonic power. It should, thus, come as no surprise that Western men have created a knowledge governance system that primarily protects the Western and the masculine. As a consequence, it is the Western and the masculine that is valorised, disseminated and built-upon, and it is men who chiefly benefit from the financial and reputational gains of patenting. Furthermore, it is mainly men who shape the development of society and politics through technology.

As noted in Chapter 3, there are more women in the patent-heavy STEM fields in 2021 than ever before and this has resulted in more females being named as inventors on patents (though still disproportionately low). It is arguable that, given time, there will be enough women in STEM who have a stake in the status quo, such that no changes to the knowledge governance system need to be made. This argument fails to address the politics and power at play. Current trends show that more and more women are entering STEM and patenting. However, there is inequity in who these women are, in terms of their racial, ethnic, cultural and social backgrounds. We observed this when white middle-class women entered the "public" workforce, shifting "private" and invisible work to women of colour. In the words of Katharine Bartlett,

> If feminism addresses only oppressive practices that operate against white, privileged women, it may readjust the allocation of privilege, but fail to either reconstruct the social and legal significance of gender or to prove that its insights have the power to illuminate other categories of exclusion.[76]

74 Laura A Foster, "Situating Feminism, Patent Law, and the Public Domain" (n 12) 332, notes that a hybridised understanding of the public and private fits Indigenous peoples' epistemologies.

75 Paul Myburgh, "New Zealand / Aotearoa" in Toshiyuki Kono (ed.), *The Impact of Uniform Laws on the Protection of Cultural Heritage and the Preservation of Cultural Heritage in the 21st Century* (Leiden and Boston: Martinus Nijhoff Publishers, 2010) 639, 661; Peter Shand, "Scenes from the Colonial Catwalk: Cultural Appropriation, Intellectual Property Rights, and Fashion" (2002) 3 *Cultural Analysis* 47, 60; and Tshimanga Kongolo, *Unsettled International Intellectual Property Issues* (Alphen aan den Rijn, Netherlands: Kluwer Law International, 2008) 31–32 and 35.

76 Katharine T Bartlett, "Feminist Legal Methods" (1990) 103 *Harvard Law Review* 829, 834.

Furthermore, because the system reflects and is controlled by hegemonic power, it might shift on the disempowered as they reach for the power that patents embody. Patentability could alter depending on gender balance in different fields. After all, those in power do not like to share their power.[77] We observed this with the feminisation of work, whereby certain fields lost economic power when women entered them, such as education, and the feminisation of poverty. And the flipside of the coin, we observed this with the masculinisation of computing as soon as it became something "public", industrial and of economic significance. Thus, the "woman question" asked must address the multiple underlying social relations, including gender, that result in biases.

More still, invention and innovation are poorer if everyone is pushed into a limited knowledge governance system, where they have to create a certain way in a certain field in order to patent. This is particularly true when we consider that the patent law-created knowledge governance system embodies modernity's binaries, which do not reflect how creation takes place for either women or men.

In this chapter, I have attempted to frame a new knowledge governance system that is egalitarian and better reflects the understanding of knowledge as situated within relational networks. It is not universalistic. It is not final, but always contested and re-created within different networks.

77 See e.g. Heidi I Hartmann, "The Unhappy Marriage of Marxism and Feminism" (1979) 3(2) *Capital and Class* 1, who explains why simply having more women in the work force has not resulted in equality. Namely, men and women do not share the same experiences under capitalism. Furthermore, men benefitted from the free and invisible work of women in their houses and having less competition in the workforce.

Conclusion

There is sexual division of labour. Dictated by the Western male capitalist model, this division has allowed men to exploit the labour of women, whether physical or intellectual. The same can be said regarding race and the non-Western. This is true with respect to free work (performed in the private sphere – the home), lowly waged work or work that is less rewarded. This affects wealth accumulation, which is a proxy for power accumulation, cementing power relations.

This division will exist, shifting as necessary to protect the hegemony, until we address the power relations at play. Thus, we need to stop talking about "women in science, technology, engineering and mathematic (STEM)" and instead focus on why women need to be in STEM in order to partake in the knowledge economy. One of the main reasons is that patent law -which lies at the centre of Western knowledge governance systems – is gendered. Laws and regulations around what is patentable reflect multiple gendered binaries to favour the masculine and men.

Binary constructions of knowledge and society arose from modernity, which sought to purify the subject from the object, the mind from the body, the public from the private, culture from nature, and the individual from the community. These binaries are deeply embedded in society, affecting the general understanding of science and invention, as well as the scientist and the inventor. They are so embedded that they have the veneer of being essential. However, more recent philosophy of knowledge and being show that binary constructions are not essential, and there are alternative ways that we can theorise knowledge and being.

These different ways of viewing knowledge and being are important because they allow us to step back from the presumption that patent law is objective and that it is unquestionable that we use property to govern knowledge together with is dialectic partner, the public domain. Postmodern, poststructuralist and posthuman philosophies generally breakdown binaries to show that there is no essential distinction between subjects and objects (humans and matter), the mind and body, culture and nature, the private and public, and individuals and communities.

The final chapter of this book suggested a possible knowledge governance system that could replace patents, with a broader and less hierarchical understanding of inventorship and invention. This included legally recognising the norms of limited common property systems, thereby creating a situated and local

DOI: 10.4324/9781003128502-9

understanding of knowledge generation and regulation. In concert with this, short-term marketing rights could protect that which is marketed, if seeking such rights would be in line with the norms of the relevant limited common property system. The marketing rights proposed would offer less exclusivity than patent rights, but the rights would be distributed across more creators and creations. It does this by flattening the hierarchy of different kinds of contributors to knowledge generation, recognising the cumulative and communal manner in which this occurs, and acknowledging the relational interdependence of individuals and the communal. Furthermore, the proposed approach would break down the culture/nature binary by removing the assessment of a product or service being marketed vis-à-vis nature. In addition, in recognising that matter and humans co-constitute one another and meaning, the suggested approach favours the sharing of materials required for invention and breaks down the upstream/downstream and public domain/privatised binaries.

The point, however, is not the exact system suggested. It is that we need to have the discussion on how we could govern knowledge in a more egalitarian and power-neutral manner. Failure to have this dialogue and to address the power relations that undergird the knowledge governance system will result in the powerful retaining their power, partly through the exploitation of the labour of the disempowered. Furthermore, it places the burden on the disempowered to operate certain ways within certain fields. However, when they do so, they are ostracised and marginalised. In other words, we set them up to fail. Finally, we want a knowledge governance system that supports and maintains a diversity of knowledge and ways of knowing, as this leads to better invention and innovation.

So, let us have that discussion. Let us ask the "woman question" vis-à-vis patent law so that we can reveal and change "the ways in which political choice and institutional arrangement contribute to women's subordination",[1] when it comes to knowledge governance and the knowledge economy.

1 Katharine T Bartlett, "Feminist Legal Methods" (1990) 103 *Harvard Law Review* 829, 843.

Index

www.ingramcontent.com/pod-product-compliance
Lightning Source LLC
LaVergne TN
LVHW011130300926
849160LV00008B/597
9781032079578